Chaplaincy and Seafarers

Chaplaincy and Seafarers

Faith at Work

HELEN SAMPSON
NELSON TURGO
WENDY CADGE
SOPHIE GILLIAT-RAY

OXFORD
UNIVERSITY PRESS

OXFORD
UNIVERSITY PRESS

Great Clarendon Street, Oxford, OX2 6DP,
United Kingdom

Oxford University Press is a department of the University of Oxford.
It furthers the University's objective of excellence in research, scholarship,
and education by publishing worldwide. Oxford is a registered trade mark of
Oxford University Press in the UK and in certain other countries

Published in the United States of America by Oxford University Press
198 Madison Avenue, New York, NY 10016, United States of America

British Library Cataloguing in Publication Data
Data available

Library of Congress Control Number: 2024903251

ISBN 9780198913269

DOI: 10.1093/9780198913290.001.0001

Printed and bound by
CPI Group (UK) Ltd, Croydon, CR0 4YY

MIX
Paper | Supporting
responsible forestry
FSC
www.fsc.org
FSC® C013604

Acknowledgements

We would like to thank all of the port chaplains, centre managers, volunteers, members of stakeholder organizations, and seafarers who took part in this study. We would like to thank the operators of the two ships that we sailed with for their hospitality and for permission to be on board. We would like to thank Jason Zudeima for access to the International Christian Maritime Association archive and the Mission to Seafarers for access to their archive in Hull. Finally, we would like to thank friends and colleagues who supported us in undertaking the research, Louise Deeley for invaluable assistance with the preparation of the manuscript, and the Economic and Social Research Council (ESRC) for making the study possible. This work was supported by the ESRC (grant ES/N019423/1).

Contents

List of Tables

Abbreviations

AB	Able Seaman
AoS	Apostleship of the Sea
ASFS	American Seamen's Friend Society
BIMCO	The Baltic and International Maritime Council
EFCS	Episcopal Floating Church Society
ESRC	Economic and Social Research Council
HMSO	His Majesty's Stationery Office
ICMA	International Christian Maritime Association
ICOSA	International Council of Seamen's Agencies
ICS	International Chamber of Shipping
ILO	International Labour Organization
IMO	International Maritime Organization
ISWAN	International Seafarers Welfare and Assistance Network
ITF	International Transport Workers' Federation
KIMM	Korea International Maritime Mission
MAIB	Marine Accident Investigation Branch
MLC	Maritime Labour Convention
MNWB	Merchant Navy Welfare Board
MtS	Mission to Seafarers
NAMMA	North American Maritime Ministry Association
NCOSA	National Council of Seamen's Agencies
OS	Ordinary Seaman
SCI	Seamen's Church Institute
ST	Seafarers' Trust
UNCTAD	United Nations Conference on Trade and Development

Introduction

The shipping industry has long-established roots and traditions and a strong, often mythologized, place in British culture. Notwithstanding its enduring appeal in British works of art, fiction, and film, the centrality of the sector declined, in the United Kingdom, over the course of the twentieth century. It has continued to do so over the last three decades. While the wider maritime cluster continues to be of strong domestic economic importance in the United Kingdom, the relative significance of the United Kingdom as a global ship-owning nation, and the numbers of UK seafarers employed in the world cargo fleet, has fallen. In 1990, the United Kingdom was listed as the seventh most important ship-owning country as judged by the cargo-carrying capacity of its domestically-flagged and foreign-flagged fleet (UNCTAD 1990). By 2021, it had fallen to tenth place, carrying only 2.54 per cent of the world's cargo by weight, as compared with 4.31 per cent of cargo in 1990. In this sense, we can say that shipping continues to be of importance to the UK economy but that the United Kingdom is declining in importance relative to other economies in relation to international seaborne trade.

The international cargo-shipping sector is vast. It is comprised of 53,973 commercial cargo vessels of more than 1,000 gross tonnes, and in 2020, it was relied upon for the transport of more than 10 billion tonnes of cargo (UNCTAD 2021, p. 36). Despite these impressive figures, across the shipping industry, an oft-repeated lament relates to the invisibility of the services that modern ships and contemporary seafarers provide to consumers across the globe and the extent to which the collective endeavour that powers the international transit of goods is unappreciated and undervalued. For the most part, consumers give little thought to how their bananas arrive on the shelves of their local supermarket, how oil gets to port-based refineries, and how toys and cheap electronics are containerized and brought across the oceans to meet what sometimes appears to be an insatiable demand. When ships do come to the attention of the public, it is usually because of some misfortune that has occurred. In 2021, one of the largest container ships in the world, the *Ever Given*, received widespread media attention when it became wedged across the Suez Canal in high winds. The public were regularly updated on the six-day salvage operation during which one person was killed. Images were shown of vessels 'piling up' in queues as a result of being unable to transit the canal, and we were warned of the potential adverse impact on supply chains. Throughout it all, the crew remained largely invisible. Their lives and conditions of work were of no particular interest to a media 'circus' fully mobilized to tell a story of catastrophe on the high seas and inclined to report, at face value, allegations from the Suez Canal Authority that the captain was to blame for what had happened. Most reports showed little understanding of the context of operations in the Suez Canal or the role played in its navigation by *pilots*,[1] who were eventually identified to be at significant fault. This is not uncommon. The maritime industry operates within a web of complex international and national regulations. The jobs undertaken on board are conducted miles away from communities ashore from which seafarers, as individuals, are also frequently isolated over time (Sampson 2005, 2013). Seafarers live and work in what may be described as total institutions (Zurcher 1965; Gould 2010). They often feel they are forgotten by shore-based communities and even their families and friends. They complain that when a vessel sinks, the public are generally more concerned about the damage done to the environment than the injuries and fatalities suffered by the crew. Such priorities also drive the concerns of vessel operators, who have been shown to be more bothered about marine pollution (for which they may be fined significant sums and from which they would anticipate significant reputational damage) than they are about the health and safety of seafarers on board (Sampson 2011, 2016).

There is little evidence in the public domain that the perceptions of seafarers or of other members of the shipping community are askew. However, amongst seafarers there is one group of people who *are* seen to care about them and about their problems. They are people who can be called upon for assistance at any time of the day or night. They are folk who bring them free gifts and provide them with free transport and safe havens while a vessel is in port. They are known as port chaplains, and they are supported by volunteers who assist in the process of making sure that seafarers are not wholly forgotten and are befriended and helped while at sea and in port. Port chaplains are most frequently found in ports in the United Kingdom, the United States, Northern Europe, and Australia but are not limited to these areas and maintain a limited presence in most regions of the world.

Chaplains are religious professionals who work outside of local congregations, in public and private organizations, in roles designed to support their members. Thus, chaplains may be found working in prisons, specific industries, ambulance services, police forces, schools, universities, hospitals, youth services, military regiments, private chapels, and even sports clubs. While they are appointed by

---

[1] Pilots are qualified captains employed by local port authorities to join vessels and bring them safely into port, making use of their local knowledge of tides, currents, underwater hazards, and seabed topography. In the Suez Canal, it is compulsory for ship operators to hire the service of the Suez Canal Authority pilots. Legal responsibility for the vessel during a transit is normally held to be the responsibility of the captain and the vessel operators, not the pilots.

religious organizations, Christian chaplains work beyond them and beyond the normal limits associated with ministry to church congregations. Ordained chaplains working in full-time paid roles are in the minority, and many chaplains are volunteers working with, and directed and supported by, a religious organization. In the United Kingdom, it has become standard procedure for Christian chaplains to work in multi-faith contexts and alongside other volunteers of different faiths. Their work is often out of the public eye and, like seafarers, they may feel that they exist unseen by the general public (Gilliat-Ray et al. 2022), particularly when they work in closed institutions such as prisons or controlled spaces, which prohibit or control public access such as ports, schools, hospitals, or industrial premises.

This book is about the work and faith of port chaplains specifically, and the life, work, faith, and welfare needs of seafarers. In writing it, we have been informed by what we have learned in the course of the conduct of a large and multifaceted Economic and Social Research Council-funded study (ES/N019423/1),[2] which took place in the period 2017–2021. The study considered various aspects of the work and lives of port chaplains, it considered the significance of both faith and the services of port chaplains to seafarers, and it delved into the theological understandings of both port chaplains and seafarers and how these played out in daily life and work. In these ways, it set out to shed light on the largely 'hidden' lives of two groups of people who work in controlled contexts that are removed from public life and scrutiny.

One of the unique aspects of the research was the way in which it was completed by a team with differing but, in the context of the study, complementary disciplinary orientations. Helen Sampson and Nelson Turgo have worked for many years on social science issues of relevance to the maritime field. Respectively a sociologist and anthropologist by background, each of them have substantial experience of undertaking shipboard ethnographic research with multinational crews of seafarers and of work with port chaplains and their organizations. Their understanding of the global shipping industry and the maritime sector helped inform the design and conduct of the study and assisted in the analysis and interpretation of findings from the field. Wendy Cadge came to the study with a detailed understanding of port chaplaincy services and their social history in the United States. Having undertaken a considerable amount of work on religion and chaplaincy in health-care settings, airports, and public institutions, Wendy's work bridges the gap between port chaplaincy past and present and chaplaincy in other areas of public life. As such, her contributions have allowed us to arrive at a broader and better contextualized understanding of our results. Similarly, the work of Sophie Gilliat-Ray on chaplains and chaplaincy in prisons and hospitals,

[2] This work was supported by the Economic and Social Research Council (grant ES/N019423/1).

combined with the study of Islam and the work of Imams in Britain, has assisted the research team in arriving at an analysis that is strongly situated in broader-based studies of religion in public life. The combined skills and interests of the team[3] have allowed us to undertake a challenging project that has delivered richly detailed empirical findings, which we have been able to situate in a broad-reaching historical, occupational, and theological context. It is these findings and their context that provide the focus and substance of this book.

The research itself was challenging. It involved fieldwork in ports and on cargo ships as well as interviews with chaplains in the United Kingdom, chaplains overseas, and stakeholders. Fieldwork was conducted in two UK ports for a total of six months to ascertain the forms of services that port chaplains provide to seafarers and the attendant issues related to the provision of such services from both a practical and theological standpoint. This involved shadowing chaplains while they undertook shipboard visits and 'hanging out' and doing observation in seafarers' centres. The two ports have been assigned pseudonyms and will be referred to here as Porton and Riverside. Porton encompassed two port catchment areas and was served by port chaplains from two national charitable organizations. The Porton chaplains operated from an unstaffed seafarers' centre owned by the port authorities and leased to one of the organizations. It was within the limits of the port and was, therefore, highly accessible to visiting seafarers. Though unstaffed, it was open twenty-four hours and had a lounge where seafarers could relax and enjoy free wi-fi, coffee, and tea. There was also a separate room for religious contemplation or worship, should seafarers require it. This prayer room was heavily adorned with Christian images and well supplied with religious reading material. The port chaplains from the two different organizations serving the port had specific geographic zones within the port limits where they undertook shipboard visits. This minimized overlap and was designed to ensure that resources were utilized efficiently and to the maximum benefit of seafarers. In the absence of a staffed seafarers' centre to manage, port chaplains in Porton solely focused on shipboard visits, and they were helped by their volunteers in this task.

The seafarers' centre in Riverside, on the other hand, was managed by two independent, faith-based charitable organizations and was not connected to any national organization. In the past, it had employed port chaplains, but at the time of our fieldwork, no port chaplain worked from the centre. The centre was run by a manager with the help of paid staff and volunteers. The seafarers' centre was close to the port and was housed in an imposing Victorian building owned by the local organizations that ran it. It had a recreation room, a lounge, a bar, and a chapel, and it was open from 10 a.m. to 10 p.m., seven days a week. Shipboard visits were conducted by centre staff and volunteers. They were of a relatively

---

[3] The team also included a theologian—Professor Graeme Smith, who provided guidance and input on theological concerns that are beyond the scope of this book.

short duration compared with the visits conducted at Porton, and sometimes the only contact that volunteers or staff had with individual seafarers was associated with providing them with transport from their vessel to the centre or to local amenities and tourist attractions.

Port-based fieldwork involved the development of close connections with chaplains, volunteers, and centre staff. Seafarers were part of the study as and when they visited the seafarers' centres and in the course of chaplains', staff, and volunteers' visits to ships and, in one case, a hospital where a seafarer was a patient. The port-based fieldwork did not afford us the opportunity to develop a rapport or an understanding of seafarers as individuals, given that contact with them was fleeting. For this reason, we included two voyages on working cargo ships in the project fieldwork. The ships were selected on the basis that they carried multinational crews and were likely, therefore, to offer us the opportunity to talk with, and observe, seafarers of different faiths and none.[4] They were also selected according to their trading patterns as some routes are prone to pirate attacks and were judged as too high-risk for research purposes. These routes largely involve traversing the Arabian gulf, the Malacca Straits, and the seas off the west coast of Africa. In order to avoid these routes, our selected ships sailed from North America to the Caribbean and from New Zealand to China.

Nelson Turgo conducted both shipboard voyages. While on board, he observed the routine practices and interactions of seafarers, including when they enjoyed brief periods of shore-leave. In some cases, while in their company, he visited staffed and unstaffed shore-based facilities that were provided for seafarers, but he did not experience an encounter with a port chaplain or volunteer ship visitor in the course of his time on either vessel. By chance, he was on board our first vessel at the time when Christmas is celebrated by Christians, and he was able to witness at first hand how this major religious occasion was handled by a mixed-nationality crew. Fifty-five formal, recorded interviews were undertaken as part of the shipboard fieldwork, and these allowed us the opportunity to explore, in significant detail, the beliefs and understandings of individual seafarers and the ways in which they expressed these while navigating the sensitivities of shipmates.

In order to fully understand the provision of chaplaincy services to seafarers, the research also incorporated recorded interviews with stakeholders and with Christian chaplains who worked in the United Kingdom and overseas. Of ten Christian chaplains interviewed in connection with the research, four were ordained and six were not. In Tables 1–4, we summarize the various elements of

---

[4] Although we targeted companies employing multinational seafarers, we were unable to request access to seafarers of specific faiths as companies do not normally record the faith of the seafarers they employ on board. Some faiths are under-represented amongst seafarers due to international crewing patterns. Chinese, Filipino, Indian, and East European seafarers dominate the international labour market, and the predominant religions in these states are therefore predominant amongst international seafarers. In this context, we did not manage to include seafarers from a large number of faiths, including Islam.

Table 1 Interviews with centre personnel at Porton and Riverside

	Porton	Riverside
Paid centre staff (including chaplains)	3	2
Volunteers	4	6

Source: authors.

the primary research that was undertaken in the course of our study, which underpins the analysis offered in the forthcoming text.

In addition to this primary data collection, the team also attempted to access and analyse secondary data from both the International Christian Maritime Association (ICMA) and the Mission to Seafarers. This information supplemented our understanding of the historical development of port chaplaincy and added fresh material to contextualize the narratives available in published sources.

We have used these combined sources of data to arrive at a relatively comprehensive understanding of seafarers' attitudes to working in mixed-faith crews, their understandings of their own faith and its role and negotiation in a life at sea, and their needs with regard to faith and more general welfare support. In addition, we have explored the daily life and work of port chaplains, how they understand their roles and their importance, and how they, themselves, work in a multi-faith environment. In doing this, we have taken into account the perspectives of relevant stakeholders and the historical underpinnings of port chaplaincy and have considered how port chaplaincy compares with other forms of chaplaincy about which rather more has, hitherto, been known.

In this book, we present the results of our analysis, and in support of these, we draw heavily on verbatim quotes from fieldnotes, documents, and interview transcripts. The book is organised into three parts. Part I, focuses on port chaplains and port chaplaincy, Part II concentrates on the experiences and needs of seafarers, and Part III contextualizes the work of individual port chaplains by considering the role of the wider community in their work, ecumenical work practices, and other forms chaplaincy.

In developing these themes, we move on from this introduction into Part I of the book and an account, in Chapter 1, of the historical development of some of the major faith-based charities that provide and support port chaplaincy in UK ports today. We focus on two organizations that have played a major role in delivering port chaplaincy services—the Stella Maris, which has also been known as Apostleship of the Sea (AoS),[5] and the Mission to Seafarers (MtS). Using archived documentation and secondary sources, we outline the ways in which

---

[5] Apostleship of the Sea changed its official name to Stella Maris in 2020.

Table 2 The nationalities and affiliations of interviewed seafarers

	Filipino	Chinese	Swedish	Norwegian	Latvian	American	Sri Lankan	Total
Atheist	0	3	0	1	1	1	0	6
Roman Catholic	37	0	0	0	0	0	0	37
Buddhist	0	1	0	0	0	0	1	2
Jesus is Lord	1	0	0	0	0	0	0	1
Iglesia Filipina	2	0	0	0	0	0	0	2
Lutheran	0	0	1	2	0	0	0	3
Baptist Church	2	0	0	0	0	0	0	2
Jehovah's Witness	0	0	0	0	0	0	1	1
Potter's House (Christian Pentecostal)	1	0	0	0	0	0	0	1
Total	43	4	1	3	1	1	2	55

Source: authors.

Table 3 Interviews with chaplains (beyond Porton and Riverside)

	Sex	Affiliation	Country
Chaplain 1	Female	Mission to Seafarers	UK
Chaplain 2	Male	Stella Maris	UK
Chaplain 3	Female	Stella Maris	UK
Chaplain 4	Male	Mission to Seafarers	UK
Chaplain 5	Male	Sailors Society	Myanmar
Chaplain 6	Male	Mission to Seafarers	Hong Kong
Chaplain 7	Female	Sailors' Society	Brazil
Chaplain 8	Male	Mission to Seafarers	Australia
Chaplain 9	Female	Mission to Seafarers	Canada
Chaplain 10	Female	German Seamen's Mission	Germany

Source: authors.

Table 4 Interviews with stakeholders

	Sex	Affiliation	Country
Stakeholder 1	Female	Mission to Seafarers	Philippines
Stakeholder 2	Male	Scalabrini	Philippines
Stakeholder 3	Female	Stella Maris	Australia
Stakeholder 4	Male	NAMMA	Canada
Stakeholder 5	Female	Mission to Seafarers	UK
Stakeholder 6	Male	ISWAN	Philippines
Stakeholder 7	Female	MNWB	UK
Stakeholder 8	Male	Mission to Seafarers	Belgium
Stakeholder 9	Male	Stella Maris	UK
Stakeholder 10	Male	Stella Maris	UK
Stakeholder 11	Male	ITF	UK

Source: authors.

port chaplaincy services have been developed in the United Kingdom, the reasons for their development, and the transformation of provision over time. Chapter 2 presents a detailed account of the daily work of port chaplains, and the challenges they face in carrying it out. Drawing upon fieldnotes and the testimony of chaplains themselves (in the form of quotes from interview transcripts), we present a rich flavour of what it is that port chaplains do, how they do it, and the challenges they face in trying to do it. Chapter 3 continues the focus on chaplains themselves, and, using many verbatim quotes, it describes why port chaplains undertake what must often seem to be relatively thankless and frustrating work, what motivates and drives them to do it, and why they frequently become so passionate about it.

Part II of the book focuses on seafarers and their faith and welfare. The shipboard work and life of most seafarers is experienced as stressful and monotonous.

In this context, working in teams that do not share a first language or culture and are composed of members of different faiths and none can be extremely challenging. Bearing this in mind, Chapter 4 draws on shipboard observations and seafarers' own accounts to describe how they frame and understand their own shipboard behaviours and how they navigate the tricky interactional terrain associated with working in strongly hierarchical, mixed-nationality and mixed-faith crews. In many cases, this involves suppressing religious expression and practice, to an extent, and, in some cases, suppressing moral codes and deviating from pious behaviours in order to conform and 'fit in'. The significance of faith is therefore obscured from 'public' view on board a vessel, yet for many seafarers, faith plays a vital role in helping them to endure the harsh characteristics of a life at sea and to process and cope with the fear that is regularly associated with what is widely understood to be a dangerous occupation (Zevallos et al. 2014). Chapter 5 outlines the significance of faith to seafarers on board, focusing not just on Christian-based faith but on spirituality of any kind. It describes how' many seafarers draw upon faith as a major source of psychological support while at sea but also how conflict between faith-based values and the occupational culture of a ship can cause disquiet. Beyond this, it describes the importance and significance of port chaplains and their services to serving seafarers.

In Part III, we focus on contextualizing port chaplaincy. We consider the relationship between port chaplains and port chaplaincy and the wider community. We examine the ways in which the charitable organizations supporting port chaplaincy have embraced ecumenism and ecumenical working practices and the consequences of this for the day-to-day work of port chaplaincy. Finally, we seek to locate port chaplaincy within the broader, well-established traditions of chaplaincy in the United Kingdom, focusing on commonalities and differences and how these play out in relation to the day-to-day work of port chaplains and the support they provide to seafarers.

Our final chapter reflects on the main findings presented in the book and establishes the contribution that it has made to an understanding of the life and work of port chaplains, the lives of seafarers, and to our understanding of broader issues relating to the provision and funding of chaplaincy services more generally. The chapter offers some recommendations for policymakers and charitable organizations in the field of maritime welfare and some suggestions for further research directed towards the academic community.

Chaplaincy and Seafarers: Faith at Work. Helen Sampson, Nelson Turgo, Wendy Cadge, and Sophie Gilliat-Ray, Oxford University Press. © Helen Sampson, Nelson Turgo, Wendy Cadge, and Sophie Gilliat-Ray 2024. DOI: 10.1093/9780198913290.003.0001

PART I

PORT CHAPLAINCY SERVICES AND THE WORK OF PORT CHAPLAINS

1
The Origins of British Port Chaplaincy

Introduction

A senior chaplain with the Anglican Mission to Seamen described his work in a 1948 report saying,

> The Royal Alfred Fund asked us to visit an aged seaman living near the Mission. He was very ill and it was arranged for him to go into the London Hospital, where he passed away soon after admission. We attended to the funeral formalities and his remains were covered with the flag of the 'Flying Angel' which he knew so well.

The report went on, 'A request of a different kind was from the Central Criminal Court asking us to retain a seamen's bag while the man was serving a 2-year sentence. However, we received a letter from the man's mother asking us to send the luggage to her and this was done' (MtS 1948).

Fifty years later, a Catholic chaplain with Apostleship of the Sea (AoS) began his report writing, 'Burmese crew on a Greek ship contacted me about their grievances on wages, safety in working conditions and allowance for winter clothing.' He continued,

> They did not want me to bring the local ITF [International Transport Workers' Federation] representative for fear of consequences. I went to discuss the situation with the ship's master. He produced a document of an agreement between their socialist government in Rangoon and the ship owners which agreed to the low wages. The master increased the winter clothing allowance but it was still not sufficient. I made an appeal in the parish for warm clothing. The seamen were very thankful.
>
> (AoS 1989)

These two chaplains, fifty years apart, along with other staff of Mission to Seamen (affiliated with the Anglican Communion and called Mission to Seafarers (MtS) after 2000) and Apostleship of the Sea (affiliated with the Roman Catholic Church) in the United Kingdom have long offered assistance to seafarers. On issues ranging from illness and hospitalization, legal difficulties, and problems with managers to the loneliness and isolation of working at sea, ship visitors and religious leaders from these and other groups have an important history of supporting seafarers passing through British ports from around the world.

Today, this welcome continues to be extended through seafarers' centres across the United Kingdom. For example, a member of our research team visited Riverside in 2019, and found that it offered billiards, a bar, a shop, and a cosy lounge with couches where seafarers can have a drink while playing the guitar or browsing on the free Wi-Fi. Ship visitors and two local organizations—one Anglican, the other Catholic—support the centre. 'I like spending time here. I feel freed from the demands of work', a Filipino seafarer told our researcher.

> Here I can slouch on the couch, even sleep if I want to, without fear of being told off by the staff. They respect us. You can leave your things with them. If you want coffee or tea, you can ask them to make one for you. They don't bother you. Alex, a staff member, will check up on you from time to time but that's fine. He offers you fruits and biscuits. I like the atmosphere here.

Many seafarers today, in centres like this, are unaware of the religious history that underpins chaplains' work. Another seafarer at Riverside explained:

> When I visit the centre, I go straight to the bar, buy drinks, find a nice place to sit down and use the internet. I think what I do is mostly done by many, if not all seafarers. We don't look for any chapel or think about going to the church. I have no idea why. So, when you told me that there is a chapel here, I was surprised. But it does not make any difference to me.
>
> (Riverside field notes)

In this taken-for-granted context, port chaplains dominate the provision of port-based welfare services in the United Kingdom. In order to better understand the work and motivations of today's contemporary port chaplains and the organizations that support them, it is worth considering how this situation has come about.

This chapter offers a short history of the support offered by religious organizations to seafarers in the United Kingdom. This support has taken place alongside the work of chaplains in the military, in prisons, and in health-care and other settings but was not described as chaplaincy per se until the twentieth century (C. Swift 2015). Chaplaincy has ranged from evangelism to welfare provision, and it has taken the form of religious services; provision of religious and secular reading materials; provision of lodging and transportation; provision of seafarers' centres and access to telephones, phone cards, and the internet; hospital visitation and more (Kahveci 2007). Here, we focus on the work of the Mission to Seafarers (renamed from Mission to Seamen in 2000) and the Stella Maris because of their status and history as two of the largest groups consistently serving seafarers in the

United Kingdom. In this chapter, we chart their transition from models premised on evangelism to a focus on welfare provision over time. Port welfare committees also support seafarers in ports, usually alongside religious groups and port chaplains (Ross 2012; Swift 2013). Nevertheless, today, the service of port chaplains— particularly their welfare support—remains much in demand. A 2017 survey of seafarers (MNWB 2017) found that just under half (49 per cent) hoped that their ship would be visited by a port chaplain or ship welfare visitor in the United Kingdom. They expected to have a few hours of leave and wanted to learn about shore-based facilities, visit a seafarers' centre, and use the internet (MNWB 2017). Today's port chaplains continue the long history of support that religious people and organizations in Britain have offered seafarers from the United Kingdom and around the world.

Background

Predominantly Christian as a group, port chaplains often date their work to the life of Jesus of Nazareth, whom they see as a fisherman who communed with people who worked on the sea. The institutional efforts of port chaplains—which, over time, have included Bethel Churches, Mariners' Churches, Seamen's Communions, Seafarers' Fellowships, Seafarers' Missions, and a range of social service efforts—typically date themselves to the Bethel Church Movement started in Methodist and Evangelical revivals in eighteenth-century England, including in the Royal Navy (Anson 1974; Kverndal 1986, 2008; Down 1989; Mooney 2000, 2019). In 1817, a flag combining a star, olive branch, dove, and the letters for *Beth-El* (Hebrew for 'House of God') was designed and flown on ships to indicate where lay-led worship and prayer meetings were held. Ship captains carried the flag (and these ideas) across the seas. Many seafarers' missions were established in the 1820s as leaders aimed to make floating 'Bethels' available around the globe to support Christians and bring more seafarers to believe in Christ (Chapman 1994).

In the nineteenth century, sea captains, described in the primary sources as 'Bethel Captains', led devotions at sea, facilitated shipboard meetings and gatherings in ports, and reached out to seafarers from other countries. Some captains drew on organizing work they had done in earlier years through bible societies (Kverndal 2008). This grassroots maritime evangelism movement gradually became institutionalized, as captains formed a range of associations for Christian support and fellowship under the Bethel flag and provided Christian witness to other seafarers. The British and Foreign Sailors' Society and the American Seamen's Friend Society, two of the earliest maritime mission groups, were committed to these efforts on Biblical-evangelical premises rather than according to specific denominational roots; the institutional organization of the work along Anglican, Catholic, and Lutheran lines became important in later years. In addition to the strong British and American origins of this work, Scandinavians—especially Norwegians—also played distinctive roles, as they created country-specific missions and had large numbers of vessels and seafarers on the seas (Chapman 1994).

Such efforts to support seafarers are emblematic of longstanding Christian efforts to go out to those ostensibly in need of faith who otherwise cannot access more traditional church communities. Dwight L. Moody, one of the most significant leaders in American evangelical history, for example, viewed this direction of activity as a necessary method of keeping the flame of religion alive: 'If people won't come to our churches, let us go for them in that way and keep the church awake [...] If people will not come to the churches, why not send others out after them, and why not have meetings outside?' (Moody 1877). Aiming to save seafarers from a long list of vices (historical sources focus heavily on prostitution, gambling, and abuse of alcohol), early Protestant reformers opened hostels or inns where seafarers lived when not at sea; offered social services, preaching, and opportunities for religious conversion in ports; and sent religious libraries with seafarers for their spiritual edification aboard. While most of this work focused on ships trading internationally, some was also designed to serve local fishing communities (Hovde 1994; Stam 2012; Knickerbocker 2014).

Over time, Christian evangelism towards seafarers shifted to include more and more social service provision and advocacy, including support for regulatory systems designed to support seafarers' welfare (Kverndal 2008). Many organizations were involved, including the groups that became Mission to Seafarers and the British and Foreign Sailors' Society in the United Kingdom; a significant number of other organizations appeared along the way, some of which have survived into the present. While they did not usually connect with chaplains working in other settings, the geographical arrangement of many ports meant that port chaplains often worked among industrial chaplains who also worked in engineering, steelmaking, and other heavy industries in the United Kingdom by the middle of the twentieth century (Johnston and McFarland 2010a, 2010b; McFarland and Johnston 2010). They remained largely Christian even as the demographic of those working at sea shifted to include many more from the global south, with a wider variety of religious backgrounds (Sampson 2013).

The work of port chaplains has always been fluid, changing in response to developments in maritime work and the rise of subsequent needs. Such developments included transitions first from sail to steam-powered ships and then to diesel-powered vessels in global shipping. The introduction of shipping containers in the 1960s also provoked major changes, as they resulted in smaller crews and a decrease in the amount of time ships needed to spend in port (Sampson and Wu 2003). As a result, the social isolation of seafarers increased significantly. Port chaplains in the United Kingdom and around the world responded by more frequently going on board vessels to serve seafarers, rather than waiting for seafarers to come to centres on land, many of which closed as they saw fewer seafarers making use of them. More ships started to operate under flags of convenience in the mid-twentieth century, working conditions changed, and port chaplaincy organizations increasingly advocated for the rights of seafarers.[1]

As globalized shipping became a more integral part of most countries' economies, groups in the United Kingdom more frequently worked with partners around the world. Such global ecumenical efforts were formalized, for instance, with the creation of the International Christian Maritime Association (ICMA), which developed out of an initial consultation in 1967 involving the International Council of Seamen's Agencies and the World Council of Churches. Paul Mooney writes that at a gathering in Rotterdam in 1969 which included more than 100 delegates from 52 Christian-based volunteer organizations, 'Those who came together in Rotterdam [...] felt a pervasive sense of God's providence at work among them. Their eyes were opened to their common calling, and they were moved to found a common organisation for working together and representing Christian maritime ministry in the shipping industry and the world' (Mooney 2019). Founded to foster 'collaboration and mutual aid amongst constituent bodies', the ICMA aimed to be the 'collective and respected voice of the association within the industry and outside of it; which can offer counsel and be heard within the councils of those bodies whose deliberations in any way affect or influence the lives and welfare of seafarers' (Kverndal 2008, p. 113). The ICMA currently has over twenty member organizations and has supported seafarers for more than fifty years (see Table 5). It has supported training for port chaplains, advocated for seafarers, built relationships with the International Labour Organization and other international bodies, and supported member organizations in their work for multi-faith and multinational seafarers around the globe (Mooney 2019).

The Mission to Seafarers

Much of the Anglican support for seafarers is provided by the Mission to Seamen/Seafarers and the British Sailors' Society. Prior to the founding of the Mission to Seamen, the Episcopal Floating Church Society (EFCS) was formed in London in 1825 as an Anglican mission for seafarers; in 1829, the *HMS Brazen* was stationed as a floating church off Rotherhithe in London. Subsequent efforts to provide support to seafarers included the introduction of a 'sailing church' and St Paul's Church for Seamen, which, in 1847, was consecrated and included a chaplain to serve former seafarers at the Destitute Sailors' Asylum and the Sailors'

---

[1] Registering a ship under a 'flag of convenience' describes the practice by which a ship's owner registers the ship in a different country. This practice almost always entails reduced operational costs due to less stringent legal requirements—including those pertaining to labour—in the 'convenience' country.

Table 5 Member organizations of the ICMA and country

Member organizations of the ICMA	Country
Association for Seafarers' Mission	Japan
Biblia Harbour Mission	South Africa
Christian Seaman's Organization	South Africa
Danske Somands-og Udlandskirker	Denmark
Deutsche Seemannsmission e.V.	Germany
Estonian Seamen's Mission	Estonia
Fishermen's Mission	United Kingdom
Indenlansk Somandsmission	Denmark
Indonesian Ministry to Seafarers/Wisma Pelaut Internasional	Indonesia
Korea International Maritime Mission (KIMM)	South Korea
LIFE International Seafarers Christian Missions	Romania
Liverpool Seafarers' Centre	United Kingdom
Mission to Seafarers	United Kingdom
Naval and Military Bible Society	United Kingdom
North American Maritime Ministry Association (NAMMA)	United States of America
Nederlandse Zeevarendencentrale	The Netherlands
Queen Victoria Seamen's Rest	United Kingdom
Sailors' Society	United Kingdom
Seemannsmission der Nordkirche	Germany
Seamen's Christian Friend Society	United Kingdom
Seamen's Church Institute (SCI) of New York and New Jersey	United States
Seamen's/Fishermen's Service Center (SCT)	Taiwan
Sjomannskirken/Norwegian Church Abroad	Norway
Stella Maris	Italy
Stichting Pastoraat Werkers Overzee	The Netherlands
Suomen Merimieskirkko	Finland

Source: authors.

Home located nearby (Kverndal 2008). Several years later, Rev. Dr John Ashley was vacationing near the Bristol Channel and offered to visit a group of sailing ships anchored off the coast. He was warmly received and continued this work, founding the Bristol Channel Mission in 1836. In 1856, this Mission joined several other Anglican Missions to form the Mission to Seamen.[2] The group employed salaried, shore-based chaplains as well as relying upon shipboard volunteers. It initially provided support on board vessels and later transitioned to more shore-based support (Chapman 1994).

The work of the Mission to Seafarers altered as shipping transitioned from sail to steam in the latter part of the nineteenth and early part of the twentieth century. The Mission to Seamen was operating in sixty-two locations in Britain in 1906 and twenty-four ports overseas. Like the British and Foreign Sailors' Society, it ministered to seafarers on sailing ships and steam cutters, conducted services

[2] See MtS, 'The History of the Mission to Seafarers', https://www.missiontoseafarers.org/about/history (accessed 23 January 2024).

on board, provided religious tracts as well as books and magazines, and offered advice. Bill Down, former General Secretary of the Mission to Seamen, describes the work as 'pastoral, evangelistic, and intensely practical' (Down 2014, p. 33). Seafarers increasingly needed places to stay while in port, and the Mission to Seamen opened centres that provided food, reading and games rooms, chapels, and, in some places, overnight accommodation. Other groups, like the Sailors' Home in London, also provided accommodation for seafarers between times at sea. By the start of the First World War, the Mission to Seamen had 150 chaplains and lay leaders worldwide as well as 80 honorary chaplains (Kverndal 2008).

Between the two world wars, the Mission to Seamen expanded its work. The British government, which had committed to accepting a recommendation of the International Labour Conference in 1936 on the Promotion of Seamen's Welfare in Ports, appointed a Seamen's Welfare Board in 1940. The Board found great need for improved shore amenities, recognizing both voluntary Christian-based efforts and the need for secular clubs. The Seamen's Welfare Board was later replaced by the Merchant Navy Welfare Board, which provided structure and funding for more professionalized efforts at providing services to seafarers (Kverndal 2008).

Reports from local chaplains in the 1940s describe how many ships were visited; how many men from the ships were visited in hospital; how many people attended religious services; how many beds, meals, New Testaments, books, games, and woollen comforts were distributed; and approximately how many people were served in total. Giving a flavour of the varied assistance offered to seafarers, a senior chaplain reported on his work, in May 1947, saying, 'twenty-five Russian seamen spent two nights at the Hostel [...] we arranged the funeral of a seaman who was found dead in a bomb crater [...] Padre Lloyd intervened on behalf of two West Africans who were in trouble on a ship and they were set at liberty' (MtS 1947). Other common tasks included informing families of the deaths of men at sea, offering services, and providing entertainment, especially at Christmas. On Christmas Day in London in 1949, a port chaplain wrote of their Christmas celebrations that

> about 140 men were present at the dinner which was an excellent meal, and the staff are to be congratulated on all they did to make the day a happy one for the seamen staying in the Hostel. The Carol Service was attended by a good number of men. Each man residing in the Hostel was given a pair of socks and a packet of cigarettes.
>
> (MtS 1949)

Many of the basic services provided by port chaplains continued and were enhanced throughout the 1950s, as described in detailed monthly reports from local chaplains. In Tilbury, social events—mostly dances—were popular with seamen, and a new television was placed in a newly refurbished lounge. Chaplains made regular visits to seafarers in the hospital, with support from translators as needed. They helped to support mariners in getting news to their families and finding places to stay once discharged. A chaplain in Tilbury in 1958 saw sea-farers in the hospital from New Zealand, China, and Greece. Providing a sense of the nature of his work, he described how, on one occasion,

> a Greek who was very ill had got out of bed and demanded his clothes so I had another chase around for my Greek interpreter. Taking him back to the hospital we did our best to make the man stay in hospital and have the operation which would put his troubles right, but he would have none of it and said he would go whatever happened.
>
> (MtS 1958)

Port chaplains also regularly dealt with death and frequently took responsibility for breaking bad news to relatives when seafarers died. In 1954, a port chaplain in Tilbury described a seafarer who had experienced an 'epileptic fit and died'. The company asked the chaplain to deliver the news to the seafarer's wife; the chaplain wrote,

> As added tragedy was the fact that they had been married ten years and lived with in-laws, and then during the voyage their turn had come for a house and the wife was busy preparing it for her husband to come to. I have had very many of these cases in my time but this one shook me badly.
>
> (MtS 1954)

In 1959, a seafarer at the Mission in Tilbury stood up from watching television, collapsed, and died: 'we saw to all his affairs and arranged for his cremation a few days later', the chaplain reported. They also arranged for the burial at sea of other former seamen who died during the decade and helped to facilitate memorials for seamen whose loved ones had died while the seamen were at sea. In notes from 1960, a report is made of how, 'One of the men received the sad news that his mother had died, and I was able to arrange a memorial service that evening in the parish church. This service was conducted by the Vicar [sic.]' (MtS 1960).

Missions continued to hold regular religious services, especially on Christian holidays. Services at Easter and Christmas in Tilbury were highlighted in reports from the 1950s, including support provided by local women that made these holidays special. At Easter in 1955, the 'Lady Wardens' surprised the men with a meal served at decorated tables, including 'gaily painted eggs, many of them painted by the men themselves' (MtS 1955). In 1957, about 125 seafarers (mostly African, according to the chaplain's reports) gathered on Good Friday in Tilbury, with fewer attending the Easter breakfast, Communion service, and Easter Monday evening gatherings.

With changes in the industry, the Mission to Seamen continued to adapt and change—what Bill Down (1989) calls 'resetting' in *On Course Together*—through the next decades. Automation, faster turnaround times, smaller crews, and other changes led the Mission to increase its focus on ship visiting, comprehensive care, collaborative work, and advocacy for seafarers when needed. The central office of the Mission to Seamen in London increased collaborative coordination between local sites in response to identified needs. The founding of the ICMA in 1969 also led to more global collaborations and expanded efforts by the Mission to Seamen in Australia, South Africa, the Middle East, and other world regions. The Mission to Seamen in London also set up a group in its London office to gather information directly from seafarers and offer advice on specific problems related to employment, poor treatment, and other industry challenges (Down 2014, pp. 58–59).

Reports from chaplains in the 1970s reflect both these changes and the continuities in provision that characterized the work of chaplains. They describe the number of seamen visiting centres, staying in centres, attending religious services, and being visited in the hospital as the mission continued to serve seafarers as whole persons. They show chaplains bridging cultural divides, like a chaplain in Avonmouth in 1975 describing how his wife helped two seafarers from Lagos use a bottle of shampoo they had purchased: 'We arranged a shampoo session for the next night [...] My wife did the shampoo successfully and I put them both under the hair dryer. They were both very grateful and went away convinced that the shampoo we sold really did work (MtS 1975).' Some centres closed, others opened, and many tried to provide more amenities such as means of communication, television, billiards, and a quiet room or chapel. While a few still offered overnight accommodation, longer-term lodging was phased out, reflecting changes in demand as a result of variations in industry practices. As one chaplain commented in a survey in 1976, 'It is the industry which writes the agenda for our work and so long as we remain adaptable to change and new opportunities as they occur [...] our ministry will remain valid in the context of seafaring life' (Down 2014, p. 87).

In the 1980s, the Mission to Seamen continued to offer support in the form of local facilities. Surveys found that seafarers looked forward to visiting centres; Bill Down wrote, in 1989, that 'Today's seafarers' centres are imaginatively laid out, attractively decorated, well equipped and furnished, and designed to be comfortable and easy to supervise' (Down 2014). The quick turnaround times of vessels and twenty-four-hour working of ports made it harder and harder for seafarers to use these facilities, however. As reflected in meeting minutes from the early 1990s,

The quick turn-around of vessels, lower manning levels, [and] the multiplicity of different nationalities and cultures amongst the crew of a single vessel created different tensions amongst seafarers than previously. At the same time many of the old problems remain, particularly those associated with the dangers of seafaring and the continued presence in the industry of a significant minority of

employers for whom safety and good working conditions and the well-being of
seafarers continues to be a low priority compared with profit making.

(MtS 1991)

Regardless of the shape of the work, the relationships between seafarers and
port chaplains have been, and remain, central to the work of the Mission. As a
port chaplain wrote in a 1999 report,

> Seafarers are like any other people. They suffer bereavements at home and among
> their companions on board ship. They worry about their children. Their marriages
> hit rocky times [...] They can be very lonely. They think about the meaning of life.
> They try to pray. They try to live good lives but often fall into temptation.
>
> (MtS 1999)

A colleague told this chaplain that he had never 'been used more as a priest than
in his ministry with Mission to Seafarers', in part because he meets people 'in a
relaxed setting' that 'often enables them to open up and to talk to the chaplains
about the deepest things in their lives' from which they both learn (MtS 1999).

In 2000, the Mission to Seamen changed its name to the Mission to Seafarers to
signal its commitment to all seafarers, women and men, from a range of religious
backgrounds in a range of countries around the globe. Records about this change
indicate that

> The President stressed that the change of name and logo was not a cosmetic
> change, it was a considered response to changing situations and changing needs:
> 'we all know that the Mission is for all seafarers, no matter who they are and
> where they come from, but we need to make sure that this is clearly recognized
> by everyone else,' that is to say by men or women joining the shipping industry,
> by the church, and by the supporters of the future.
>
> (MtS 2000)

This work—started in English in the United Kingdom and countries where the
British flag flew—expanded and contracted with the British Empire and now
includes people from a much broader range of racial, ethnic, linguistic, and religious backgrounds. The pastoral and practical orientation of chaplains continues
to be central to the Mission's work as they provide emergency and longer-term
support to seafarers.

Stella Maris (Apostleship of the Sea)

Catholic support for seafarers in the United Kingdom (and around the globe)
has been provided primarily by the group called Stella Maris (Latin for 'Star of

the Sea', a title applied by Catholics to Mary, the mother of Jesus, in devotional contexts related to the ocean), also known as the Apostleship of the Sea (AoS).[3] Like Anglican support, Catholic support for seafarers emerged in the late nineteenth century. Catholic orders, including the Brothers of St Vincent de Paul, the Jesuits, and the Augustinians of the Assumption, started Catholic centres and ship-visiting programmes in the 1890s. In 1894, the Augustinians founded the 'Société des Oeuvres de Mer' in France to bring medical, religious, and material support to seafarers, especially those working in deep-sea fisheries off Iceland, on the Newfoundland Banks, and around the Faroe Islands.[4] Paul Chapman reports that, in 1895, British Jesuits started a Seamen's Branch of the already existing Apostleship of Prayer, which enlisted thousands of seagoing members (Chapman 1994).

The impetus for the establishment of Apostleship of the Sea, according to Bill Down, came from the Benedictine community on the island of Caldey off the coast of Wales. The lives of the monks were closely linked to the sea, and they prayed daily for those at sea. In 1917, an Oblate Brother of the community, Brother Richard (Peter Anson) revised the list of Catholic churches offering services near ports and visited the Catholic Seamen's Home in London. He was concerned about the limited support available and wrote of his hope that local Catholic efforts would one day 'be joined up in one great Society of Catholic Mission to Seamen' (Down 2014).

After the First World War, Brother Richard helped to facilitate a meeting of Catholics who came together in Glasgow to start AoS. The group planned to visit ships in ports, distribute Catholic literature, provide recreation for Catholic seafarers, and keep Catholic seafarers in touch with the church. AoS was defined at the time as 'A society of Catholic men and women united together in prayer and work for the greater glory of God, and the spiritual welfare of seafarers throughout the world'. Leaders, including priests and laymen, aimed to be apostles to seafarers, bringing them the word of God.

Great Britain had one of the world's largest merchant fleets in the early twentieth century; a number of the fleet's sailors were Catholic. Catholic leaders were aware that little welfare provision was being provided for, or by, Catholics at the time. Between 1920 and 1932, the number of chaplains, places with sleeping accommodation, and committees for ship visiting organized through AoS expanded around the globe. A branch of AoS was formed in Hull in the early 1930s and rooms were set aside in a church near the port to provide refreshments and a place for seafarers to relax (AoS 1931–1942). AoS branches were started in other British ports by Catholic ship visitors who served Catholic seamen (AoS 1940–1960). Staff and volunteers connected to AoS served fishing, industrial, and

<hr />

[3] Apostleship of the Sea changed its official name to Stella Maris in 2020.
[4] See Stella Maris, 'Our History: 100 Years of Supporting Seafarers', https://www.stellamaris.org.uk/our-history (accessed 23 January 2024).

passenger ships, and priests sometimes offered Mass on board. Archival materials describe a range of efforts in the United Kingdom as well as in Europe organized by Ladies' Committees, Council Ship Visitors, Guilds of Our Lady of the Ships, Hostel Committees, and Samaritan Work.

By the end of the Second World War, AoS had eighty centres around the world and a Council in Rome under the authority of a department in the Church's organizational structure. Formal headquarters were established in Rome in 1952. In 1970, Pope Paul VI established the Pontifical Commission for the Pastoral Care of Migrant and Itinerant People to provide care for those away from home, including seafarers. AoS operated under its guidance until 2016, when Pope Francis reorganized the department into the Dicastery for Promoting Integral Human Development.[5]

The work of AoS expanded, contracted, and shifted in the second half of the twentieth century, like that of the Mission to Seafarers. Leadership in the United Kingdom in 1970 described efforts in the works by writing,

> Stella Maris, Bootle is the latest Apostleship of the Sea club in this country built at a cost of almost a quarter of a million pounds. Embodying all the know-how acquired over the years, it is the spiritual and temporal home of the world's seafarers arriving in the northern complex of Liverpool's docks. Also acquired last year in Liverpool was Gatenears Grange, a splendid property standing in more than four acres of grounds which is to be a home for retired seafarers who have, during their seafaring lives known no other home but the clubs of the Apostleship of the Sea.
>
> (AoS 1970)

Subsequent reports described the opening of additional residential and social clubs, some in collaboration with non-Catholic seafarer groups, as the shipping industry continued to change. A 1977 report from a port chaplain in Immingham stated,

> During the year, I celebrated Mass on 22 ships. In addition, many seamen from all over the world attended Mass here. Usually, I took them back to their ships afterwards and occasionally I fetched seamen who had difficulties in finding the place. I also visited the local hospitals where seamen are detained.
>
> (AoS 1977)

---

[5] See 'Apostolic Letter Issued Motu Proprio by the Supreme Pontiff Francis Instituting the Dicastery for Promoting Integral Human Development', https://www.vatican.va/content/francesco/en/motu_proprio/documents/papa-francesco-motu-proprio_20160817_humanam-progressionem.html (accessed 23 January 2024).

Shipboard visitors, some local parishes, and schools, also supported the work of AoS with donations to seafarers, especially around holidays (Montemaggi et al. 2018).

By the 1980s and 1990s, the number of British seafarers had decreased, the number of seafarers from the developing world had increased, and ships operating under flags of convenience were common. Financial pressure and short turnaround times for ships led more AoS centres to close, even as port chaplains argued that their work was more needed than ever. Reports from the late 1980s and 1990s show port chaplains adapting, and meeting seafarers where they were. Chaplains visited on board, brought needed items, and arranged for the celebration of Mass, especially at Christmas. They continued to support seafarers with personal difficulties. In a report from the early 1990s a Catholic chaplain wrote,

> I was called to comfort a Filipino seaman who had just heard that his father had died. He was greatly distressed because the captain would not allow him to return home for the funeral. I spoke to the captain, and he told me that he had a severe shortage of crew. The Filipino insisted on giving me a one hundred dollar note. I forwarded it to the family.
>
> (AoS 1991)

Collaboration among organizations for seafarers in the United Kingdom continued to increase as more residential facilities closed. International reports show AoS leaders considering ways to make Catholic worship more accessible to people from different backgrounds, speaking different languages.

Port Chaplaincy Today

Today, seafarers who are mostly from the global south, have little time in ports, spend long months away from their families, and at times struggle with their labour conditions (Cudahy 2006; Sampson 2013). Port chaplains remain largely Christian but serve a more ethnically, and religiously diverse, group of seafarers than at any time in the past. Individuals affiliated with the Mission to Seafarers work in 200 ports in more than 50 countries around the globe. In 2013, for example, Tim Tunley, a chaplain with Mission to Seafarers, described how he and colleagues visited crews in seventy-six ports in Scotland, offering hospitality to people of all nationalities, ranks, and beliefs (Brown 2013). In 2016, the Mission to Seafarers launched a corporate partnership portfolio to encourage the maritime industry to embrace corporate social responsibility. Lay people and priests with the AoS—some paid and some volunteers—continue to visit seafarers on board vessels in the United Kingdom as well as in ports around the globe. The ICMA remains an important collaborative group, helping organizations to join together in service provision.

Contemporary studies show how British port chaplains connect with seafarers to provide welfare services, facilitate access to phone cards and ways to communicate with home, welcome seafarers to centres, and more. These centres give seafarers the opportunity to meet and talk with others and occasionally to attend religious services, which also sometimes take place on board vessels. In a recent study, Catholic chaplains spoke about 'being like Jesus' by tending to the physical and emotional needs of seafarers. Their narratives show hospitality based on compassion, openness, and the acceptance of others (Kahveci 2007; Palmer and Murray 2016; Montemaggi 2018; Montemaggi et al. 2018). Chaplains continue to advocate for seafarers and work with the International Transport Workers' Federation (ITF), port welfare organizations, and local port authorities as needed (Swift 2011; Viljoen 2011).

The wide variety of seafarer needs and capacities to serve from centre to centre results in only vague agreement on what makes port chaplains successful and what success even means. In 2010, the ITF partnered with the ICMA on a report focused on twelve successful seafarers' centres around the world. They argued that love makes a centre successful, evident in friendship, personal touches, ship visiting, celebrations of birthdays and holidays with seafarers, offers of entertainment, and respect for the decisions seafarers make about whether and how to engage (La Grange and Homden 2010). In this, port chaplains participate in the broader sense of professional spiritual care today in all settings, putting seafarers' needs above all.

Chaplaincy and Seafarers: Faith at Work. Helen Sampson, Nelson Turgo, Wendy Cadge, and Sophie Gilliat-Ray, Oxford University Press. © Helen Sampson, Nelson Turgo, Wendy Cadge, and Sophie Gilliat-Ray 2024.
DOI: 10.1093/9780198913290.003.0002

2
The Work of Contemporary Port Chaplains

Introduction

The charity and voluntary sectors have never been more important in people's lives (Lambie-Mumford 2015; McKay and Lindberg 2019). From global behemoths like Oxfam, Amnesty International, and Greenpeace to more geographically bounded organizations serving the needs of very specific groups and localities, their work has a significant impact at both global and national levels, promoting and leading humanitarian causes in many parts of the world (Eyeman and Jamison 1989; Bardarova et al. 2013). In the context of the growth of neoliberalism and the associated shrinking of the welfare state, these organizations have either supplemented or taken over some key responsibilities previously assumed by government agencies, from food distribution and racial justice to the protection of the environment. Many charity and voluntary-sector entities have a global profile. However, some organizations, and the people who work in them, have been less well-understood, despite their work being known amongst the people that they serve. This is generally the case for those organizations that work with seafarers. They are readily recognized by the world's 1.9 million serving seafarers across the globe but may be unheard of by members of their local communities.

When it comes to port welfare services, the human faces of this sector are port chaplains. They are the most common providers of welfare services to seafarers, from shipboard visits to the management of seafarer centres.[1] In this chapter, we will look at the welfare services that port chaplains provide; the challenges that accompany the work that they do in ports, including the financial constraints they face; and the emotional labour that is involved in their work with seafarers. We will also look at the challenges faced by port chaplains in their pursuit of sustained welfare work with seafarers and those associated with working alongside port chaplains from different organizations.

---

[1] It is worth noting that they are largely invisible to personnel working ashore and are almost exclusively known by seafarers and ex-seafarers as their focus is on ship visiting and providing support to seafarers' centres.

The Services That Port Chaplains Provide

The welfare work that port chaplains undertake with seafarers is often referred to as a ministry of presence (Zuidema and Walker 2020). The concept of a ministry of presence is not unique to port chaplaincy, and it has often been attributed to chaplaincy in different settings, including schools, the military, hospitals, and prisons (Avery 1986; Holm 2009; Otis 2009; Sullivan 2014). Among port chaplains, however, the concept of a ministry of presence gains particular traction given the nature of their work and the social isolation of seafarers working at sea. As seafarers' contact with people ashore is limited (a situation that was exacerbated by the COVID-19 pandemic and the associated denial of shore leave), ship visits by port chaplains have become even more valued and appreciated, even though contact may be fleeting and relatively impersonal. In the course of our research, port chaplains understood this and would often highlight the importance of providing a ministry of presence, explaining that this was a form of welfare service in itself.

During shipboard visits, we witnessed some port chaplains spending a considerable amount of time talking with seafarers over coffee and shared meals. Conversations covered a variety of topics, from problems encountered in the last port of call to family issues and other more personal matters shared by some seafarers. During these encounters, port chaplains patiently listened to the stories that seafarers told them, only offering observations and encouragement to continue, from time to time. They allowed seafarers to talk freely and gave them the space and time to raise whatever subjects they wished. The port chaplains we interviewed believed that such encounters were important in breaking the isolation and monotony experienced by many seafarers on board. One port chaplain explained,

> The biggest part is that you showed up, like if nobody comes to visit a ship then seafarers are even more isolated, even more lonely but even if I come on the ship and I don't have what I feel is any sort of meaningful conversation and I feel totally unwelcome then I leave the ship feeling like that's a bad ship visit. So, I think it's even worth it that I showed up you know and that's the way you have to look at it because it's not every visit that you have where someone's going to cry and tell you about their life story or you're going to see pictures of this new baby, you're not always going to have a great story every single time. So, every single ship visit is equally important to the crew just so that even they know that someone is thinking of them, it's someone's job to take care of them.
>
> (Chaplain from the United Kingdom)

A more detailed account of their ministry of presence was shared by another chaplain in a different port. He talked about an occasion when a seafarer had just ended his contract and was waiting to be picked up by the agent at the seafarers' centre for his flight back to China. The port chaplain kept him company while he was at the seafarers' centre, making sure that he was well looked after. This is how the encounter was described by the port chaplain concerned:

> So, I was just gonna hang with him at the Mission. I didn't want him to be alone. So, I got there and he was sleeping, but I brought food for him. So after about an hour, two hours, working away in my office. And he woke up and sort of wandering around because the lights were on. He said, 'What's going on?' I told him I had food for him. So, we sat and had dinner together. And he's taking pictures out with his iPad, and he's taking pictures of me, and he's sending them home to his mother. And I said, 'So what are you gonna do when you go home?' I said, 'Are you gonna take more courses?' 'Oh no, I'm done with the sea. So I'm gonna open a restaurant, I've saved all my money.' And he and a buddy were opening a restaurant. And I said, 'What are you gonna open?' 'We're gonna open a noodle house. In China.' I said, 'really?' He said, 'Yeah, but where we're from, all they eat is rice. We're making noodles.' So I said, 'Okay. You know what you're doing.' So, he was a happy guy. But he was really excited that he had somebody there to talk to and share his food with and hear stories about his family. [...] They get to talk to somebody who treats them like a human being. That's where their appreciation comes in. I appreciate the opportunity.
>
> (Chaplain from Canada)

However, despite its centrality, the welfare services that port chaplains provide to seafarers go beyond a ministry of presence. The presence of port chaplains on board in recent years has also become synonymous with the provision of local SIM cards and internet data to seafarers. The importance of SIM cards to seafarers arises because even though more ships today have some kind of internet access, a significant proportion do not, and even those that do, may offer a poorservice, which does not support video chats or stable connectivity (Sampson et al. 2018). With the growth in internet services, today's seafarers generally maintain contact with family members using the internet. The provision of SIM cards in ports is therefore very popular. In recent years, the use of free portable wi-fi devices has also been made available in some select UK ports. In Porton and Riverside, for example, we were told that portable wi-fi devices had been lent to ships on extended stays in the port.

Our research also revealed that after the provision of SIM cards, free transport was the most popular form of welfare assistance provided by port chaplains. Free transport is frequently provided by seafarers' centres to assist seafarers in accessing them. However, in Porton and Riverside, free transport was also made available to seafarers who wished to visit the town or city centre, to undertake some shopping, or to visit famous tourist attractions. Where seafarers are on vessels that cannot berth, chaplains will often find a means of visiting ships. In one case in the United Kingdom, a chaplain visited ships that were laid up in the River Fal and crewed with skeleton crews who were confined to their vessels anchored in the midst of the river. In order to do this, he made an arrangement with the seafarers on board one very old vessel, which had been laid up for a long time and which had a small tender that the seafarers were permitted to use, from time to time. When he wanted to visit this vessel and the others that were anchored nearby, the chaplain would ring the seafarers on board the old ship and arrange to be picked up and ferried about from ship to ship to make his calls. In Hong Kong, this approach has been taken even further. Seafarers on ships that are at anchor for significant spells are unable to get ashore. This has led the local mission to run their own launch to get from ship to ship. The chaplain explained,

> We have our own boat, our launch. That is going out six days a week from Monday to Saturday, not Sundays or public holidays. That one, normally we go out in the morning. Also we take turns to go out there as well, on our boat, to visit ships that are in anchorage, or in a dry dock.
>
> (Chaplain from Hong Kong)

Organizing religious services on board or making arrangements for seafarers to visit places of worship ashore are also services that are performed by port chaplains. In Porton and Riverside, there were dedicated spaces for religious observance within the seafarers' centres, although they were not well-used. In addition, seafarers calling at either area were given assistance by port chaplains and volunteers if they wished to attend religious services in nearby churches/houses of worship. On special occasions like Christmas, the port chaplains we interviewed also organized activities such as gift-giving to seafarers as part of their welfare activities. A member of the research team experienced this himself when the ship he was on called at a port in New Zealand. To his surprise, he and the seafarers on board were provided with gifts of candies, chocolates, and toys (presumably intended for seafarers' children) by the port chaplain. In one port, during Lent, shipboard visits were also organized by the port chaplain, together with the local vicar, to administer the anointment of holy ash to Christian seafarers. However, port chaplains don't just offer services to Christian seafarers; they also help seafarers with other religious beliefs to find suitable places for worship or the performance of their religious obligations. As one chaplain explained,

We'll call an Imam or whoever they spiritually need. We'll put them in touch with them. [...] That's not an issue. In actual fact between [organization] world-wide our port chaplains...we do have port chaplains of Muslim, Buddhist and other religious backgrounds as well. So, our Port Chaplains are not necessarily all Christians or ordained Pastors. We have people from all other faiths and religions on board our team.

(Chaplain from Hong Kong)

One of the things that stood out in our fieldwork was the extensive use of the services of chaplains in the procurement of merchandise. Prior to the COVID-19 pandemic, this was usually requested when seafarers were at the end of their contracts and were going home or, indeed, when such items were not readily available in the ports that they had visited. Popular requests for assistance with shopping were associated with the purchase of devices (like mobile phones) and items such as perfume. While requests were usually planned ahead of any potential visit by the port chaplain, in some cases, they could be made in response to a whim. For example, on one of the visits made by a Porton chaplain, the chief cook took a liking to the port chaplain's after shave/cologne and asked for the brand name. The port chaplain could not remember its name, so on the next visit, he brought a bottle of the one which he thought he had worn that day for the seafarer to smell. Field notes of the interaction that followed indicated that

From the rucksack, [name] took out an almost empty bottle. [...] The chief cook had to smell and confirm whether it was really the scent that he liked. The chief cook was delighted to confirm that it was the one that he wanted. He asked for the price. [Name] checked it on his phone. If the price would not be that steep, the seafarer said, he was planning to ask the port chaplain to buy one for him and deliver it to the ship next week.

(Porton field notes)

Similar accounts in relation to helping with merchandise were also shared by other port chaplains who we interviewed. Sometimes, chaplains take pleasure in locating more unusual items for seafarers who simply don't have time to find the specialist retailer they require. At a port in Brazil, for example, one chaplain described how they helped one crew member find a guitar for use on board. More prosaically, they were frequently asked to buy bars of chocolate or groceries, particularly in cases where ships' chandlers were not appointed by the ship operator, and crew could not leave the ship to restock their food provisions.[2] In our fieldwork, therefore, we observed how, on many occasions, port chaplains could be

---

[2] This is most common on smaller coastal vessels and would be unusual in the international, 'deep-sea' cargo fleet.

found conducting shipboard visits with boxes of goods for the seafarers onboard. While some of these goods were purchased at the personal request of seafarers whose vessels regularly called at the port concerned, and who had met the port chaplains in person, others had been ordered online by seafarers who had arranged for the delivery to be made to the seafarers' centre. Seafarers would then notify the centre of their purchases, and port chaplains, in turn, would deliver them during their ship visits.

Serving seafarers usually have the option[3] of having the bulk of their wages paid into nominated bank accounts ashore and a portion of their wages taken as cash on board. When additional funds are required by families, or in the event that a seafarer has accumulated more funds than anticipated because he has been unable to go ashore, seafarers may use remittance services to send money home. Some seafarers' centres have therefore established remittance facilities on their premises, administered by centre staff. Riverside, for example, had facilities for money transfer, which were frequently used by Filipino seafarers. If they were unable to get ashore, some port chaplains would also facilitate such requests in the course of ship visits. On top of this, port chaplains may agree to post gifts to seafarers' family members. These combined practices cause some port chaplains to wryly refer to themselves as seafarers' personal shoppers and couriers; however, the services are rendered willingly and in the context of strong, trust-based relations.

Mutual trust was most apparent when large amounts of money were involved. For example, we observed seafarers entrusting chaplains with a considerable amount of money to send home on their behalf or for the purchase of goods to be collected on their next visit. No receipt was demanded by seafarers from port chaplains, but such informality also left some chaplains wary of rendering assistance. While some port chaplains were comfortable rendering financial/material assistance to seafarers, others were not, and these chaplains and volunteers would tell seafarers that they needed to visit the centre and undertake the transaction formally and in person.

Some ports serve vessels that are involved in what are termed 'liner' trades. In contrast to 'tramp' vessels, these liners have a regular schedule of port calls, which remains stable over many months so that, in the course of a nine-month contract, a seafarer might come to visit a port nine times. Chaplains are therefore afforded an opportunity to form stronger relationships with seafarers working on board liner vessels that regularly call at their ports. Such regular contact between port chaplains and seafarers often occasioned the provision or demand for more bespoke services. These opportunities to form firmer relationships were valued by chaplains, and in some cases, they went so far as to invite seafarers into their own

---

[3] This is compulsory for Filipino seafarers, who are required to remit 80 per cent of their basic wage to a nominated bank account in the Philippines.

homes. One port chaplain described an experience that she shared with a regular visitor to her port as follows:

> My colleague took them from the port and took them to my house; picked them up, took to my city, and we had lunch together. I knew them already, and they were there for the weekend because sometimes they depart before the weekend and then I ask if captain if he would like to have a meal with my family and he said yeah that would be great!

It is estimated that not more than 2.5 per cent of the global supply of seafarers are women, and the majority of them work on cruise and passenger ships. A minority work on merchant vessels, and the majority of them are officers (BIMCO 2021). Women seafarers often meet particular challenges on board cargo vessels, where, even in the twenty-first century, their needs are poorly catered for (Belcher et al. 2003, Sampson 2024). When women seafarers met with women port chaplains, a special connection was frequently forged as they felt able to ask for assistance with gendered services and goods in a way that they did not feel able to do when male chaplains visited their vessels. One woman chaplain recounted an unusual experience when she found several women seafarers on board a vessel that she visited. She said,

> I was on one ship [...] where three of the five senior officers were women. I've only ever [previously] met, like cooks and cleaners. But there were quite a few women officers in [name of port], last summer in particular, and they were so thrilled there were women chaplains to give them some help. Oh, they were overjoyed. A hairdresser, for crying out loud. 'Gotta go to the hairdresser. Can you help me with the hairdresser' ... 'Yeah, we can help you with the hairdresser.' So stuff like that which was just so sweet.
>
> (Chaplain from Canada)

On top of such everyday services, port chaplains also play an important role in assisting seafarers who face serious difficulties on board, including bullying, physical violence, dangerous working conditions, and delayed salary payments. In the constrained environment of a ship, where seafarers are not free to disembark (Markkula 2021; Sampson 2022), they may feel they have very few pathways to access help. Sometimes, as a vessel approaches a port, a seafarer might take the opportunity of a moment alone with a ship's pilot[4] (accompanying him or her to or from the bridge, for example) to ask them to ask a port chaplain to visit

---

[4] A ship's pilot is generally a port-based, specially qualified captain who is hired by ship operators to board a vessel and provide expert knowledge of tides, currents, underwater terrain, and weather to the crew to facilitate the safe arrival and berthing of the vessel.

the ship while it is in port. On other occasions, chaplains who have become aware of a problem on board may seek to directly intervene and may ask a colleague based in the next port to visit the vessel concerned to see how things are for the seafarers. In such cases, sensitive details are often shared by seafarers with port chaplains in the belief that they are on the side of seafarers and will help them in dire straits. While not all interventions were successful, and chaplains had to take care not to alienate ship operators or exacerbate problematic situations, our research revealed occasions where chaplains had played a positive role in resolving seafarers' shipboard concerns. In one such case, a port chaplain had helped a seafarer get home for Christmas. The chaplain explained:

> So…we get this email from this guy saying, 'Can you please help me? My contract extension is up, and they just told me they're not gonna let me go home for Christmas. I just want to go home.' In his fifties, Filipino, retired. He'd done all he's supposed to do, but now they just told him arbitrarily he can't go home because he's a fitter. And fitters are few and far between, so they wanted him to stay. And they weren't listening to him. So he sends an email and says, 'Can you please help me? You know me, you brought chocolates on our ship.' So that was the identifier, we brought him chocolates. So, we got in touch with him and he sent us pictures of his contract. And his contract information extension information, which I forwarded to a colleague, [name]. And [name] just—in a week—he got a hold of everybody, magically, the president of the company—and said, 'You let this guy go home. He's done his stuff. You're telling me you can't find a fitter? No. You just don't wanna look for a fitter. And you need to do that. Now!' And so when he got to [place], the Chief came in and said, 'You're going home.'
>
> (Chaplain from Canada)

In these myriad ways the welfare services that port chaplains provide to seafarers range from the seemingly ordinary and everyday acts of providing a listening ear to solving complex issues related to employment and living conditions on board. In the context of the modern shipping industry, the work that port chaplains do has become integral to the well-being of seafarers, and, at this time especially, in the aftermath of the COVID-19 pandemic, their welfare work in ports has never been more important or more appreciated by seafarers.

Emotional Labour in the Delivery of Port Welfare Services

Port welfare services may be provided free of charge, but they do, of course, carry a cost. Not only does the provision of such labour require an infrastructure with financial costs, but it also takes an emotional toll on chaplains. Emotional labour has generally become increasingly important in the constitution of work in modern society (Hochschild [1983] 2012). The concept of emotional labour refers to the ability of workers to induce or suppress feeling in order to sustain the outward countenance that produces the proper state of mind in others (Hochschild [1983] 2012, cited in Butler and Russell 2018, p. 1670). In recent years, the idea of emotional labour has come to frame our understanding of contemporary work in various settings (Walsh and Bartikowski 2013; Mauno et al. 2016; Butler and Russell 2018; Kim et al. 2018; Turgo and Sampson 2021). The management of emotions has become part and parcel of the work effort involved in the delivery of services, especially in environments that demand regular social interaction. This is certainly the case with port chaplains, who deal with the needs of seafarers from different parts of the world on a daily basis, as well as managing relationships with a variety of others such as funders, volunteers, and parishioners.

Port chaplains interact with seafarers in seafarers' centres and on board during their ship visits. They place themselves at the service of seafarers, willingly act on their requests, answer their questions, and listen to their stories. Such interactions are almost always constrained by differences in first language. UK-based chaplains are most frequently English-as-a-first-language speakers interacting with seafarers for whom English is a second language. In non-UK ports, chaplains and seafarers may interact in English (which is the international language of the sea) when it is not the first language for either party. This places an additional strain on chaplains, who seek to be understanding and to be understood while communicating across language barriers. During one of our ship visits, we took note of how this can play out in everyday encounters between chaplains and seafarers. A field note recorded how

> Our third ship was a Russian vessel, full crew. It took the officer on duty some time to come to us. He was on the deck keeping an eye on the operations. When he came over to us, he looked puzzled and asked who we were. 'We're from the mission', the chaplain said in his usual upbeat manner. The man was unmoved. He did not share the chaplain's enthusiasm. The chaplain ran through his usual repertoire of questions. However, 'Okay' was the only answer he was given to all his questions. I thought it was very awkward as a 'bystander' looking on as the chaplain did his best to connect with the guy. We were not invited to come in. There was difficulty in the language.
>
> (Porton field notes)

Language difficulties are inevitably exacerbated by cultural differences, which, at times, proved to be a hurdle in relation to happy interactions. One port chaplain elaborated on his difficulties as follows:

> Then I think like the culture barrier and language barrier that ship visitors face is a big, like not a problem but something to really consider, especially like

Eastern Europeans and Chinese. I find they have a really difficult time understanding what you're saying and the Eastern Europeans are really suspicious.
Like I know I'm stereotyping a lot here but once you do hundreds of ship visits
that's kind of just what you face over and over again.

(Chaplain from the United Kingdom)

Our fieldwork in Porton and Riverside revealed that port chaplains habitually
faced this kind of challenge. However, many of them demonstrated resilience and
mental agility in handling situations which, at times, were extremely challenging.
While there was usually goodwill on both sides, exhibiting patience and equanimity at times of a breakdown of communication was draining for port chaplains seeking to avoid misunderstandings and upset. Emotional labour always
figured, therefore, in the work of port chaplains. One explained, for example, that

[It is] spiritually, physically exhausting because it is, because you're taking out of
yourself a practical, physical thing as well as an emotional one because you have
to keep going on board the next ship, 'Hello, how are you, what do you need,
blah-blah-blah' and that is tiring.

(Chaplain from the United Kingdom)

In accompanying chaplains making ship visits, we ourselves experienced taxing
emotional labour. We also witnessed the emotional labour demanded from port
chaplains when confronted with different scenarios during ship visits. For
example, the simple act of making an approach to a ship populated with strangers
can be emotionally challenging. This is particularly the case given that a ship is
both a place of work and a place of residence for seafarers. This was sometimes
made apparent in the way that the seafarers encountered by chaplains were
dressed. Seafarers who were working might be attired in boiler suits or officer
uniforms, but chaplains might also meet seafarers in the accommodation section
of their vessel wearing clothes resembling underwear, such as shorts and vests.
Inexperienced chaplains had to rapidly normalize such encounters, despite the
fact that they made them feel as though they were barging into the private spaces
of people's lives. As one port chaplain explained,

I see so many seafarers like wake up from homes, nap, they're all sleepy with
their hair sticking up and you know [laughter] but that was like a big factor to
get over just like that sort of I'm barging into their lives so what's the best
approach to that?

(Chaplain from the United Kingdom)

Inevitably, it is not just chaplains who sometimes feel as though, in rolling up to a
ship unannounced, they are intruding. In some cases, chaplains are not received

enthusiastically by seafarers. In shadowing chaplains, we witnessed at first hand how some visits could feel like a tremendous effort, in the face of encounters with grumpy and adversarial seafarers. One such example is recounted below:

> The port chaplain boarded the ship first. I followed him. [...] The duty officer looked at us with surprise. 'Who are you?', he asked us. 'We are from the mission', the chaplain said. 'We want to know if you need anything', he added. The guy shook his head, 'No mission, no', he said. I thought that when the chaplain said the word 'mission', the guy suddenly frowned and made a face. 'Why, we are here to know if you need anything', the chaplain asked. It felt very uncomfortable. The guy clearly did not like us to be on board. We were not welcome. 'No', the guy said, 'no need, no mission, leave', the guy said again. His face was not really angry, but he was smirking, his voice was taunting. 'Okay, no problem if you don't need us, maybe you want to get some woolly hats for yourself and the crew?' I opened the black bag. I thought that maybe the offer of woolly hats would change his mind. [...] When the guy had a look at what's inside, he shook his head again. He pointed to the gangway. 'No mission, no like, no like hats', referring to the woolly hats. Okay, the chaplain said, in his calm voice whilst I was already very upset.
>
> (Porton field notes)

In this kind of situation, the chaplains' emotional labour was manifested in the calm and cheerful demeanour they maintained throughout even the most awkward interactions. They showed no ill feelings towards anyone who denied them access on board; they were calm in the face of thinly disguised aggression; and we observed how, after a challenging interaction, they simply proceeded to the next ship with the same enthusiasm that they had showed in their last encounter. However, once back in their offices, 'backstage' as it were, some port chaplains expressed their disappointment with interactions that had not gone well. One described how

> I've had several times I go on board a ship [...] I'll go on board and I'll be like, 'Hey I'm from the seamen's club', like 'Is there anything I can do for you' and 'I've brought you top-ups and I've brought you information about the centre and I'll drive you if you want' and they're just like, 'No we don't need anything thank you'. So, it's just really crushing because sometimes it's like logistically it's difficult to get around the port and a lot of times security puts a lot of barriers in your way.
>
> (Chaplain from the United Kingdom)

Some of the port chaplains we interviewed in the research spoke of how, in some cases, they felt that they were not treated well or with due respect by some seafarers. Some seafarers' tone could be abrasive and brusque, demanding and expecting service rather than appreciatively accepting it. When this happened, port chaplains could find it disconcerting, and it sometimes led them to generate stereotypes, which inevitably constructed another emotional barrier to be overcome in the future. One said,

> Yeah, I think there's been some [nationality] crew in the past who kind of just expect you to do this for them. It's more in the way that, maybe it's a cultural thing, and it's just the way they speak to you about what they want you to do for them and giving them a discount for top-ups and things like that.
>
> (Chaplain from the United Kingdom)

This port chaplain also lamented the fact that there had also been occasions when they were not seen as people who came on board to provide help but as business-men, wanting to profit from seafarers. Such misconceptions had understandably provoked ill feelings:

> And you're just, I think they sometimes, it's a confusion then because they think you're a businessman. And it's like saying, 'Well no, I'm bringing these here because I know it's something you might need, but I'm not a businessman, I'm not making any money off this.' So yeah, that's happened a few times that, and it's just, it gets frustrating. Because you've having to explain yourself to a few people at the same time, it's not just one person.
>
> (Chaplain from the United Kingdom)

In cases when port chaplains felt let down by their negative experience with sea-farers, they tried to attribute it to a variety of causes, thereby rendering it more understandable and less personally offensive as a result. This also entailed the management of emotions as port chaplains attempted to rationalize their difficult encounters with seafarers and to imagine that, despite everything, their visit was worthwhile. One chaplain explained,

> but then you have to think like maybe the pamphlet that you left on board, one of the seafarers that's not there to greet you he sees that later and he has a big issue in his life or even he needs to go shopping because he's going home and he doesn't have any chocolate for his family. [...] You always have to consider like I don't see the results of the ministry that I do a lot of the time, which can be difficult, like when you're a parish priest or something you build relationships that are consist-ent and you can see the development and things like that. When you're a ship visitor, often you're very anonymous and you meet people once for five minutes and you never see them again in your life, like fortunately at [place] it's some-thing that I like is that we have ships that come back every week or even every day.
>
> (Chaplain from the United Kingdom)

As discussed earlier in the chapter, one of the major activities of chaplains when they visit a ship is to sell SIM cards at little or no profit. This provides seafarers with ready access to reasonably priced SIM cards from a source that they trust. On the face of it, this would appear to be a relatively simple transactional matter readily facilitated by chaplains. However, our port-based research, shadowing port chaplains, indicated that it was a little more taxing than might be expected. As described by a chaplain earlier, despite being keen to develop empathetic relations with seafarers, chaplains can find themselves cast as street vendors being hassled by seafarers keen to make a quick purchase and leave. The field notes from two separate visits give a sense of patience and tolerance exhibited by chaplains when performing a function that was ancillary, in some respects, to their core 'mission'. We noted:

> Soon other crew arrived inquiring about top-ups and SIM cards. They milled around [the port chaplain] and asked for help with SIM activation and loading top-ups. It would have been quite difficult for [port chaplain's name] if he had been there on his own as there were incessant questions and requests for help. Luckily, I was there to help him. For more than half an hour, we were busy helping the crew activate their new SIM cards.
>
> (Porton field notes)

> In a matter of minutes, we were inundated with seafarers wanting to buy top up vouchers. However, topping up required [name] and myself to help seafarers as doing it was oftentimes confusing to the uninitiated. Imagine ten to fifteen seafarers, coming down on you all at the same time, all wanting to be the first one to be served. Imagine all asking questions at the same time. So, on this ship, we had to politely tell the crew to wait, and since the signal in the ship's office was weak, we had to leave the room and find a place where the signal was strong so that we could do the top-up. Then once it was done, we would go back to the ship's office, transact with another seafarer, and then go back to the place where there was a strong signal and do the topping up again.
>
> (Porton field notes)

Dealing with the demands of such interactions was experienced as challenging by chaplains. Being surrounded by seafarers all wanting their phones to be loaded with internet credit at once could be both unnerving and infuriating, especially for the uninitiated. One chaplain put it like this:

> You can be surrounded by phones sometimes for the top-ups. There was, no idea what ship it was, but I just remember someone, he was the cook or the messman or something and he kept trying to shove his phone in front of me. And there was other people waiting, and it's like just wait a second, I'll get to you in a second. So it's more people trying to rush you and things like that.
>
> (Chaplain from UK)

Although such matters may seem relatively trivial, the regularity of their occurrence could be taxing for chaplains with regard to emotional labour and the maintenance of a patient welcoming front at all times. Occasionally, however, they came across situations that were even more disturbing and unsettling. These required chaplains to draw on their reserves of emotional labour and also made considerable demands on them in relation to emotion management. Issues related to physical violence inflicted upon seafarers by their fellow seafarers, deprivation of employment rights or lack of decent living conditions on board, and worse still, shipboard deaths. These were all encountered by port chaplains and had to be dealt with. At such times, chaplains described being sucked into a vortex of complex emotions generated as a result of empathy with individual seafarers, an understanding of broader issues and contexts that could be impacting on seafarers' experiences, and an awareness of their own limitations in relation to the capacity to help. One chaplain, for example, shared their experience of encountering seafarers who asked for help to be immediately repatriated back home because Ebola virus had been on the rise in their next port of destination, and they were understandably afraid of catching the disease. The chaplain recounted that

> They spoke to me and they were like, 'It's [the schedule] been changed to this [port], and we don't know what to do, we don't know what it's going to be like.' They were really scared for their lives. So it was the first time I had to contact ITF, and he [an ITF inspector] came on board, and it was right at the start of MLC [Maritime Labour Convention] as well. So he, because they didn't want to pay for their, there was a few of them that left the ship and went home, but they didn't want to pay for their flights and stuff. They were just scared for the safety of their lives really. And they managed to argue that, they got the company to pay and ITF said that it was, it was like because there was a risk to their lives, and you could argue with the MLC that it was for the company to, if there was substantial risk to their lives then they should repatriate them for free. And yeah, and they were really grateful, but there were some guys who had just arrived, and they were like, 'Well, we can't leave the ship now'; they'd only just got there and no money yet. So they had no choice. And the company said they were going to provide everything for them, like all the safety stuff and whatever they had to wear. But yeah, it didn't take away from, I remember because I went back there with the ITF guy and was in the mess room when all the crew were there. It was so, there was so many emotions in the room, I think because I was only just starting out I felt like I could have cried. I was just like, 'You're the one who's meant to be strong here, you keep it together.' But it was so, people were so emotional, so worried that they were going to go to [country in Africa].
>
> (Chaplain from the United Kingdom)

In such highly charged and emotive situations, port chaplains felt that they were expected to provide a sense of normality. They had to work at managing their emotions in order to appear calm and collected in the presence of seafarers. Some port chaplains reported that they had to completely suppress their emotions in the midst of such circumstances and engaged in the performance of surface acting (Hochschild [1983] 2012). However, their work was not finished once they left the ship or in the case of resolution. Once they were on their own, they continued to feel the effects of the sometimes traumatic interactions and to deal with their own emotions by themselves. Their experiences paradoxically highlight the dangers to the emotional well-being of people like port chaplains who are tasked to look after the well-being of others. A port chaplain described the impact of being taken into the confidence of a group of seafarers involved in a case of physical abuse. He explained how

I've only had it a couple of times. And you do, when you get off you think...'Phew, let's go and have a coffee.' And it's one of those things that when I had that physical abuse case...it's one of those things afterwards I just wanted to be left alone. I needed some time to process it for myself. Because people were processing the event for themselves through me. I then needed a bit of time to process what I had heard. You know, I had a very, very, very detailed conversation with this one particular officer who told me about the things he'd done in a previous life which...were horrific really. When I got off that ship (I'd been there four hours talking to him). I just needed time to process it, 'cause I'd been told all sorts. I didn't go back to the centre, didn't go back to the office, didn't go to any more ships. I took myself—in [place]—down to [place], to Starbucks...and I got a cup of coffee and I went for a walk. Because I just needed time to think about what I'd been told. Because if you just keep going, you...you need—you're caring for people, but you need to make sure you're caring for yourself.

(Chaplain from the United Kingdom)

As a repository for seafarers' problems, chaplains could find themselves unable to shake off their human emotional responses to the trauma of others. The accounts that seafarers gave them could leave a lasting impression on port chaplains, particularly in situations when they felt at a loss in terms of the assistance they could offer. One such occasion was described by a port chaplain as follows:

You do...well...maybe not disturbed sleep, but you're sitting there at night thinking about it. There are times when, you know, it's...I still remember it to this day. That he was a cadet on a container ship [...] in [place]. I said, 'So how are you doing, mate?' You know, signing in...'Oh, not very good.' I said, 'Why, what's up?' And at that point, the Officer came to collect me to take me and he said, 'Oh, I'll tell you later.' And I went in, did what I needed to do, and I came out, he was still on watch, I said, 'Right, come on then. I'm in no hurry, What's up?' And he was telling me how his girlfriend of goodness knows how many years had cheated on him. And the love of his life he'd lost and...and he was talking probably for half an hour, just standing on the gangway talking. And you know, I can remember it to this day, that story, really. And I think it was that...it does strike you. And I think it's almost...almost frustrating in one sense. No matter what I said, it wasn't going to make that situation any better for the guy. And I think it was...maybe he needed someone to listen. I think he did—he wanted to get some things off his chest. But I could sense almost in a sense...he wanted something. There wasn't a lot really I could give, because I couldn't change that situation for him, and it was a very unfair situation, and I felt for him because it could be any of us really, in that situation...you know, and...he was a lovely chap and you could tell he was very committed to his relationship, and now it had broken down.

(Chaplain from the United Kingdom)

There were comparatively few women chaplains involved in our study, and in this way, the demographic profile of port chaplains seems to echo the global demographics of seafarers. Just as women seafarers are known to face considerable challenges working in heavily male-dominated shipping industry, so too do female port chaplains. Like their male colleagues, they are presented with complex issues in relation to managing emotions when they undertake ship visits but, at times, they also face additional issues as a result of their gender. Women chaplains described how their presence as a chaplain could be denied or rudely snubbed and, in some cases, they were subjected to sexual violence. This lengthy quote gives us an insight into the emotional struggles that women port chaplains may grapple with:

[I]t comes with a load of disadvantages like I'm not as respected, I think, when I go on board a ship or like, for example, yesterday, when I went visiting with [name], they come and they shake his hand and they ask to see his ID and it's like I'm just ignored, you know. I'm not really seen as important enough to take my ID or shake my hand, I'm kind of like the one accompanying them, and I think this does come also with cultural differences because different cultures view women in different ways, and a lot of cultures don't think that women can be priest ministers or any sort of religious leader so that can be a challenge for me as well. It's easier because I'm not ordained so I'm not like you have to respect me. I'm a priest or whatever, and there's also instances like where seafarers are not so genuine with me because they only want to ask if I'm married, like, 'Oh ma'am are you married, are you single, do you have a boyfriend?' It's like, 'Dude, I'm not here to talk about that. Tell me what you're doing, how you are, right?'

So, there's always that initial like hurdle or barrier and there's been a few times when I don't feel safe on board the ship too, where I know I'm not necessarily in an environment where I'm going to be like thought of as a person and more thought of as an object. Like I did have one time I went on a [...] ship [...], there was like a lot of smoke in the air and it was really weird and then the chief cook came to me and he was like, 'Here, come in the galley with me' and he just pulled me in the galley and then he tried to touch me so I had to run away.

(Chaplain from the United Kingdom)

Thus, for both male and female chaplains, the task of providing welfare services to seafarers is physically and emotionally exhausting. From a physical point of view, chaplains move around large port areas most of the time, sometimes in adverse weather conditions (particularly during the winter season), with their heavy rucksacks loaded with items to be distributed or delivered to seafarers. They negotiate long jetties in oil terminals and struggle with unsteady gangways on their ship visits. These realities can be seen and observed plainly with the naked eye. However, emotional labour is another significant aspect of welfare services in ports, which is often under the radar of the general public but was observed by our research team and widely shared by port chaplains in the course of our research. These are stresses associated with the provision of welfare services in ports, which are mostly silently absorbed by port chaplains and yet are a dominant part of successful welfare work with seafarers.

Other Challenges Faced by Port Chaplains

The shipping industry has changed over the years, and the United Kingdom is not the maritime centre that it once was. Not only are there fewer successful British shipping companies than there were in the twentieth century, but they are also structurally different. Family-owned businesses, which frequently had a philanthropic edge, have largely been replaced by strongly profit- and dividend-driven shareholder companies (Sampson 2013). This has had consequences for the relationships between shipping managers and seafarers, and it has also impacted on the revenues of maritime-orientated charities such as Mission to Seafarers. These changes have created challenges for port chaplains associated with both a need to raise funds and a need to cut costs. This has changed the ways in which they work, requiring them to spend more time attempting to raise funds and also making changes to their daily activities. In today's financially challenging context, port chaplains may find themselves without a base from which to work, or they may be required to share office space and related facilities with other organizations. In some ports, chaplains effectively job-share with chaplains from other organizations and are required to find ways of working with them in sub-optimal circumstances.

The Challenges of Fund-Raising

Seafarers' centres all over the world face unprecedented challenges in relation to their finances. Many have seen traditional sources of income, such as those associated with legacies and grants from welfare charities, reduce or dry up altogether. This has had consequences for the delivery of welfare services to seafarers, and it has restricted the development and adaptation of services to new needs and a changing context. One chaplain provided a good example of this when describing the ways in which restricted resources were limiting the ways in which local service provision could adapt to changing circumstances and new needs. He told us,

> There are things I would like to do but I can't, and I think part of it, like everything, is down to finances. At the minute, I would like a third car for [place]. But the reason is, I have a car for the team on [place] and I would like a car for the team on the North side of the [place], which we're developing. But we can only have an effective Ministry if we have the resources. And I think sometimes getting the resources can be a struggle.
>
> (Chaplain from the United Kingdom)

In our interviews with port chaplains, the impact of financial difficulties on the delivery of services to seafarers was frequently highlighted, and we were told how even some basic services, such as providing free transportation from seafarers' ships to the seafarers' centre, had been affected:

> As I said, because of our time constraints and our limitation in our resources, sometimes we couldn't really respond to even very basic requirements like free shuttle service because of the time they come into the port, you know? We couldn't do anything more, or because our centre opens at this time every day and sometimes you can see a ship has just called in and they need a place to go and again, because of…these is our opening hours. Okay. Now we couldn't do anything. We would love to do more but, again, we are limited by our resources.
>
> (Chaplain from Hong Kong)

The uphill battle of securing finances to support the provision of welfare services to seafarers was exacerbated by the COVID-19 pandemic, when seafarers' centres had to temporarily close, and yet charities were badly needed by seafarers, who faced multiple problems on board. These included the denial of shore leave (Sampson and Acejo 2022), a lack of access to medical treatment, and the imposition of longer contracts (Devereux and Wadsworth 2021), which sometimes resulted in seafarers serving over twelve months on board.

In the trying time of COVID-19, many port chaplains were at the forefront of securing resources to fund their work with seafarers. Seafarers' centres were no longer able to make even small amounts of money from the sale of sundry goods, and with many churches closed, traditional fund-raising events, such as 'Sea Sunday', could not take place. There were special initiatives taken at an organizational level to raise funds to support seafarers, such as the Mission to Seafarers (MtS) 'Crew Welfare campaign', which raised funds from the shipping industry to support chaplains' work with seafarers, and chaplains themselves continued with their efforts to raise funds. Even prior to the pandemic, fund-raising was a weighty problem for port chaplains. Our research uncovered stories of chaplains juggling their busy schedule of ship visits in order to attend social events to raise funds for centres. Indeed, such was the scale of their fund-raising that many complained that they were unable to focus on their (proper) work with seafarers:

> Because, in the last couple of years, the fundraising has sucked up all the oxygen in my personal room. And that's really difficult. I don't get on ships as much as I used to. I need to do more training with my volunteers. And I'm trying to build relationships between the organizations and the people in the port, the port harbours, the harbour masters, the port authorities.
>
> (Chaplain from Canada)

Inevitably seafarers' centres differ in size and levels of financial support. Those with broad-based support, or with premises they can use to raise an income, lean less heavily on chaplains and volunteers for help in raising funds. Conversely, where centres are on shaky financial ground, staff have to be bold and creative in securing funds to allow them to meet the costs of the centre and, sometimes, to pay their own salaries. Some of the port chaplains that we interviewed discussed the great lengths that they had been to in order to secure funding for their work. They were conscious that the survival of their centres rested squarely on their shoulders, and they constantly tried to identify innovative ways of raising more funds. One described how

> I'm just a small centre, and my resources are limited, and I have to survive, so what do I do to make it? So maybe they have to pay for coffee, maybe they have to pay for phone card. And then, as a centre, you can go and negotiate with phonecard providers for example, you know. Or, wi-fi, free wi-fi, but you can have a contribution: 'Would you like to contribute?'. Like, a lot of those open-source projects, right, even Libre Office and other open source, it will say 'Would you like to donate $10?', and surprisingly, I just did a search online, so if you put out 'Please donate', even the *Telegraph* newspaper in the UK, you know, you can go online and read, you know, we need to keep going in order, 'Would you like to donate something to the Telegraph?' It is surprise that people really do donate the £5, £10, you know. So maybe, maybe the independent centres can say, 'Okay, if we try this, then can it work or?' Because the doors must be kept open, you know.
>
> (Chaplain from Australia)

He went on to describe how

> I took the initiative, [...] And I almost had to do it single-handedly, you know, from A to Z, you know. I have no support from my boss. Early morning, 8, 9 o'clock I start going up, knocking at doors, make phone calls, okay? On top of that, he still rosters me to work. So I would have worked 12–14 hours a day. He didn't give me time off, okay, still expect me to work. By the way, I went to sea. Knocked at doors and said, 'We are doing a fund-raising, we are doing an auction, live auction, would you like to donate some of your product for us for live auction?', you know. So I got this and that and [name] donated things and, you know. So we have put products up and, things... And then we got one agent, auctioneer from the, from selling the house. Real estate agent, auctioneer, he volunteered to be our auctioneer for the night. [...] And then I organized, we have dinners, you know, sit-in dinner. We have 150 people that night, okay? My wife was in [place] for the dinner [...] we sell tickets, raffles, and that night we raise more than $10,000, for that night, okay. And what happened was, I met this Aussie guy who designed, yeah, designed mobile phone. And he donated two mobile phones, brand new, and at that time, that kind of waterproofing that didn't really come out yet, so you can drop it in pool and come out. Donated two phones. Of course, very supportive of us!
>
> (Chaplain from Australia)

Fund-raising had become almost a norm for the majority of port chaplains that we interviewed during our research. Accounts like that of the port chaplain in Australia (cited above) highlight the extraordinary lengths to which many port chaplains go in order to make the delivery of services to seafarers a reality.

In some cases, port chaplains are faced with situations where they either raise more funds from donations to allow for their work to continue or they accept a pay cut and a reduction in paid hours (often without a corresponding reduction in hours worked). This led some to form the view that their roles had become more about fund-raising than the actual provision of welfare services to seafarers. This was not especially welcome, but it was recognized by most chaplains as an inevitable part of the financial landscape and something they simply had to accept. The observations of the following port chaplain illustrate the combination of pragmatism and despondency that was characteristic of the outlook of many port chaplains in the study:

> So, this year we all had to take a 50 per cent cut in pay. And that was incredibly difficult. For all of us. I'm being paid half-time but I'm certainly working well over my limit. And that's been really difficult because my job actually grew this year because of the third station. I've opened that, that's my baby, I put that whole thing together, got all the funding, found the trailer, moved the trailer,

painted the damn trailer. I mean it's just…I did everything in there. I spent hours on the floor on my belly picking dry paint off the vinyl tiles. Yeah, it's been really rough this year, it's been a really tough year for us. And I know it's rough for everybody. We've been around for a long time. At one point, we had a lot of money. We don't have that money any more. When I came on, it was like we were on the downslide. So, we are keeping our head above water. It's been incredibly difficult. We've worked, all of us, very very hard to make sure that happens. But we're literally taking it a few months at a time.

(Chaplain from Canada)

Thus, the challenges faced by port chaplains who were trying to keep their centres financially afloat were amongst the greatest trials that they described. Not only did this often represent a significant change to the context in which their work took place, but it also put a great deal of pressure on them above and beyond the emotional and physical stresses already entailed in their regular work.

Ecumenism and the Sharing of Resources

In response to the financial pressures faced by many charities and a reduction in footfall associated with broader changes in the industry (which mean that fewer seafarers come through the doors of seafarers' centres), there have been various measures taken by organizations providing port-based welfare to seafarers to increase efficiencies in service provision while decreasing costs. As part of this drive, there has been a move, in recent years, to consolidate the welfare work being performed by different organizations in ports under one roof or in a single seafarers' centre within a port. Such ecumenical work is in tune with the theological underpinnings of port chaplaincy and the ethos of the charitable organizations who provide it. Working together in one single seafarers' centre in a port was thought to rationalize the use of limited resources and complement the various services available to seafarers. However, while this seemed a natural extension of the theological foundations underpinning chaplaincy, we found that it was often challenging for the port chaplains working together on the ground. Their difficulties belied the strongly held belief that chaplains are willing to sacrifice themselves and their interests in the service of seafarers. Ecumenical working sometimes laid bare competition between chaplains, the limits to their selflessness, and their human frailties, which could result in resentments, metaphorical backstabbing, and blatant conflict.

In some cases, ecumenical working took the form of one organization assuming the running of a building that they might own or lease while other partners provided additional personnel in the form of drivers and volunteers. In some seafarers' centres shared by different organizations and faith traditions, resources such as service vehicles were also shared. In some ports like Porton, zones were created for each port chaplain to facilitate better coverage for the seafarers visiting the port and to avoid inefficient use of time in the duplication of ship visits. While this could augur well for some seafarers' centres and port chaplains, at least resource-wise, for others, it resulted in strained relationships.

The case of Porton provides a good example. At Porton, the seafarers' centre was shared by two different organizations, and informal expectations had grown up amongst them around certain operational protocols. These proved contentious at times and were a source of irritation for port chaplains, who found that their relationships with their opposite number came under strain. The situation also led to confusion arising amongst volunteers. Both port chaplains had volunteers to help them with their work (especially with paperwork, answering emails, and ship visits), and although they identified with one specific chaplain, volunteers could find themselves answering to both chaplains rather than just one. Some volunteers found such situations uncomfortable, and they could become fraught with ill feeling. A volunteer in Porton, for instance, reflected as follows on their experience:

> I think the relationship with [organization] here has deteriorated, it became about territory and power and I confided to [name] saying that it's making me feel uncomfortable, that I'm being asked all these questions. I have to make myself accountable to [organization], and I have to inform them when I'm going to be in the office.
>
> (Porton field notes)

What was supposed to be an ordinary and mundane act of coming to the seafarers' centre to do some work had become a stressful and complicated activity owing to divergent expectations and unclear rules set by the managing organizations. The same volunteer continued,

> [Name] agreed with me that I do not report to [other name]; I don't have to let [them] know anything. [Name] knows when I'm coming in the office, and the majority of the time, I try and meet up with [them] here, so that's not a problem. But there has been times when I've come in on my own, [name] knows I've been coming in, I always inform [them] when I'm leaving as well, so [they] know that I've left the building. But there are times that I've been in on my own and then [other name's] been prying, wondering what I'm doing. And it just…I was like, 'What's it got to do with [them]?' There's no need for [them] to be asking me this; [they are] not my boss but [they] treated me as if [they were], and I didn't appreciate that because I report to [name].
>
> (Porton field notes)

The port chaplains involved were not insulated from the difficulties experienced by their volunteers. As a result, the research team noted how tensions came to the fore from time to time, revealing the frayed edges of the relationships between port chaplains. When tensions surfaced, other issues that were sources of resentment were brought up, further complicating the shared port chaplaincy. We witnessed a certain amount of 'needling' between chaplains and a degree of impoliteness, which could be surprising given the degree to which they aspired to be 'good' and kind people. A field note captures Nelson's observations of an instance that took place in Porton:

> I chanced upon two other port chaplains serving in Porton. [...At the time] We [myself and a volunteer] were preparing for our shipboard visit. [Name of port chaplain] was carrying a chair, which he was planning to take to his other office. Out of the blue, one of the two chaplains that we had run into said in a joking tone: 'So, here you are, the port chaplain, another chair to sit on all day, and giving all the hard work of ship visiting and visiting the sick seafarer in the hospital to [name of volunteer].' I froze. I looked at [name of port chaplain]. He smiled and said, 'Yes'. The other two port chaplains walked past the door and vanished into the frigid temperature of the port.
>
> (Porton field notes)

Port chaplains who worked together and were from different faith traditions could also find that differences in theology fuelled misunderstandings. This issue also emerged at Porton when a seafarer was admitted to the hospital and was visited by [name of port chaplain]. The seafarer's denomination was different from the denomination of the port chaplain who paid him the visit. When the other port chaplain was appraised of this, they asked [name of port chaplain] if the seafarer wanted a service particular to his religious affiliation. The port chaplain who visited the sick seafarer did not like the intervention that was made, especially when the query was repeated. The incident added further stress to what was already a strained relationship between the two port chaplains.

In another example of the problems that could be caused by theological differences, a chaplain described his experience of working with a chaplain from a different maritime charity. On the surface, there appeared to be a simple difference in view about the selling of SIM cards to seafarers. However, this difference of view was rooted in theology. While one chaplain thought that selling SIM cards to seafarers was part of his chaplaincy work with seafarers, the other one considered that it should not be.

While differences in theological traditions (which we return to in Chapter 8) could sometimes underpin tensions between port chaplains, the act of sharing limited resources also proved to be a source of conflict. In Porton, for example, one of the chaplains noted, rather wryly, that they were the only ones paying for the maintenance of the facilities of the centre.[5] While this financial arrangement had been forged at the management level of their respective organizations, port chaplains could still feel that such a burden should be shared equally by organizations making use of the facilities of the centre. In the course of our research, we found this problem in other seafarer centres where space and resources were shared. A chaplain we interviewed explained their own experience as follows:

> So like in [place] we had like [maritime charity] was owning the centre but [maritime charity] chaplains were part of it as well and like when they didn't pay for I don't know, they didn't want to put in money for the rent, or they didn't want to put in money for the air conditioning, or whatever they said, 'Well, why should we? You guys own the centre.' So then [maritime charity] would say, 'Well, you guys use it, and you guys are doing your photocopying here', and you know, it just got into this small bicker, bicker, bicker things and it's like, 'Open your mind and think about the fact that we're all here to do the same ministry and the same job essentially', but that's human nature to get caught up in these small squabbles like this. So that, and that was really hard for me.
>
> (Chaplain from the United Kingdom)

Seafarers' centres face unprecedented challenges in managing their resources at a time when they also face mounting pressure to provide more welfare services to seafarers. One way to address this is to work alongside other maritime charities in order to conserve and rationalize the use of resources to better serve the needs of seafarers. However, while this arrangement helps in the attainment of such goals at an organizational level, at an interpersonal level, on the ground, it can create difficulties and challenges as chaplains try to deal with differences in theology and quirks in personality.

Conclusion

The charity and voluntary sector serving the welfare needs of seafarers continues to survive and adapt to developments in the maritime industry and to the needs of seafarers. Within organizations providing welfare services to seafarers, port chaplains serve as 'a kind of linked safety net that spans the globe' (Cadge and Skaggs 2019, p. 98) for seafarers coming from different countries. However, just

---

[5] There was an inference that this meant that they should be regarded as the 'lead' organization and the leader in the shared chaplaincy arrangements. This feeling was not shared by the partner chaplain, and we considered that the difference of view was likely to be at the root of many of the interpersonal tensions between the chaplains concerned.

like others in the welfare sector, maritime welfare charities are facing unprecedented challenges. They experience difficulties associated with the changing complex environment that they operate in. In some ports, the physical buildings that used to house the seafarers' centres, which were once a symbol of kindness to strangers (Turgo et al. 2023), have closed down, while others have made staff redundancies. Some centres only offer free wi-fi and tea and coffee facilities for seafarers, in contrast to the facilities that they used to offer, and that are still offered in a limited number of areas. Even these centres had sometimes become a drain on maritime charities' finances and were under threat of full closure.

The reasons for these challenges and issues are complex, and they are often beyond the control of organizations that maintain and run seafarers' centres. As ships have become bigger and more technologically advanced, logistics and operational processes in ports have become more complex and automated. Vessel turnaround time has increased rapidly, and as a result of these changes, seafarers spend less time ashore. This has had a substantial impact on the economic viability of seafarers' centres, many of which are now threatened with closure. In addition, donations in the form of legacies are dwindling, and grants from funding institutions have also become less available in recent years. All in all, seafarers' centres are becoming more precarious, notwithstanding the fact that (as we will show later) seafarers continue to place great value on them.

Amidst all these challenges, port chaplains continue to 'hold the fort' and constantly find ways to continue to preserve services to seafarers. Their work in ports is both physically and emotionally challenging, and the extra work of raising money for welfare services has made their work even more complex and difficult. In recent years, the need for ecumenism as a way to consolidate resources and foster cooperation between organizations working in the same port has opened up opportunities and, at the same time, presented challenges. Regardless of these factors, welfare services in ports continue to be provided. Port chaplains press on, strengthened by their belief in the cause of their work and the very reasons and motivations that initially brought them to provide welfare services to seafarers. They are not put off by the less welcome aspects of their 'new' roles but continue to be enthusiastically driven to serve the needs of seafarers, regardless of their background. This enthusiasm and motivation will be explored further in Chapter 3.

Chaplaincy and Seafarers: Faith at Work. Helen Sampson, Nelson Turgo, Wendy Cadge, and Sophie Gilliat-Ray, Oxford University Press. © Helen Sampson, Nelson Turgo, Wendy Cadge, and Sophie Gilliat-Ray 2024.
DOI: 10.1093/9780198913290.003.0003

3

The Motivations and Aspirations of Port Chaplains and Volunteers

Introduction

Several decades ago, a port call was associated with a buzz of excitement amongst seafarers, who could normally look forward to a chance to explore a new town, visit a bar or a restaurant, and walk without restriction. Today, port calls are often associated with stress (Sampson 2024). Ships turn around in port very rapidly. In 2017, the United Nations Conference on Trade and Development (UNCTAD) Maritime Review (UNCTAD 2017) reported on data originally collected by Marine Traffic. The data indicated that in 2016, container vessels were able to turnaround (i.e. enter a port, discharge and/or load cargo, and leave) within less than twenty-four hours. On average, Marine Traffic suggested that container vessels spent 0.87 days within port limits. This is a fall from the average 2.62 days that it took a decade earlier, in 2006. The fall represents something of an economic and environmental triumph as a rapid turnaround ensures that vessels optimize profits and minimize emissions (Poulsen and Sampson 2020). However, for seafarers, such efficiencies come at a price. In most cases, they create fatigue amongst crews, whose normal shift patterns are disrupted and whose hours of work increase in port, and they increasingly result in many seafarers being unable to go ashore (Sampson et al. 2018). This latter issue is something that has been exacerbated in the course of the COVID-19 pandemic.

In this context, for many voyage-weary seafarers, the visits of port chaplains and volunteers bearing goods and gifts is a welcome relief. After weeks and months at sea with the same 'crowd' talking about the 'same ole, same ole', the visit from a seamen's mission allows them to interact with people from outside their own circle, to break the monotony, and to splash out on some treats, such as SIM cards. These allow them to call home for uninterrupted conversations with loved ones, perhaps face-to-face by video call and with the exchange of images—photos of the kids at a sports competition or in their new school uniform and pictures of the last port. For seafarers who are struggling on board, the visit of a chaplain allows them the opportunity to reach out to someone who they can trust and perhaps find solutions to their problems. If they need to attend a religious service or have one on board, they can ask for assistance. All these welfare services provided by port chaplains, either in seafarers' centres or on board during their shipboard visits, have been well described in Chapter 1. We have seen how these welfare services—in their varying forms—address the needs of seafarers. Furthermore, we have described the emotional and financial costs of such provision and the kinds of challenges that port chaplains face in their day-to-day work. What we have yet to consider is why it is that such welfare services are provided by port chaplains and the organizations that employ them, at all.

Port chaplains' work with seafarers has been the subject of a select number of studies (Montemaggi 2018; Cadge and Skaggs 2019; Zuidema and Walker 2020), which have explored the history of chaplaincy and the changing contours of welfare services in ports. However, when compared to other forms of chaplaincy (Beckford 1999; Otis 2009; Cadge et al. 2011; Grimell 2020), port chaplaincy remains relatively unexplored. Very little is known about what motivates and inspires port chaplains to do what they do. There are various possible reasons for this. One of the most likely is that welfare provision to seafarers is often performed in remote locations and under strict security (Goulielmos and Anastasakos 2005; Mazaheri and Ekwall 2009; Grillot and Cruise 2010), with the result that the public is rarely given a glimpse of how it is conducted or why. In this chapter, we will look at some of the personal narratives of port chaplains and volunteers, and we will explore their reasons for their commitment to this particular field of work.

The Motivation to Work as a Port Chaplain or a Volunteer Seafarers' Welfare Worker

Port chaplains and volunteers often see their work as something of a vocation. The interviewees we included in the study came from a variety of backgrounds, although many shared a common interest in, or attraction to, the sea. The majority of the port chaplains we interviewed were ordained, and all were Christian. All of the chaplains were attached to, and were employed by, major maritime welfare organizations, which were, in turn, connected to recognized faith groups. Volunteers were mostly locals living close to the port that they served or were part of a church congregation to which a port chaplain was connected. The majority of volunteers were retired professionals, and many had a prior connection to the maritime industry. This was not invariably the case, however, and we also met young and employed volunteers and some who had never had any connection to seafaring whatsoever. Volunteers have become quite central to the operation of most seafarers' centres in the past decade or so. For financial reasons, many of the welfare services provided by seafarers' centres depend on the input of volunteers, who are entrusted with considerable responsibility. Our fieldwork in Porton and Riverside revealed that volunteers had recently taken on more responsibility for work such as shipboard visits and running bars, and our interviews with other chaplains confirmed that this was a fairly typical scenario in terms of seafarers' centres and their reliance on volunteers.[1] In this chapter, we will outline how both port chaplains and volunteers have come to work with seafarers' welfare, and we will explore their understandings of their role and the meaning of their work from their own personal perspectives.

Port Chaplains

Chaplains described various ways in which they came to be involved in the provision of seafarers' welfare services in preference to running their own parish or engaging with other kinds of chaplaincy. Some described how they had been brought to port chaplaincy by accident, while others had a more complex journey. In the course of our research, we were given accounts of some chaplains coming to chaplaincy in the later years of their lives. Working with seafarers was not an endeavour that they had imagined in the early years of their career; rather, it came to them fortuitously, after many years of doing pastoral work in their parish. One chaplain told us about various secular jobs undertaken prior to becoming a priest, doing parish work, and then in later years becoming a port chaplain:

> I left the parish and, through a series of serendipitous events, became attached to the Mission. I was doing odd jobs and bits and pieces and things and covering while my predecessor was away. He was travelling, so I stepped in. But there was a need for somebody because he had a chaplain who had been working for him, who was leaving, and then, um…he himself was gonna retire. So then I took over the position of Executive Director. He was the Chaplain, I was the Executive Director. And then he retired, and I became the Executive Director to the Mission to Seafarers.
>
> (Chaplain from Canada)

This chaplain was not alone in feeling that it was the unfolding of events in something of a random fashion that led them to become a port chaplain. A chaplain we interviewed from Australia told us that he had helped a pastor run a Christian rehabilitation centre in his youth. Over time, he had moved on to establish churches in different countries and had then become a port chaplain:

> I was very young when I sensed God's calling into the ministry, and my first full-time ministry was in 1980 when I was only nineteen years old. I ended up helping my church pastor, who runs a Christian rehab centre to end drugs dependency, for two years. […] So, I was with my pastor for one full year, after which I went to a school and […] since then I've been in the church planting

---

[1] The increased reliance on volunteers has occurred in the context of considerable financial challenges and can be seen as one response to these.

[start-up] ministry. [...] You know? Start a new church. [...] and then I moved on, then I moved on [again], you see, after a few years.

(Chaplain from Australia)

Another chaplain, in a different port, was mainly drawn to youth chaplaincy, and it was by a random act of faith that he progressed to working in a different chaplaincy altogether. He felt that his journey was also an interesting one and he told us:

Yeah really, so then after that I did youth ministry, which I've always said made me interested in chaplaincy as a whole. Because I used to see a lot of school chaplains coming into the retreat centre and things like that. So I started to think, 'Oh, I could be a school chaplain at some point.' And then I volunteered [in the port], or started to volunteer back in 2012 with Father [name]. And then after that, I was, well I was volunteering for a tiny bit before I moved to [place], and I was doing, I was a support worker, community support worker for an autism charity. And then, yeah, it was only when the [seafarer] centre got flooded, and they were really looking for, at first it was an extra pair of hands to get to the ships because they hadn't got, the seafarers didn't have anywhere to come. So, I was taking the wi-fi units back and forward a lot. That's when I started this work, or this side of chaplaincy, which I never really thought I would end up in after, like I say, I thought school chaplain would be where I was heading.

(Chaplain from the United Kingdom)

Our interviews also revealed stories of chaplains who first volunteered in seafarer centres before taking on the job as chaplains. In one port, another chaplain was a volunteer at the seafarers' centre for years before applying for the job of chaplain when it became vacant:

I came over here and I met our existing chaplain, and I did a bit of volunteering over here and then just carried on doing that, and then the chaplain who works, who worked here prior to me, left in 2007, and his job became vacant, so I applied for it.

(Chaplain from the United Kingdom)

For others who participated in our research, although port chaplaincy was not their specific goal, their educational background led them to it. This was the case for a port chaplain in Myanmar, who finished a degree in theology. Looking for a job after graduation, they were informed of a vacancy in port chaplaincy in their district. Their educational background landed them the job.

By way of contrast, we also talked to chaplains who said that they had their sights on chaplaincy in general even in the early years of their theological education. Chaplaincy had always attracted them, and when they found a chaplaincy opportunity in port, they went for it. For some chaplains, any form of chaplaincy would be pleasing to them, and it was happenstance that took them to chaplaincy work with seafarers. One chaplain, who had experienced this general calling to chaplaincy, liked port chaplaincy so much that he planned to return to it at the end of his religious education:

> [R]ight now I feel my calling is at very much a mission-focused vocation. So I can see myself coming back to chaplaincy, and I'd love to come back to the Mission. Um, if not, the other thing would maybe be naval chaplaincy with the Royal Navy. But the Mission is certainly attractive to me, and so much so that as I'm going through the sermon process for ordination now, or ordination training—we're looking at maybe part time training, which would allow me to stay with the Mission and train at the same time.
>
> (Chaplain from the United Kingdom)

In our research, we were also made aware of port chaplains who used to work as chaplains in different settings but ended up working with seafarers as they sought new experiences and challenges in their ministry. One chaplain, for example, explained how they found work in port chaplaincy after many years of challenging work providing pastoral and practical care to the sick in hospitals:

> I was working at a hospital for a long time, and I wanted to change, because this is very hard, to be at the hospital for many, many years without any break, and then I was asking the Lord to give me a chance to change, and then [name] was in [place] visiting my colleague and he ask if my director in [place] from the Baptist Convention if he knew a person who could take place in the port of [place]. And then my director [...] , called me and told me '[name], please come', that I have something new for you. And then I had a meeting with [name] from [maritime charity] and he invited me to join him.
>
> (Chaplain from Brazil)

They further averred that their previous work prepared them for the demanding work in ports, and after years of ministering to seafarers, they reflected that they found port chaplaincy to be enjoyable and dynamic work, which they did not regret choosing over other forms of chaplaincy.

Some chaplains were recruited to work in seafarers' welfare as a result of a particular skill set—for example, being fluent in another language. In one case, a chaplain was invited to help strengthen the presence of maritime welfare work in a place where their facility in the local language could be beneficial. Once firmly established, they were asked to stay on and run the centre:

> I kind of started being involved in the Ministry since the end of 2016. Then our senior chaplain invited me to join in the Mission there as someone helping the Mission. Hopefully, we can establish some kind of services inside China. That was the very first kind of contact or involvement in this kind of ministry. Then

I started to travel inside there, to talk to certain people, especially local author-ities, their officials, kind of hoping that we can have their kind of permission to set up these certain type of services. As most people might be aware, it's not that straightforward to get that kind of approval from inside. I mean that's why we call it a Chinese project. We're still kind of trying our best to do it. Later on, [name] said, 'Why not you . . . come in as full-time?' But before I really entered full-time I started doing part-time as a port chaplain, so they also registered me to take part in an online course and ship visitor course in [country], so that was my proper training as ship visitor. Since February this year, I became full-time. They said, 'You'd better come in as full-time to be the port chaplain' and also as someone that can more relate with the seafarers as I speak their languages.

(Chaplain in China)

For others, it was merely their fascination with ships that attracted them to port chaplaincy. One chaplain, for example, went out looking for work in the sector because of what they called their obsession with ships. They explained how

I'm just obsessed with ships, and I think they're really cool, so I just went on Google and I put 'ship ministry' in to see if anyone does that, and then I was like, 'Oh, wow it's a thing; people do ship ministry and they go and talk to sailors and stuff', and so I was like, 'Alright then, let me see if I can do that.' So, I did some more researching and I found out there was going to be a position offered in [place] on an intern-type basis, and I was like, 'Well, you know, I've already done the intern thing.'

(Chaplain from the United Kingdom)

Volunteers

While some ordained chaplains were led to port chaplaincy by a random act of fate, a decision to shift career, or, in a small number of cases, a long-held aspir-ation in the early years of their religious education, among most volunteers, we discovered a more purposive trajectory in their choice of welfare work with seafarers.

More often than not, people tend to assume that working in the voluntary and charity sector is rooted in a desire to enact munificence to others. However, some of the volunteers that we interviewed were quite blunt about making their deci-sion to volunteer with their own self-interests in mind. In cases where volunteers had long retired from employment and had time to spare, they thought that volunteering would help them, as this allowed them to be physically active and to be more socially engaged. One volunteer explained,

[It is] Something, out, you know, doing...Otherwise I would be doing nothing. [...]
It helped me, I supposed, mentally that I am keeping myself occupied. [...] And
I think it's nice talking to seafarers when they come in. [...] It's very interesting
talking to them; sometimes it's just talking about nothing, but it's still interesting.

(Riverside volunteer)

The same reason was shared by a retiree volunteer in the same centre:

I get a lot of satisfaction. I suppose, being retired it gets me out of bed twice a
week for sure.

(Riverside volunteer)

Some volunteers came from an experience of profound personal struggle, and
they saw volunteering as a way of dealing with their sense of loss. In one case, it
was the loss of friends, family, and their own community that drew them towards
port chaplaincy. The rejection that they suffered from people closest to them had
scarred them, and it was their volunteer work with seafarers, and the people who
worked alongside them, that helped them get on with life. Their recovery came
from their work in another community—this time, with a community of people
working for the welfare of seafarers:

What do [I] get from it? A feeling of belonging to a helping community.
Although it's like a few, it does become like a little family; you get to know each
other. He's not just a ship visitor, he's a friend. And as you walk along and get to
know each other's background a bit more, that's great. You've got to put yourself
in my position if you can. Sixty years of friends were shut out one evening [...],
and they never look at you or speak to you, you're a dead man basically. Or to
put it in their words, 'You've been handed over to Satan.' So, you've got to have
the determination to make new friends [...] And this is, for me, quite a break-
through, and satisfying on a personal level. So, I suppose that's the best benefit
for me. The new friendships that share a common goal for the welfare of somebody else. There are other benefits too, but that's, I suppose, the key one.

(Porton volunteer)

However, these volunteers were quick to add that they soon discovered the sheer
joy of helping seafarers, and as a result, many of them had elected to devote more
time to the centre and actively help in the recruitment of new volunteers. Their
commitment to this voluntary work was further affirmed by accounts of long
years of service to the centres in Porton and Riverside. Some went above and
beyond the call of duty, one might say, by providing chocolate and sundry items
to seafarers, which they bought with their own cash.

There were some volunteers who had a personal connection with seafaring that
led them to do voluntary work in seafarer centres. Two volunteers had experience

of working in the maritime industry and, as such, had a detailed insight into life at sea. In these cases, the motivation to do voluntary work was, in a sense, to do with repaying the kindness that they felt had been shown to them by others. One of the volunteers explained that they became a volunteer because

> I really feel I wanted to give something back for all the hard work that the seafarers do. They do a lot for me on board, as well, and I think a lot of it goes unnoticed by the cruise lines and how hard they work. A lot of it is under-appreciated. I've seen how the crew kind of, not suffer, but they're not greatly appreciated as, from not every cruise line is as good as the other from appreciating the crew.
>
> (Riverside volunteer)

The same reasoning was described by another seafarer, who still worked at sea but volunteered at the centre whenever he was home on leave. He said,

> I've been at sea for nearly twenty years now. I know what it's like to be away from your family and your friends, oh God, only having a few hours off to enjoy yourself or have a bit of downtime before you've got to go back to the ship and be on duty. It's nice just to give a little bit back to them, you know? And seeing how much they appreciate it, all different crew members from all nationalities, is a really nice feeling.
>
> (Riverside volunteer)

In our interviews, we were given the impression that a desire to help was an over-riding factor for many in their decision to volunteer in seafarers' centres. This overriding desire was paramount, but volunteers also enjoyed their unpaid work for other reasons to do with maintaining a connection with the maritime environment. This was particularly evident when they had previously worked as seafarers. The seafarers' life, the sea, and the memories associated with many years of sailing and interacting with seafarers drew them towards work in a seafarers' centre. A chaplain, for instance, related the story of how they were able to recruit a former seafarer to work with him as a volunteer. He told us,

> Well for one of them, he was a merchant seaman. He was a captain, he was a master mariner. And now he works in IT in criminal investigations for a bank. [...] So, he [the senior chaplain, who I know personally] was at a barbeque, and he [the present volunteer] was chatting with one of his neighbours, and the guy said, 'You do what? You get to go on board the ships?' [Name] says, 'Yeah that's what we do. Hard hat and a safety vest', and he said, 'Can I go with you some time?' [...] So, he went on the first ship [...] So I think it's an opportunity for [name] to have a little taste of his old life without the stress of when he was doing it. Family at home and this kind of thing. We all know about the stresses of seafaring. And offer the guys a really deep appreciation of what they do and how they do it.
>
> (Chaplain from Canada)

A similar reason was given to us by a former seafarer, who volunteered together with his wife at Riverside. He described how it is his way of 'keeping in touch with the life that (he) had' (Riverside volunteer). The couple worked in the centre three days a week for four hours each, usually in the morning. He drove seafarers from ships to the centre, or to the town centre for shopping and sightseeing, while his wife worked in the bar selling drinks and snacks to visiting seafarers. These volunteers were some of the longest serving at Riverside, clocking up an impressive ten years in the centre. They said that the only times they had missed working in the centre were when one of them was unwell or when they were both on holiday. Their dedication in their voluntary work was greatly appreciated by the management, to the extent that they were trusted to run the centre on their own in the mornings.

For some other volunteers, family connections had brought them to the seafarers' centres. In our interviews, we were made aware of volunteers who had grown up in seafaring families and had become acquainted with romanticized sea stories and yarns from a young age. As a result, they saw their involvement in providing welfare services to seafarers as a natural progression, a logical development in their life in the context of the environment within which they were nurtured.

Sometimes, it was different kinds of family connections that motivated volunteers. In one case, a seafarer working in the domestic shipping sector had volunteered to work in the centre while on leave because of his father's activities there. His father had been volunteering in the centre as a driver for twenty years and was one of the most long-standing volunteers that we learnt about in Porton and Riverside. He told us,

> Well, I'll be honest, I think the main reason was my father has been driving here, […] 20 years? Yeah. You know, he said, 'It's nice', and I was thinking about it, and sometimes, even though a lot of people might think having all this time off is great, it can actually be quite boring at times. You can only do so much with your time off, so my dad spoke to me.
>
> (Riverside volunteer)

The involvement of family members seemed to draw others to work as volunteers in centres. The family members were able to act as a bridge between the centre and the would-be volunteer, and as a result, potential volunteers were more confident about the welcome they would receive and the kind of work that was entailed. In Porton, there was a mother-and-daughter team that came to the centre once a week. The mother described being encouraged by her daughter to join her in her volunteering work with seafarers.

As we have previously described, many seafarers' centres in the United Kingdom are run by religious charities and have been run by these organizations for many years (Cadge and Skaggs 2019). It is to be expected, therefore, that some volunteers had prior involvement in church activities or had been recruited from parishes close to the port or from churches where port chaplains were affiliated. This was the case with a volunteer in Porton, who had just returned to the United Kingdom after many years of working and living overseas. As the centre in Porton was run by a major religious organization, she saw her voluntary work as a continuation of her church work. In the United States, where she had worked and lived for many years, she had been an active member of her local church, raising money for church projects and other charitable causes:

> So that combined with my, you know I have been involved in churches and I do like to give, so put those three together, I saw the advertisement on the website and that's where I felt that would be a good thing, you know. I mean you, well you're not really giving to the community, but you're giving in a different way, you know, because obviously the community is wider because it's ships, but it's a way of giving with an underlying church baseline but then have an interest in the sea.
>
> (Porton volunteer)

A very similar reason was given by a second volunteer in the same centre, at Porton. Having worked for the church as a volunteer in various different capacities, they had come to a point when they felt that they needed to do something different. They felt that their new role should also centre on helping others and that it should be related to their faith, but not within the confines of the church. They explained that

> I suppose how I found my way into the Mission is I had a feeling of being bored for maybe between six, seven, eight years and couldn't identify what it was. All I knew is that my faith was telling me that whatever it was wasn't within a parish, it wasn't within a church. [...] I started looking around, and I'd always had a soft spot for the Mission, in my days it was the Seamen's Mission, the Flying Angels [...] So I'd been into a few of those around the world, always had a great welcome and some good social activities, and it seemed a fantastic way of putting something back in the system and also doing something that dovetailed with my faith.
>
> (Porton volunteer)

Working and volunteering with seafarers is not a particularly popular branch of the volunteer sector. In part, this results from the relative invisibility of the maritime industry in the eyes of the general public. However, there are also other factors that act as a deterrent. Not everyone recognizes seafarers' welfare as a 'worthy cause'. In addition, the remoteness of seafarers' centres and the health-and-safety issues associated with boarding ships and driving within port limits are likely to put some volunteers off. The volunteers who we came across and who had found their niche in the maritime charity sector often had an underlying interest in ships, or life at sea, or a personal or indirect connection with the shipping industry as a former seafarer or the relative or friend of a seafarer. These specific factors, coupled with their desire to be of help to others (which was often linked to their faith), brought them to seafarers' centres. Having found their place amongst seafarers, many have not looked back and continue to work and volunteer in seafarers, centres for very many years. The next section of the chapter explores the ways in which chaplains and volunteers understand their long-service records and their associated, deep, commitment to the maritime charity sector.

Understanding Long-Term Service to Seafarers

Contemporary society and workplace relations are no longer constructed around notions of a job, or even a specific career, 'for life ' (Boswell et al. 2001). The fast turnover of workers is common in many occupations(Siefert et al. 1991; Taplin et al. 2003; Di Pietro and Bufquin 2017), and even institutions such as universities have come to be so familiar with issues of staff turnover (Gandy et al. 2018) that they reference 'churn' as a regular feature of employment dynamics. In this context, loyalty to one's employer, or indeed employee, has become a complex issue (Roehling et al. 2001; Sajeva 2007; Linz et al. 2013). In contrast, in seafarers' centres, we found workers and volunteers who were deeply committed to their work and to their 'clientele' and who had no intention of changing role.

Port chaplains were usually employed by faith-based organizations, and consequently, they faced some limits with regard to decisions about where they worked. Some of the port chaplains involved in our research had served in their respective ports for many years. For instance, we were informed that it was not uncommon for chaplains to work in their assigned port or seafarers' centre up until they were required to retire, or they were asked by their religious organization to transfer to another role. In Porton, the previous chaplains from two different religious organizations only relinquished their posts upon reaching retirement age. Notwithstanding his formal retirement, one of these chaplains continued visiting the centre every week as a volunteer. We found a similar pattern with volunteers. Many had worked in their respective centres for long periods of time and demonstrated great reluctance to stop. One of the volunteers in Riverside, for example, had been there for twenty years.

In many parts of the world, providing welfare services to seafarers is strongly associated with Christian ministry (Palmer and Murray 2016; Cadge and Skaggs 2018, 2019; Montemaggi 2018), and in the United Kingdom, the biggest maritime welfare charities are run by Christian organizations. It is no surprise, therefore, that the Christian faith was described by many chaplains and some volunteers as initiating and sustaining their work in the sector, regardless of the challenges and difficulties that they faced on a daily basis. One chaplain, for example, described how:

Personally, I think like without my Christian faith my ship visiting would be really different like, it's my Christian faith that allows me to believe that my impact goes beyond my little ministry, and also it's sort of like the driving, motivating factor. Like I said, I got into ministry and stuff because my faith was really important to me, so I would say sort of that's with me behind everything I'm doing.

(Chaplain from Canada)

Another chaplain explained how he felt called to his work, saying,

I always felt I wanted to do something different, but I didn't really know what I wanted to do, and I felt like a calling, I wouldn't say a vocation because that's probably too, but I felt a calling to do something [...] One might say it's the power of the Holy Spirit.

(Chaplain from the United Kingdom)

However, faith and calling might be a double-edged sword, in a sense, when it comes to chaplains and their work with seafarers. The role of the port chaplain has several dimensions to it that might militate against a person of faith feeling contented and fulfilled in the role. Port chaplains were very clear that, in working with multinational groups of seafarers, they should not be proselytizing. Furthermore, they did not have many opportunities to engage in religious rituals with seafarers or, indeed, to discuss faith or religion at all. In our research, we found out that although there were times when seafarers specifically requested assistance in attending religious services or visiting churches when on shore leave, these situations were not the norm. Similarly, the conduct of religious services on board had become infrequent. The degree to which this was a loss for port chaplains was highlighted by their delight on the rare occasions when opportunities to offer communion or other religious services arose. On these occasions, chaplains described how the conduct of the religious service had bestowed upon them a different kind of fulfilment. Some suggested that it made them realize the importance of their work and the value of their ministry to seafarers. For example, one chaplain had a vivid recollection of their experience of conducting a religious service on board and told us how this affirmed his belief in the importance of his work:

And there was something about being there in the presence of Christ...and it was an example of being in the midst of all the dirt, the noisiness, the chaos—you know, doing the small part of the service that I did in the engine room, you know, running off to turn that alarm off. And I thought..., 'This...is where Christ would be.'

(Chaplain from the United Kingdom)

Although such religious services are seldom held on board contemporary vessels, their rarity seems to lend them an increased significance. They become very special moments for chaplains in the daily conduct of their work and one of the many ways of affirming chaplains' Christian ethos and identity.

Beyond the limited opportunities to minister directly to seafarers via the provision of religious services, chaplains have found myriad ways in which they are able to enact their faith on a daily basis via the practice of kindness to strangers (Turgo et al. 2023). This takes on an immediate significance when chaplains are called to an emergency on board. In our research, we were provided with numerous accounts of shipboard emergencies where chaplains played an important role in bringing calm and reassurance to the frayed nerves of seafarers who had experienced a tragedy onboard. Recognizing the stress experienced by seafarers in circumstances where official investigations may be underway and where they may feel profound sadness at the loss of, or serious injury to, a colleague, chaplains often found moments of affirmation on the occasions when they attended a vessel following an accident. Being able to respond to a clear and obvious need amongst seafarers reminded them of the huge significance of their role, something that was not always as apparent to them when engaged in their more routine tasks of distributing gifts and selling merchandise on board. One chaplain shared their experience of an occasion when they were asked to visit a ship where a seafarer had gone missing:

> So, we had a report from the police saying like, 'Listen, you'd better go on this ship when it comes in because we have this issue' and so we went on board this ship, and it was like, wow, if the chaplains hadn't been there nobody would be there for these guys who are feeling this hurt, this loss, this confusion. So, it was a special moment to be there to support because these guys, they were processing, and they just wanted to talk, you know. I don't know that we really helped them solve anything, but it was just the fact that they had someone to vent to, they had a listening ear, they had someone who was open because they were going through a lot. Like this guy, they were all questioning themselves like, 'What was the last thing I said to him?' or maybe it was, 'If I had just done this or if only I had asked him to have breakfast with me or something like it all could've been different' because they're all thinking the worst. So just to be there and like listen to their frustrations and their sadness and their confusion, I think it's really important that they have things like that.
>
> (Chaplain from the United Kingdom)

They went on to say that by being there, they were able to support the crew, and through their presence, they were able to help the crew come to terms with this tragic event. They drew inspiration from this to continue with their work.

There were other infrequent events that gave chaplains a similar sense of fulfilment. In cases when seafarers were hospitalized, chaplains were often called upon to visit them and offer whatever service might be of value. These occasions affirmed chaplains' sense of usefulness even when such affirmation was not immediate, as in the following example, when a chaplain reflected that:

I remember having one situation with a chap that was injured. He was in hospital quite a long time and I didn't, never really felt that I was getting through to him, but I kept visiting all the time, and then when he came back [home], he sent me a lovely letter saying, oh, because he was in hospital quite a long time and he said, 'Oh, thanks very much for everything you do' [...] I think that was lovely.

(Chaplain from the United Kingdom)

Port chaplains often referred to their work as ministry of presence (Zuidema and Walker 2020), and many would highlight the importance of their mere presence on board in relation to their provision of welfare services to seafarers. However, their presence was not always allowed and was not always wanted. For instance, there could be port inspections, deliveries, or cargo operations going on that prevented visits by chaplains. In other cases, crew members on the gangway could be lukewarm or even outrightly antagonistic when receiving requests to visit from chaplains. In some respects each ship visit was a game of chance. However, this seemed only to increase the positive impact that successful ship visits had on chaplains' morale and sense of purpose. When positive encounters with seafarers took place, they offered many chaplains a sense of fulfilment, which allowed them to keep going and to continue to believe in the value of their own work despite the hurdles and barriers with which they frequently met. One described how

I would say as long as you've made it onto the ship, and you've not just been, you get put in a mess room and then you don't see anyone kind of thing. That's when you think, well, there's probably a better use of your time. But then even in those situations, there's been times when you've sat there and then thought, 'Oh, this has been a waste of time', and then someone comes in, and then you end up speaking with someone. So yeah, I think that's one of the things, just knowing that you've had a conversation with someone that might have been just a bit of fresh, like a breath of fresh air for them. And when, they're always very thankful for you, if someone's said thank you for visiting us, then I always think I've done something, even though it might be very little.

(Chaplain from the United Kingdom)

In Chapter 2, we described how port chaplains facilitated seafarers' communication with others either via the sale of SIM cards or the provision of portable wi-fi facilities (Montemaggi 2013). In fact, their, sometimes controversial, trade in SIM cards and internet data[2] was so characteristic of their visits that seafarers would refer to chaplains as 'vendors of SIM cards'. Regardless of such a deficient depiction, it was the provision of SIM cards that brought some chaplains immediate and regular

---

[2] Not all chaplains felt that this is what they ought to be doing when visiting ships.

satisfaction in their work, as evinced by the experience of the chaplain quoted below. In this encounter, the chaplain described how being able to help seafarers connect with their families was what kept 'them doing what (they) are doing':

> It's when, after sitting there for goodness knows how long, sorting out the bloody SIM cards...but after that when you're sitting with the seafarers and you can see them talking to their families, and they turn their phones with their wife and they wave at you. That's why we do what we do!
>
> (Chaplain from the United Kingdom)

The idea that they were of great help to seafarers, and often in a compelling and immediate way, provided chaplains with the impetus to continue their welfare work with seafarers. In addition, there were special occasions and religious festivals where chaplains, once again, felt that their work was valued. Christmas was one such occasion, and chaplains were aware that at times like Christmas, Christian seafarers (and, indeed, others too) may feel particularly isolated from the world and their families and communities. Some chaplains shared their experience of bringing gifts to ships and bringing seafarers ashore during the Christmas period. The fact that they might be the only people to give seafarers a gift or a treat in the season of 'goodwill' gave them an intrinsic sense of satisfaction that was only enhanced when seafarers were moved by their care. Two chaplains from the same port shared their different experiences with seafarers in relation to past Christmases, as follows.

First chaplain:

> You give them gifts, and I remember one Polish ship [...] we gave them a lot of boxes from a parish that I had quite close contact with and then I said, 'Send me some pictures' and he sent a long email about how the Polish crew celebrate the tradition of Mass on Christmas Eve and the meals that they have and a lot of pictures of them opening presents, then he said, 'I'd like to thank you and all the people that have contributed to these presents for remembering us' and that was about two years ago, so that was lovely because sometimes it's nice to get feedback.
>
> (Chaplain from the United Kingdom)

Second chaplain:

> One of my regular ships I know very well...the Chief mate phoned up and said [...] 'Captain's asked can you go and buy 23 tubs of Roses?' 'Yeah, but why?' 'Cause it hadn't clicked at that point. I was thinking, 'Captain's got a sweet tooth.' And he went, 'Oh it's from our Christmas fund money that's the leftover.' It was Christmas!
>
> (Chaplain from the United Kingdom)

However, it is not just during special occasions such as Christmas or Easter that chaplains went the extra mile to show their care for seafarers. Going above and beyond what was expected of them did not require a special occasion or excuse, and there was a sense in which chaplains valued such opportunities and were particularly uplifted when they were appreciated. One chaplain described an occasion when he accompanied a Russian seafarer to do some shopping and was able to help him out with a short-term 'loan' of some cash. He told us,

> For example, one Russian Captain asked me for a favour. 'Could you take me to the local supermarket? I just need 20 minutes to buy something, some goodies or something for the staff and then I will go back to my ship.' I happily say, 'Yeah, no problem.' Then after that, also, he asked would they accept credit cards? I said, 'I'm not quite sure whether the local small supermarkets would.' Then he said, 'Where could I go and change money?' I said, 'Our club. We do provide this service.' I said, 'Well just go to the supermarket anyway', and then I just pull out some cash from my own purse. I said, 'Just go and get yourself something first, then we just go to our club and then you can change the money and just pay me back.' Yeah, so then, at the end he said, 'You really made my day. I'm really happy, you know, and I'm enjoying getting all this stuff that I needed.' Yeah, I think this small thing I rather enjoy.
>
> (Chaplain from Hong Kong)

Sometimes, chaplains recognized that they might be of particular benefit to specific seafarers on board, and they felt of value when they were able to reach these individuals. One chaplain described how he gained pleasure from dealing with seafarers who he deemed to live a particularly solitary existence, like captains or chief cooks. He felt that, in these roles, as people who usually take decisions (the captain is in charge of the ship and the chief cook prepares meals on a daily basis), some positions on board could be more challenging than others and, accordingly, lonesome. For these reasons, he took time to seek cooks and captains out and check on whether he could be of help to them. He said,

> Sometimes, I do like to try and target the captain and the cook. Because those are two very lonely positions, I think. One, the captain's got quite a lonely role, and he can only…you know, the captain talked to me about sacking one of his crew and sending him home, and the difficulties. And he was—he said, 'The guy's a nice guy but he's just not good at his job.' He said, 'I want to give him another chance, but if something goes wrong it falls on me.' Sometimes, captains don't have anyone left to talk to. And also the cook, because 'I…wake up in the morning— "Morning Cookie"—have your food and off you go.' Cook's left there preparing lunch, preparing coffee break, preparing afternoon coffee break, preparing dinner, cleaning the dishes. Especially if you're the only cook on the ship (you don't have a mess man or anything), it'd be quite a lonely position if you're on your own all day.
>
> (Chaplain from the United Kingdom)

In these many ways of helping seafarers, chaplains were quick to highlight the fact that being able to serve seafarers was a reward in itself. They did not expect anything in return. However, we found that chaplains and volunteers nevertheless found it gratifying, and highly motivating, when expressions of gratitude came their way. A chaplain recounted his own experience in this regard and explained,

> Quite often they always say, 'We really appreciate you coming on board. We're really thankful for caring for us even with those newspapers, the football dividends, or small gifts.' Most of them, I would say the majority of them, are really welcoming us. Of course, sometimes, we understand, they are busy on board and that's why, of course, we try not to get in their way but there's a certain…really most of them, especially those officers, captains want something. It's always very welcoming. Thanking us for coming on board, visiting them. Some of them…in fact, most of them will say, 'Would you like to have a meal with us on board?' It's quite often. I enjoy having a meal with them. That's also a way to get closer to, more of a personal contact with them. What is number one during one visit, one achievement, he offered me a bottle of…a can of soft drink, which I don't normally drink soft drink. I said, 'No, thank you. I don't drink soft drink.' He said, 'No, no, you must take it', you know. 'You always come and visit us and give us this and that. This, I insist you must take this.' So, this is the way I…of course…even I'm not a person to look to have a soft drink, but you know this is a kind of cultural education for me as well.
>
> (Chaplain from Hong Kong)

The expression of appreciation by seafarers is one thing that, although it is not expected, is welcomed and relished by chaplains and volunteers. Seafarers manifested their appreciation to the chaplains in our study in a variety of ways. Words of appreciation and offers of hospitality were quite common, but there were occasions when seafarers went beyond this in their efforts to relay to chaplains how highly their work and efforts were valued. For example, one chaplain explained how, during a visit to a ship, the crew surprised him by presenting a special memento. The gesture made a great impression on the chaplain. It had taken place many years ago, but the memory and attendant emotion remained vivid:

> I think it would be [name of ship], the ship that gave me the life ring.[3] And it's not just one seafarer, but a group of them. And it was…because I used to visit them when they were running back and forth between the US and Mexico, but then they went into dry dock, and after a month, Customs took their shore passes, so after that, I was doing their grocery shopping. […] And I remember when they first went in to dry—their Customs took their shore passes in dry

---

[3] A life ring is a buoyancy aid carried by ships to assist seafarers who have fallen overboard into the sea.

dock—on their last night, they said, 'You will still keep coming to visit us, won't you? Because we can't go ashore now—you're still going to visit us?" I said, 'Yeah of course I will.' And then...you know, I did services on board. And then one of them said to me, um...when they gave me the life ring after that service, they said, it's—they said, 'You're like one of us.' And that touched me. They said, 'Although you're not a seafarer, you're like one of us.' And that, for me, was like the acceptance into that little family on the ship. Because I was always there, to be honest. Um...and that really touched me. Because although I didn't really do anything, there was no major welfare issues or anything like that. You know, doing the odd bit of shopping at Victoria's Secrets, or bringing a couple of basketballs, or whatever it was. It made a difference to them, and it made a difference to me. And I think sometimes we seek to be a blessing to those we serve. But sometimes those we serve end up being a blessing to us.

(Chaplain from the United Kingdom)

The show of appreciation by seafarers could also come in more personal ways. Another chaplain experienced hospitality from the family of a seafarer they had helped when they visited the home country of the seafarer in connection with their work. At the time, the seafarer was sailing, but the seafarer's wife nevertheless met with the chaplain and welcomed them to their home. The chaplain described how

When I visited the Philippines, I was at a captain's house. I went to Boracay, but first I went to Aklan. [The captain] was sailing. [...] His wife introduced us to all the community, to their family, to the church. We [spent] four days in their house [...], it doesn't happen always you see?

(Chaplain from Brazil)

Some encounters with chaplains and volunteers were remembered by crews for very many years. This was affirming to chaplains as it reinforced just how significant their simple actions could be. One chaplain described how she was contacted by the agent of a ship when it paid a repeat visit to 'her' port. The first visit had been at a time when the seafarers were in crisis due to the conditions and treatment on board. By coincidence, officers that she had helped on that initial occasion were on board when the ship returned, and their second encounter gave her great pleasure. It was a warm reunion, and the chaplain was clearly moved by the crew reactions. She explained,

So, I get this phone call saying, 'Guess who's back in Canada, and they wanna see you?' and I said, 'I have no idea.' And the agent said, 'It's the guys from the [name of the ship].' And this company bought the ship, it was in terrible shape. They completely refitted it to MLC [Maritime Labour Convention] 2006 specs, and they hired all five officers to be the same officers on the ship—different name. Can't remember the name. But they wanted to see me. They were in [name of port] and I happened to be at the Mission. And they were like at pier 12, and I was around the corner. So, I drive up, I get out of the car, and I hear all this whooping and hollering. And I look up and they're all on deck. And they're yelling and waving at me. And I climbed up the gangway and there's hugs and kisses all around. […] It was just wonderful to be able to see these guys again and see them in a better place than they had been before. So, I think of them with so much affection and think about their hopes and dreams for their families and how bad their lives were for a brief period of time and how much better they are now.

(Chaplain from Canada)

Chaplains and volunteers also spoke about the sheer joy and value of meeting people from all over the world. They described how ministering to seafarers from different cultures allowed them to broaden their understanding of the world and of the world of seafarers. As meeting and contact points for different cultures, chaplains and volunteers felt that ports and seafarers' centres made work enjoyable and, in some respects, unique. They described,

So, I've kind of got this interesting perspective of like working half in the old docklands kind of side with the ancient world of seafaring and the British traditions with all these ex-seafarers, and then I see the other side of it with the modern seafarers who are mostly Asians, mostly young, mostly yes, so I get the best of both worlds.

(Chaplain from the United Kingdom)

And,

You know, I enjoy meeting the different cultures and so I, yes, I get a lot out of meeting the different cultures, you know, being around people of the same mind set who like to give, and it brings joy to my day too. You know, I guess it is work but it's something you enjoy, and if you enjoy it then, which I do, it's not really work is it?

(Porton volunteer)

Sometimes, such cultural and religious diversity was also reflected in the delivery teams associated with welfare delivery in their locale, and this was also described to us as having the potential to make work in seafarers' centres particularly interesting. A chaplain described this when he said,

It helps me also to have like all these ecumenical colleagues from different backgrounds and different like denominations as well because that helps me to have that mind set of like, 'I'm culturally open, I'm tolerant.' Like I have a German colleague, a Polish colleague, an Indonesian colleague, and a few British colleagues as well and then there's me from [place], so we reflect in our ministry our different cultures and our different backgrounds. So, we have a Lutheran, a Presbyterian, a Catholic, like Irish raised Baptist working for the Anglican, it's like you know, there's already that mix, which helps us to approach the job in a more open way.

(Chaplain from the United Kingdom)

Conclusion

The pandemic provided a further unexpected opportunity for the important work of chaplains and volunteers to be revealed. Although our fieldwork in ports and interviews with chaplains were largely complete when the first 'lockdowns' were introduced, we received updates from chaplains by email explaining how they were continuing to provide a lifeline to seafarers who were unable to leave their vessels. The pandemic emphasized the degree to which port chaplains and volunteers continue their service wherever possible, regardless of the everyday challenges they meet and the risks attendant to their work. Our research revealed how they came to the sector via different routes and for different reasons and the myriad motives keeping them working and volunteering on a long-term basis in seafarers' centres. In a world where work is mostly ruled by monetary reward, port chaplaincy and volunteering in seafarers' centres stand out as a remarkable testament to the continuing belief that many people have in the value of service, kindness, and generosity. For this work by chaplains and volunteers seems not just to be connected to religious faith or the idea of a calling. Much more than this, it seems strongly rooted in everyday human exchanges predicated on trust, optimism, empathy, and warmth—an invitation to share drinks and a meal, a warm hug, a memento or hospitality when abroad. In their relationships, both welfare workers and seafarers gave something that was uncounted and unquantifiable, and it was this exchange that was ultimately the foundation for the motivation of all the chaplains and volunteers we encountered.

In Part II of this book, we move from a focus on chaplains and volunteers to consider the daily realities of the seafarers they seek to serve. We consider religious faith amongst seafarers in more detail and describe how seafarers holding different beliefs are able to live and work together in very challenging circumstances while maintaining largely equable social relations. We then describe the significance of faith to some seafarers in the context of the challenging working lives that they endure.

Chaplaincy and Seafarers: Faith at Work. Helen Sampson, Nelson Turgo, Wendy Cadge, and Sophie Gilliat-Ray, Oxford University Press. © Helen Sampson, Nelson Turgo, Wendy Cadge, and Sophie Gilliat-Ray 2024.
DOI: 10.1093/9780198913290.003.0004

PART II
SEAFARERS' FAITH
AND WELFARE

4

The Negotiation of Differences in Faith on Board Cargo Vessels

Introduction

It is likely that amongst any crew, on board any deep-sea going vessel, trading anywhere in the world, you will find individuals of different faiths and none. The 2021 *Seafarer Workforce Report* (BIMCO/ICS 2021) estimates that the global supply of seafarers stands at 1,892,720 certified officers and ratings. The same report describes the five largest suppliers of internationally certified seafarers as the Philippines, the Russian Federation, Indonesia, China, and India. These five countries are believed to supply 44 per cent of the international workforce, with the remainder coming from a broad range of countries across the globe, that is from Europe, Africa, South America, the United States, Canada, Australia, and Asia. Given the dominant religions in just the top five labour supply countries (Roman Catholic, Russian Orthodoxy, Muslim, Buddhist, and Hindu) it is readily apparent that mixed-nationality crews will represent a variety of faiths. Many also comprise individuals with no faith and/or a variety of folk beliefs and superstitions.

The research underpinning this book involved eighty-nine days spent on board two different vessels with seafarers of various nationalities and religious affiliations (see Introduction, Table 2) Filipinos are regarded very highly by many international shipping companies as a result of their facility with the English language, overall skill sets, and because of widely held stereotypes regarding behavioural characteristics (Lamvik 2002; Amante 2003; Acejo 2013). It was no surprise, therefore, that our vessels were dominated by Filipino seafarers who were mainly, but not exclusively, from a Roman Catholic background. Their presence resulted in thirty-seven Roman Catholics[1] being amongst the overall total of fifty-five seafarers from seven different countries involved in the shipboard fieldwork (see Introduction, Table 2).

---

[1] We identified eight different religious affiliations plus the category of 'atheist' in our sample of shipboard seafarers.

Diverse Shipboard Beliefs

Despite this Roman Catholic dominance, our interviews revealed very diverse beliefs held across crews. Even those sharing a religion were found to subscribe to very different elements of their respective theologies. For example, amongst our Roman Catholic participants, we found a significant number of seafarers who believed in 'heaven' but did not believe in 'hell'. Interviewees were not always able to explain their reasons for this, but there was little doubt that their beliefs were firmly held. One told us,

> Of course, you have God, there is Christ, there is heaven, and you have to do good things so that when you die you go to heaven. [...] [I believe] mainly that [hell] is based on stories. We read about it but no, there is no hell.
>
> (*New China*, Able Seaman (AB), Filipino, Roman Catholic[2])

While another stated that

> All that I believe is that there is heaven but no hell. That's it.
>
> (*New China*, AB, Filipino, Roman Catholic)

A third was more articulate when he described how he did not believe in either heaven or hell as he knew of nobody who had been to either 'place':

> I think there is really no heaven. When I was a kid, I used to believe that there is heaven, but when I grew up, I started to question that belief. It seems that there is really no heaven, right? Then I ask myself, 'So where is heaven? Nobody, so far, is able to return from heaven. There should be an evidence for me to be convinced that there is heaven.' [...] I also do not believe in hell. It's the same with heaven, no one has seen it yet.
>
> (*New China*, Ordinary Seaman (OS), Filipino, Roman Catholic)

However, on the very same vessel, there were also Roman Catholic Filipino seafarers who adhered more closely to the teachings of their churches, regardless of how these had been passed on to them. One explained that

> That's what I learned from my parents, from my grandmother. They said that good people go to heaven, and heaven is a nice place. Those are the stories of my parents. I grew up in that belief so that's the reason why I believe in heaven. [...] Yes, I also believe in hell.
>
> (*New China*, Chief Cook, Filipino, Roman Catholic)

---

[2] All quotes provide a refence to the participant's vessel (a pseudonym) rank, nationality, and religious affiliation.

The Causes and Avoidance of Conflict

In some respects, differences in beliefs held by people of the same religion may have more potential to cause conflict, on board a ship, than differences in beliefs held by people of different faiths. This is because people of the same faith are likely to feel challenged by alternative interpretations of teachings associated with their own religion. In comparison, individuals without faith, or of a different faith, may choose to simply accept and respect the beliefs of others while remaining untouched by them. One captain, who was an atheist, explained this kind of perspective when he described his attitude to the faith of others, including his parents. He said,

> I don't believe. […] I respect your belief. I respect your belief. […] I respect, no problem. Also, I go inside in churches, have a look, no problem. In China, my mother is a Buddhist. Also, I sometime accompany her to temple, make prayer. I respect their belief.
>
> (*New China*, Captain, Chinese, atheist)

This strategy and attitude was noted amongst a small number of individuals; however, most seafarers recognized that negotiating religious differences on board had the potential to be extremely challenging. Unlike most workers ashore, seafarers live together for the duration of their contracts, and the living and working conditions they experience are extremely stressful. Cargo ships are dominated by men. Shift work involving long hours and nights is characteristic of the working conditions on board (Oldenburg et al. 2009; Jepsen et al. 2015), and this, combined with environmental factors such as noise and motion, results in endemic fatigue amongst shipboard workers. On container vessels, crew members have very limited access to outdoor deck spaces and are largely confined to the vessel accommodation block when not working. Shore leave is seldom experienced by seafarers on some routes (e.g., to/from West Africa), in some ranks (e.g. Chief Officer), in some trades (e.g. oil), and with some passports (e.g. Myanmar). In the period of the COVID-19 pandemic, most seafarers found that they could not access shore leave at all, and this added to the usual burden of stressors associated with their occupation. While some seafarers enjoy their work on board, others do not, and almost *all* describe extreme difficulty as a result of being away from their families and communities (Carotenuto et al. 2012; Iverson 2012; Swift 2015). Typically, they describe life at sea as a sacrifice undertaken for the economic rewards that are used to support families (Sampson 2024). One seafarer put it this way:

> I have no choice when it comes to job. I have been doing this kind of work for quite some time and this job sustains my family. Back home, I won't be able to find any job that pays well like what I have now. What I receive from this job is

way better than what I will receive from any available job ashore, that is, if in my age they will still find me suitable. This job is difficult, I tell you. Our work environment is dangerous. We have restricted mobility on board. If we get bored, there are very limited options to kill time. Once we are done with work, where do we go? Well, we end up either in the lounge, in the coffee bar, or in the cabin. We can't just say, well, I want to go to a mall. We are in the middle of the ocean. But what can I say? I need to sacrifice for my family. But regardless of all the hardships, I am still very lucky that God has given me this job. Back in the Philippines, many would wish to do the kind of job that I have. Many people in the Philippines are poor and need a job, a decent job. They want a good life for their kids, for their family, but they can't do it because they don't have the means to do it. That's what I tell myself whenever I feel daunted and tired of what I do on board: that I am still lucky because I work at sea and the pay is good.

(*Caribbean Dream*, Bosun, Filipino, Roman Catholic)

Another told us,

For many who have no idea of life on board, their perception is different when they hear about life at sea. They don't see the kind of work that we do here. What they only see is the amount of money that we earn and the places that we visit. They base their understanding of life at sea on that. So, they have no idea of our everyday routine here. And even if you tell your friends that this is the kind of work that we do on board, they will not believe. In a way, for them to believe, they need to see or be here to experience first hand what we experience on a daily basis […] You are away from your family. In my case, and for other seafarers, it is even more difficult because my only child is only two years old; she is a girl, and I think she does not remember my face. So, when I come home, and she sees me, I am just an ordinary man for her and not her father. So even if there is a video call, it makes a lot of difference if you are there with her as she grows up. Secondly, here on board, it is 'work, cabin, work, cabin', whereas if you work ashore, it is different, and therefore you are missing a lot, especially if you are the extrovert type of person. So ashore, you could go out with your friends, with your family. You can choose to be with your male friends, whereas here on board, for nine months, you are restricted to what is possible and available on board. So, it is only when you are back ashore that normal life returns, if it is still normal.

(*Caribbean Dream*, AB, Filipino, Roman Catholic)

In this environment, where seafarers are conscious of the risks they face on a daily basis (Zevallos et al. 2014), where work dominates (Sampson 2013), where boredom, monotony, and fatigue prevail (Jezewska and Iversen 2012; Hystad and Eid 2016), it is easy to understand how conflict may arise as if from nowhere. One participant emphasized how the most trivial occurrence could result in conflict and physical violence when he gave us an example of how some colleagues came to blows over some homemade soup. He explained that

> This one guy was really into making soup; it was his hobby. So, one night, whilst we were having a drink, it was a Saturday night, this guy decided to do soup for us. So off he went to the galley and whipped up this soup. Done, he went back to the lounge and served the soup to everyone. Then there was this other guy, who, at that time, was already drunk, who said something bad about the soup. We knew it was just a joke and everybody laughed. Then before we knew, the guy who made the soup was already at him, holding him by the neck, pouncing at him. So, we had to intervene. So that conflict was just because of a bowl of soup!
>
> (*Caribbean Dream*, AB, Filipino, Baptist Church)

In this context, where work is desperately needed and valued, even if disliked, and where stress levels may be high (Oldenburg et al. 2009, 2013; Mellbye and Carter 2017; Oldenburg and Jensen 2019), with anger and frustration bubbling just beneath the surface of some shipboard interactions, it is extraordinary that seafarers are as adept as they are at avoiding conflict. In becoming so, they have developed a strong set of norms, which serve to govern life on board. These underpin an occupational culture that is inculcated into neophyte seafarers on their first voyages, whether as cadets (Gould 2010) or ratings. It emphasizes rubbing along together, avoiding intrusion, respecting others' views and beliefs, not expecting special treatment, and de-escalating conflict where possible. Much of this behaviour is driven by the knowledge that work is precarious and that any seafarer can be sent home by the captain at any time (see also Dutt 2015). One seafarer described a situation where he considered himself lucky not to have been sent home when he was implicated in a confrontation between a chief cook on board a vessel and one of the crew. He described how

> There was a crew who was so picky with the food that he ate. So, if he did not like the food prepared by the chief cook, he would make it known by making noise using the cover of pots. He would bang them loudly. So, I informed the chief cook that somebody was making all these noises every time he did not like the food. The chief cook advised me not to mind him. He said that back home, he might not even have the chance to have three dishes on offer for lunch and dinner. He was just being a spoiled brat on board. Then one day, it was lunch, this guy was doing the same thing again, creating noise and making clear that he did not like the food that the chief cook had prepared. I was in the galley. The chief cook went out, and before I knew it, there was already a commotion in the mess. The chief cook apparently manhandled the crew out of frustration and anger. Then when I came out, I was accused by another of feeding false

information to the chief cook. Then he hit me in the face. It was very chaotic, with all plates and pans and pots scattered around. And so I thought when that ended, everything would be fine already. But no, the following day the chief cook ran after the crew who was making all the noises with a knife in his hand, he was going to kill the guy. Those were scary times. The captain got fed up and ordered the repatriation of the chief cook and the AB. I was lucky I was not asked to leave the ship.

(*Caribbean Dream*, Messman, Filipino, Roman Catholic)

As a fundamentally important aspect of shipboard life, food is known to be a potential flashpoint on board, and personal issues such as politics and faith are also considered to be potentially incendiary. While described to us as relatively unusual, it is therefore unsurprising that we were also given accounts of situations where disagreements over faith had arisen between seafarers and where these had, in a small number of cases, escalated into physical violence. In an illustrative example, one seafarer told us about a row between two colleagues that spiralled into a physical fist fight. The seafarers involved were fortunate in being given a second chance by the captain but were warned that any recurrence of their behaviour would result in summary dismissal. The seafarer told us,

The Iglesia ni Cristo[3] believed that their church founder, Felix Manalo, was chosen by God to found his church in the Far East, something like that. The born-again Christian disputed this until the debate became so ugly that they ended up throwing punches at each other. So, they were called to the captain's office and were told that if this incident would happen again, they would be sent home. I thought that was funny because they were buddies before this happened. [...] Well, the two of them were really scared out of their wits. Their wives would beat them to a pulp if they would end up cutting short their contract. After that, they avoided each other, and nothing more happened, but the relationship between the two had been damaged beyond repair.

(*Caribbean Dream*, Fitter, Filipino, Roman Catholic)

While conflicts did, periodically, arise over religion and other issues, such as alcohol (see, e.g. MAIB 2012 describing the drunken assault of a second officer by a captain), seafarers talked of how conflict had been more frequent in earlier times. They explained that in the contemporary period, seafarers were more in control of their actions and emotions and had learned to fear dismissal associated with

---

[3] Iglesias Ni Cristo is one of the biggest homegrown Christian churches in the Philippines, founded in 1913 by Felix Manalo. It has branches in 156 countries and territories and has more than 3 million members worldwide. It is a politically influential religious congregation in the Philippines as a result of its block voting of endorsed candidates at both national and local levels.

policies of zero tolerance to violence that have been implemented by many companies. Retaining their positions on board, whatever it takes, has become a priority.

While conflict could arise over mundane, sometimes unexpected, issues pertinent to daily shipboard life (such as food), it was considered more predictable in relation to deeply held personal views and beliefs. Consequently, many seafarers described feeling that, in order to avoid conflict, it was best to avoid discussing religion with colleagues altogether. This seemed to apply regardless of whether or not workmates shared the same religion. Several observed that there were pitfalls in discussing religion regardless of the context—of shared or differing faiths. As a result, seafarers were often in the dark about the religion of their co-workers, only making informed guesses, or assumptions, based on the observation of particular behaviours. As one explained,

> We don't ask each other. We sometimes get to know during special occasions like Christmas, right? If the seafarer refuses to attend, that means he has a different faith. That's the time we get to know. Or voluntarily, some share information, they personally say what their religion is. Then sometimes, you get to hear it from a workmate because he was close to another, and he was informed of his religion. Say he would say, 'Don't ask him to join the party; he is a born-again.'
>
> (*New China*, Third Mate, Filipino, Roman Catholic)

Among some seafarers, previous negative experiences of the public shipboard discussion of religion had led to them becoming particularly wary of conversations in this area. One seafarer recalled that on board a previous ship, he had become drawn into a discussion of religion that ultimately became quite heated. In spite of the passage of time, his description of the argument was highly detailed, conveying the depth of his original feelings. He described how

> I did have an argument with somebody before about religion. I argued with somebody because he told me that his religion did not believe in iconographies, like statues and pictures of saints. He asked me why I believed in the sanctity of these religious artefacts. But he himself believed in God and had his own religion. I did not know what his religion was, but he did not believe in statues and pictures of saints. I shot back at him. I told him that I don't go to church often and I am a bad person, but even if I am a bad person, I still believe in the sanctity of the pictures of saints and Christ. I told him that it's easier to pray when you see a picture of God or the saint that you are praying to. There is an image of Christ, then pray to him. I gave him an example. You have a picture of yourself, then a picture of your wife, a picture of your children, isn't it that you always look at the picture of your wife? I then made a comparison. You have a picture of your children, isn't it that sometimes you talk to the picture of your children?

Here is the picture of your children. Isn't it a lot easier to talk to them when you hold a picture of them in front of you? When you wake up in the morning, it's nice to see the picture of God. I really argued with them when they questioned why we put our faith on statues when they were mere wooden artefacts. So, I told him that it's much better to pray in the presence of statues of saints and Christ. Look at Christ, it's better to pray to him when he is represented by His statue than nothing. That's a personal belief, though.

(*New China*, Motorman, Filipino, Roman Catholic)

The view that religion should not be discussed on board was expressed in different ways by different seafarers. Most recognized the inflammatory potential of discussions of religion even when they were new to the job. One inexperienced seafarer cadet speculated about how he would react if he were drawn into conversations on board that he felt challenged, or ridiculed, his religious beliefs. Although he had not encountered a situation where such behaviours were displayed, he acknowledged that some 'crazy ones' might behave inappropriately in relation to the beliefs of others and that this could cause trouble for him, given the strength of his own feelings. He reflected that

I think if the person I am arguing with is disparaging my religion, I would really fight for what my religion stands for. But I think seafarers know better so they would not argue with each other bitterly over something, and I think only the crazy ones would do that. I think no one would have an argument over religion with somebody just for fun. That he would be pleased with himself making fun of other people's faith. I think no seafarer would be like that.

(*New China*, Deck Cadet, Filipino, Roman Catholic)

On the same ship, a seafarer explained that, in his view, the significance of faith to particular individuals meant that discussion of religion was high risk and something it was wise to avoid. He felt it was reasonable to expect people who have grown up with a faith to seek to explain this to others, encouraging them to change or refine their own views in response. He felt that in a multi-faith context, this posed a danger to harmonious relations. He told us,

I grew up with these beliefs. You were baptized to Christianity and you don't stop there; you wanted people to do the same. That's the usual cause of argument, so people should really stop talking about religion because there are so many religions that people believe in.

(*New China*, Chief Mate, Filipino, Roman Catholic)

In this context, a large number of seafarers preferred to restrict public discussions with colleagues to light-hearted topics. They considered that these could or should be based on favoured subjects such as 'women' and tall stories about 'shore leave' or previous ships. One seafarer explained that

> You see, […], religion is not usually talked about on board; it is a very personal thing. You might have noticed it, most of the time we talk about women in the lounge [laughs[4]]. The talk is fun. When you discuss something which is fun, you avoid talking about things that could lead to conflict.
>
> (*New China*, Fitter, Filipino, Roman Catholic)

This view was endorsed by a seafarer on a different ship, who emphasized the extent to which work dominated almost all social interaction on board and who said that on the (increasingly rare) occasions when seafarers engaged in social events and enjoyed a drink together, it was particularly important to avoid discussing potentially contentious topics such as religion. He expressed the view that alcohol could lead to people being less inhibited and becoming more volatile, leading to some topics becoming higher risk in terms of discussion. He described how he had experienced one such occasion when seafarers, sensing a danger of conflict, had shut down a discussion that was becoming too animated. He said,

> Based on my years of experience at sea, I have not witnessed yet or became involved in any discussion of religion on board. You see, even during coffee break, we still talk about our work, what we do, problems we encounter in maintenance work, that kind of thing. In fact, when we are resting and have time to come together for a chat, we most of the time talk about nonsense, some funny stuff, nothing serious. There was a time, I remember, we were having a drink and then one mentioned something about religion, so other joined in, and we discuss religion for a while then we stopped it because we were drinking, and people were getting excited. But that only happened once. […] we don't want that. We were drinking to enjoy our free time and not to stress ourselves.
>
> (*Caribbean Dream*, AB, Filipino, Baptist Church)

Another seafarer outlined the safe topics and practices that he was comfortable with when socializing with colleagues and the kinds of unsafe topics and actions that he tried to avoid. Acknowledging the dangers of gossip and the misuse of so-called 'jokes' in the high-tension environment of a cargo ship, he again emphasized fears about dismissal. He told us,

---

[4] There is clearly an assumption here that all men find it acceptable to talk about women in a particular manner and that no women will be found working on board. Such assumptions are, of course, inaccurate.

You know what, [in our free time] we still talk about work [laughs]. And that is wrong, I think. Talks should revolve around plans for shore leave, or happy memories of shore leave, those things. But what transpires, unfortunately, is still about work, who does not work faster, who does not work enough, those kinds of things. Then of course, when this chit chat reaches the ear of the person concerned, tension follows. So, when I am in the coffee bar and then the crew start to talk about their own mates, making fun of them or mocking them, I excuse myself and leave the place. I don't want to be part of that. Whenever that happens and the potential for trouble is huge, I find ways to make myself vanish. I don't want to be entangled in talks like that. I have a family to feed. They depend on me. You see, if someone becomes very violent and knives are drawn, your never know, that could happen, and I get caught in the swirl of events, what will happen to my family?

(*Caribbean Dream*, Messman, Filipino, Roman Catholic)

It is evident, then, that there is a range of topics which can lead to tension and conflict on board and that religion is only one of these. In general, seafarers described avoiding contentious subject matter, but there were inevitably times when boundaries slipped, and seafarers transgressed in relation to the shipboard norms. In the course of the research, we were told about, and in one case witnessed, the behaviour of some specific seafarers whose commitment to their faith led them to intentionally, or unintentionally, overstep the usual limits that were informally observed by most seafarers, most of the time. This took the form of pressing the topic of religion onto people who preferred not to discuss it, of sharing religious videos or texts, or pressurizing others to join a religious discussion or prayer group. In the main, such cases were tolerated even when seafarers felt irritated, or 'put upon', by their colleagues. However, many of these interactions seemed particularly finely balanced. Seafarers often had a strong sense of appropriate behaviour on board while, at the same time, trying very hard to avoid conflict and to exercise as much tolerance towards others as they could muster. One seafarer reflected on the challenges of interactions about religion on board and concluded that where seafarers want to try to organize discussions of religion (as sometimes happens), or similar activities, the best way forward might be to simply provide information (by putting up a notice, for example) to those on board relating to a planned activity, and this would allow people who were not interested to avoid it without causing any offence. He explained,

I've heard of instances where there are seafarers who would be knocking on your door and ask you to discuss religion with him. In your cabin, he will read with you religious literature. My take on that is this: people doing that should ask first if you want to talk about religion, but again, there's another problem. Even if you are asked, he is already there. So, you can't say no; he might feel offended if you reject his offer. I think it is not a good practice knocking on everyone's cabin. What he could have done is to set a schedule and then let anyone come if they want to in the bible study.

(*New China*, Electrician, Filipino, Roman Catholic)

The idea that seafarers should be free to organize religious meetings on board was one that most seafarers seemed to support, so long as these did not impinge on people who did not want to be involved and so long as they did not result in conflicts or arguments. The appetite for such activities was said to have diminished somewhat with the arrival of the internet on many vessels, and we were also given examples of when such open discussion of faith had led to offence and caused seafarers to cease involvement in religious activities on board. One seafarer explained how he avoided one-to-one discussions of faith but had no objection to bible study sessions or similar activities. However, he qualified this observation, stating that this was providing they did not give rise to conflicts, and he provided an account of a situation where some grave offence had been given in a discussion amongst Christians of some Roman Catholic practices. He described how

I would rather excuse myself [from public discussions of religion], unless of course, it's about bible study, something like that; that is fine, okay. It is fine when you just read passages from the bible and there is no arguing with one another. I remember one of my captains, in one of our bible study sessions, he mentioned about Catholics going on pilgrimage and praying to false idols. [...] I was just silent. I did not [...] respond to his tirade. But the chief engineer who was present at that time got offended. He stopped attending after that. He told me, 'What kind of captain is he? He does not believe in so many things. But look, so many devotees flock to Quiapo. Then he is going to convert me?' So after that, the chief engineer stopped attending. He was really offended because the captain told some of the officers to stop believing in some of Roman Catholic practices.

(*New China*, Chief Mate, Filipino, Roman Catholic)

This example emphasizes the extent to which conflict over religious issues and interpretations of teachings and written texts had been experienced by seafarers with others of the same nationality and of the same or similar religious persuasions. Within the research, there were others, and several seafarers reflected on the practices of some Nigerian colleagues who they had sailed with on other vessels in the company fleet. One seafarer described how astonished he was at the degree to which they [the Nigerian seafarers] engaged in the public and private display of their religion. He described this as leading to frequent arguments and heated debates but emphasized how, at the end of a week where contentious points of view may have been aired, the colleagues had gathered together as though unified and harmonious in their weekly Sunday acts of worship. He exclaimed that

> I tell you, if you are on a ship with Nigerian crew, you will be amazed by their religiosity and the many different Christian denominations that they have. There are times when heated discussions would ensue because of their present religiosity. [...] and when they have unsettled issues, they would continue their discussion at work. I find that really funny [strange] but that's the way they do it. But every Sunday, they come together, though they come from different Christian churches in Nigeria, and hold a Mass presided over by maybe a senior member of their group. So, they sing a lot in these services.
>
> (*Caribbean Dream*, Electrician, Filipino, Iglesia Filipina Independiente)

Thus, while we were given many examples of seafarers who avoided religious discussion because of fears of conflict, and some of seafarers who had witnessed the development of conflicts or resentments as a result of religious discussions, there was also a small number of examples where seafarers welcomed approaches from others who wished to discuss faith and religion alongside examples of conflict, which could be contained and effectively controlled, resulting in little harm.

Conformity on Board: Blending with the Crowd and Avoiding Ridicule

It was interesting that seafarers also described other reasons for personally avoiding engaging in discussions of religion. Sometimes, they shelved their own religious practices and hid their own beliefs on board in an effort to get on with their colleagues. In the small, confined, and institutionalized environment of the ship, seafarers were aware that singularity had the potential to provoke bullying or stigmatization. There is a great deal of pressure to conform on board a cargo vessel, and seafarers were conscious of how this impacted on them on board. One explained,

> You are surrounded by people who don't pay much attention to their religious practices. That is a big influence, I think. When everyone is outside making fun, playing cards, why would you stay in your cabin and read the bible? I remember on one of my ships, I discussed with another messman my plan to have a bible sharing with the crew, but he sounded uninterested and so did the people that I spoke to. So, I gave up. I lost my interest also. I also thought that if I really pushed it, if I tried hard to convince people, they might poke fun at me. I don't like that. Then, of course, back home, I have a family which will remind me of my religious obligations. Here, we are on our own. No one reminds us.
>
> (*Caribbean Dream*, Assistant Cook, Filipino, Roman Catholic)

This view was endorsed by a colleague, who told us,

> I think [...] when some people do not follow certain traditions and practices, there seems to be an effect on others, they soon become very relaxed in honouring their practices, say religious practices. They are influenced by others.
>
> (*Caribbean Dream*, Chief Cook, Filipino, Roman Catholic)

Seafarers also recognized that within a very small crew, there could be risks associated with claiming too much in the way of piety. Over a period of months, seafarers who lived and worked together in such small groups were readily caught out when failing to live up to standards they had been foolhardy enough to proclaim. In such cases, they frequently felt shamed and ridiculed and could become the butt of relentless 'jokes'. One seafarer gave an example of such an incident when he recalled that

> On my last ship, there was a seafarer who was very serious about his religious belief. He was a born-again Christian. He wanted to spread the word of God on board. [...] I think many of us were feeling uncomfortable, others were annoyed. We thought that what he was saying, all these religious acts and all, do not reflect his true personality. I myself noticed that he was different. And then with the two born-again Christians, they had a quarrel between the two of them. It was work-related. Each one of them thought that he was being taken advantage of by the other. So later on, when they would talk about God, we would snigger. They have lost credibility. We would just laugh at them. They would enjoin us to be patient with people and yet, they themselves were not patient with one another. They were not helping each other.
>
> (*Caribbean Dream*, Cargo Engineer, Filipino, Roman Catholic)

Another seafarer observed that a façade of piety could easily be shattered when enjoying shore leave. Knowing that they themselves might wish to engage in behaviours that would transgress their own religious teachings while enjoying shore leave, they learnt from experience that it was risky to espouse morality on board, and they tended to downplay their own religiosity as a result. They understood that apparently hypocritical indiscretions could be harshly 'punished' by crew members, who disliked others assuming superior airs and graces. A seafarer explained that

> Everyone keeps his religion to himself. They don't talk about it in public. Also, I think seafarers find it a bit uncomfortable being seen praying in public places. And when seafarers are perceived to be religious, they could be laughed at. Maybe that's one of the reasons why seafarers do not express their religious sentiments and practices in public. And then you could have a seafarer who is very religious and yet when he goes ashore, he could also be joining his compatriots

to brothels. He could become a laughing stock. So that's the reason I think why seafarers prefer to be quiet about religion.

(*New China*, OS, Filipino, Roman Catholic)

Thus, fear of conflict and fear of ridicule worked both in combination and alone to encourage seafarers to maintain some privacy with regard to their own religion and some sensitivity and discretion with regard to the practices of others. In this context, many revealed how they had come to experience the ship as an environment where they felt temporarily released from the observance of religious obligations and duties. This led them to engage in a range of proscribed behaviours on board that they would not countenance ashore. Most commonly, these related to the consumption of food and alcohol and to seeking commercial sex.

Deviating from Pious Behaviour

In relation to food, many of the Roman Catholic interviewees described how at home they would normally avoid eating meat on Good Friday. However, on board their vessels, where food is an extremely important part of life, serving to break up the monotony of institutional living, few seafarers continued to observe the practice.

One seafarer described how it was only when he started working at sea that he broke with the practice of avoiding eating meat on Good Friday. He explained that on the very first occasion when it happened, he questioned his actions and felt as though he was transgressing in relation to the teachings of his religion. However, he did not want to stand out from the crowd and reassured himself that, since everyone else around him was eating meat, then it couldn't be important. In an interview, he went on to reflect that perhaps these behaviours indicated that despite the cultural practices which he engaged in at home, his behaviour, and that of his colleagues, probably indicated that they didn't really care about these things. They displayed strong tendencies to conform with the behaviours of others around them and were not driven by their own strong beliefs. He said,

Actually, sir, it was my first time to eat meat on Good Friday on my first ship. I was taken aback and kept on telling myself, why did I do it when old people back home were very clear that it's not allowed to eat meat on Good Friday? But you know, I was not supposed to eat meat but I saw the crew eating meat so I told myself, 'That should be fine. They are doing it so I might as well do it too.' You know, had I not eaten meat, I would be the only one. But I really checked it with everyone. I saw them eating meat, so I told myself, 'Ah, it is okay [laughs].' But you see, it is up to the galley. If the galley did not prepare meat, then we would not eat meat. [...] I was not alone in eating meat. We all ate meat. I think if I was the only one, then I would feel guilty. And I think sir, because we are at sea, I don't know, when you are at sea, you don't pay attention to all these practices already. And maybe we don't care anymore about all these things? But of course, if the person is particularly religious, then he will still do his religious practices on board like not eating meat on Good Friday.

(*Caribbean Dream*, Wiper, Filipino, Roman Catholic)

In an interview with a chief cook on board the same vessel, it became apparent that the galley crew had not usually been met with demands from seafarers for meatless meals on Good Friday. Catering staff on board are generally quite receptive to crew feedback as ignoring it can lead to conflicts and complaints and, in extreme circumstances, can lead to their dismissal, given that captains and many companies recognize the importance of keeping crews relatively content vis-à-vis food. The chief cook explained how, on Good Friday,

We prepare meat dishes. [...] I tell you, on board people do not adhere 100 per cent to their religious beliefs and practices. So, if there is meat, everyone eats meat. [...] I have become used to doing it here. Maybe those who have a sacred vow [panata], they are the ones who are steadfast in not eating meat on Good Friday. [...] I think it is because when some people do not follow certain traditions and practices, there seems to be an effect on others, they soon become very relaxed in honouring their practices, say religious practices. They are influenced by others.

(*Caribbean Dream*, Chief Cook, Filipino, Roman Catholic)

In relation to the contravention of meatless dining on Good Fridays, there was very little evidence of seafarers experiencing regret or feeling that they had committed any 'offence' in relation to their religious beliefs. Rather, we encountered some relish in relation to accounts of eating meat, as the following example illustrates. An OS was quite gleeful when he described how

I remember when I am in the Philippines, we don't eat meat, that's for sure. Here on board, what I remember is we ate congee, and sometimes we also ate meat [laughs...] The chief cook cooked meat dishes and when I saw them, I forgot that it was Good Friday [laughs...] The dishes were very good [laughs]!

(*Caribbean Dream*, OS, Filipino, Roman Catholic)

Gambling was another practice that some seafarers regarded as prohibited by their religion and that was avoided ashore. This and the telling of lewd jokes and watching pornography was regarded by some seafarers as sinful. There seemed a strong sense amongst some seafarers that these actions were highly transgressive, and these seafarers retained a commitment to the belief that they should be avoided. Once again, however, we were told of how, on board, their reservations dwindled as they sought to blend in with their crewmates and pass off the boredom and monotony that characterizes the life at sea. A seafarer explained how

> We are not allowed to do gambling, but on board I do it. It's mainly because it is boring, you can't do much on board. Watching movies and videos, all those recorded tv shows, they get tiring, you get fed up with them. You keep on watching the same shows all the time. Then you see your workmates playing cards, they are happy; they laugh a lot; you stand there watching them. You feel like joining; you feel envious of the fun they're having. Then you join because you can't resist the fun. There are times you just like to watch and not participate, but your workmates will ask you to join them, and you can't say no. At first, there is no money involved but, as time goes by, you don't notice that you're already spending money. [...] And I should add green [in the United Kingdom the term used would be 'blue'] jokes; if you notice, we are so fond of making indecent jokes. Then because you are with them and want to join the fun, you contribute your own. You tend to forget that it's improper. [...] Yes, so we play cards, you do things which you are not supposed to do. You do them because you want to get rid of stress, to relax, to have fun.
>
> (*New China*, AB, Filipino, Jesus Is Lord)

Another observed how the communal life on board a ship differed in the extreme from life ashore in his community. In each instance, on board or ashore, there was a tendency for seafarers to conform, even if this involved engaging in behaviours that, at heart, they regarded as 'wrong'. A seafarer told us,

> Of course, on board, you have all the mischief, all this banter, green jokes and all. If you think about it, every day we are committing sins. Here, you commit sin with all the lewd jokes, rude words. Back home, I am always in the house, I hardly go out, I don't fraternize much. I keep myself busy at home. And when you're at home, you don't communicate much with other people, and you keep yourself away from having a big mouth, with bad words to say all the time. But on board, you can't stay away from that. [...] You tend to forget that what you're doing is wrong.
>
> (*New China*, Chief Cook, Filipino, Roman Catholic)

Conformity and trying to cope with monotony and boredom dominated the explanations provided by seafarers for these transgressive activities. When asked about practices that contravened the teachings of his religion, one seafarer explained that gambling and commercial sex were wrong, according to his beliefs, but that boredom drove many seafarers to engage with them. He said,

> I think it's paying women for sexual favours and gambling [is 'wrong'], but you know, it's difficult if you stay all the time in your cabin, you will go crazy.

Remember the dog—if you don't set if free for some days, it goes crazy. How much more for us? [...] Those things help you cope with loneliness and boredom. The life of a seafarer is difficult.

(*New China*, Electrician, Filipino, Roman Catholic)

Another described how one seafarer who claimed to be very pious was ridiculed on a previous ship because although he regarded alcohol as prohibited, he nevertheless joined in with Saturday drinking sessions. Although he, himself, had been involved in laughing at the seafarer and making fun of him, he recalled the experience and described how, in actual fact, he could quite understand why his colleague behaved as he did. He could relate to his reasons very well. He recalled that the seafarer concerned was

very religious, of course, and he was telling us that drinking was prohibited in their religion. But every Saturday, he would join us for a drink. So, we would make fun of him, asking him why he was drinking. That kind of thing. [...] He said he wanted to join the fun; and that he wanted to shake off the boredom, the loneliness of being at sea. I perfectly understand him.

(*Caribbean Dream*, OS, Filipino, Roman Catholic)

Boredom and alcohol also featured in the accounts given to us by many seafarers of their experiences of commercial sex. For some seafarers, commercial sex was treated as something of an entitlement and was a feature of the life at sea that they had looked forward to when first working on board. Many seafarers regarded engaging in commercial sex as completely inconsequential, explaining that it was 'part and parcel of our life on board' (*New China*, Fitter, Filipino, Roman Catholic) and 'very common for seafarers, almost like a natural thing for them, to visit brothels' (*Caribbean Dream*, AB, Filipino, Roman Catholic). Several seafarers described how they had no negative feelings or regret about such practices at all, and one made very light of it, suggesting that 'I did not feel anything because it is said that go forth and multiply. God said that, isn't it? So off we went' (*New China*, Bosun, Filipino, Iglesia Filipina Independiente). Roman Catholic seafarers did not suggest that there was anything improper, in religious terms, in wearing condoms when engaging in commercial sex, but neither did they describe opposition to contraception as a motivating factor in not wearing condoms. One seafarer, who felt there was nothing wrong with commercial sex from the point of view of compatibility with his religious beliefs, described how he did not always use a condom with sex workers and that, having practiced unsafe sex, he felt anxious but not sinful. He explained,

I felt scared after. I think that's once we were back on board, when the realization that you contracting infection was a big possibility because that time, we were not using condoms. The women in Brazil, when they had sex with Filipinos, they did not want us to wear condom because according to them we were clean. [...] when I did that, I did not even think about God, or anything [laughs]. I don't think it is a sin. No.

(*Caribbean Dream*, Motorman, Filipino, Roman Catholic)

Generally speaking, any feelings of remorse or guilt described by seafarers in relation to commercial sex were linked to feelings of spousal betrayal. Several seafarers described giving up commercial sex because they had got married and they did not wish to betray their wives' trust or spend the family income on selfish pleasures. Some also described how they had lost interest in commercial sex as they had got older. One explained that 'nowadays, I don't have the liking for that anymore. I am so over that. But it's part of life at sea' (*Caribbean Dream*, Chief Engineer, Norwegian, atheist). Whatever their current view and practice, however, it was clear, in the accounts given to us, that commercial sex was widely regarded not only as 'normal' and permissible for seafarers but also as an entitlement and attraction of seafaring. A strong occupational culture placed commercial sex, and tall tales about sexual encounters ashore, centre stage with regard to seafaring, and neophyte seafarers were often encouraged to pay for sex in ports almost as an initiation into the culture. Peer pressure was described, in many cases, as very strong, and some examples were given of seafarers' bills being paid by other crew members when they first engaged sex workers ashore. One explained how he had first engaged in commercial sex, having been goaded by a senior officer, who subsequently paid for his experience. He described how

I was prodded by our chief officer. When I went with them, I only wanted to watch; there were women dancing on the stage. He told me to get a woman and he would pay for it. When I refused, he told me that maybe I wanted a man. So, I felt insulted, I felt challenged: 'What does he mean?' So, I told him, 'Okay!' That's it. The two times I did it, our chief mate was the instigator. He paid for them. I did not want to spend a penny. I only wanted to watch women perform on stage, and I did not have any plan to get a woman.

(*New China*, Chief Cook, Filipino, Roman Catholic)

The strength of the occupational culture and a lack of concern about religious deviance in relation to commercial sex were described by another seafarer. He described how not only did his crewmates engage in banter about his initiation into this occupational practice, but they also went so far as to borrow a term from their religion to discuss it. There was no sense in his account that this might be inappropriate language or behaviour, given the religion he and his colleagues shared. His words confirm the extent to which he regarded this as simply taken-for-granted aspects of being a seafarer. He recounted that

On my first ship, I was asked by some of my workmates to come with them for shore leave. And because it was my first ship, they were saying, 'Let's *baptize* [name of interviewee]. So, we also brought with us the two cadets. We were with the old timers; they were working at sea for quite long already. So, we went to this place. As we were novices, we were just observing, and as it turned out, we were never able to get any woman because our companions, the old timers, just jumped into it. There were not too many women there, so we were left with no one to get. [...] On my second ship, finally, I was able to.

(New China, OS, Filipino, Roman Catholic)

Conclusion

In many respects, seafarers display a remarkable capacity to rub along with others of different beliefs. This seems particularly notable given the stressful, confined, boring, and physically exhausting conditions encountered when working on board. However, close consideration indicates that there are several factors that assist seafarers in relation to the preservation of tolerance and open-mindedness. Perhaps the most significant reason for seafarers' patience and forbearance with others, and their beliefs, while on board is the certain knowledge that any shipboard conflict risks possible dismissal. In this regard, the stakes are incredibly high as, once sent home for bad behaviour, a seafarer may find that he or she never works at sea again, thereby losing his/her access to an unusually lucrative line of work. Along with fear of dismissal, seafarers were assisted by a strong occupational culture on board, which discourages discussion of sensitive topics, rendering many seafarers silent on a range of issues that might be regarded as intrusive and personal. In this way, religion was simply not discussed on board a great deal, and instead, many had a marked preference for light-hearted topics, banter, and the exchange of lewd jokes. However, what also emerged was a tendency for seafarers to conform with the behaviours of their crew mates regardless of the teachings of their own religions. This assisted in building group cohesion and masking differences in values and beliefs. While this practice caused some seafarers to feel conflicted (as discussed in the next chapter) others felt that, at sea, they were released from religious obligations and could park these at the bottom of the gangway when they joined a ship. In some cases, they quietly revisited them in the private realm of their cabin but in others, they seemed to simply parcel religion and its practice together with 'life ashore' and throw themselves into a different kind of life at sea, where they conformed with the expectations of crewmates and the norms of a strong shipboard occupational culture.

Chaplaincy and Seafarers: Faith at Work. Helen Sampson, Nelson Turgo, Wendy Cadge, and Sophie Gilliat-Ray, Oxford University Press. © Helen Sampson, Nelson Turgo, Wendy Cadge, and Sophie Gilliat-Ray 2024.
DOI: 10.1093/9780198913290.003.0005

5

The Significance of Faith and Support Services for Seafarers at Sea

Introduction

Religion at work has been an important area of inquiry to social scientists. There has been a significant amount of work undertaken on the activities that are specifically linked to religious employment, for example, pastors (Hall 1997), Imams (Schmid 2020), vicars (Hansson and Andersen 2001), the wives of clergy (Finch 1980), etc. Beyond this, however, there is also a well-established literature on the wider world of work and its connections with faith. There is nothing new in the suggestion that faith and religion have important connections to work and economic behaviour. Early sociologists Karl Marx and Max Weber both recognized the significant links between religion and employment. Marx was particularly interested in the role of religion in encouraging workers to accept and endure poor, and often inhumane, working and living conditions, while Weber was concerned to establish the relationship between religion, values, and attitudes to work, most notably in relation to the development of a 'work ethic'. Their work has continued to inform this field of interest to the present day, with some authors, such as Sullivan (2006), echoing Marx when describing how, in her research with women in low-income jobs, people drew on their faith and religion to help them endure menial tasks associated with their jobs and stressful daily interactions at work. Others, such as Uygur et al. (2017), use Weber's notion of *Lebensführung* to explore the impact of workplace religious beliefs.

Chapter 4 outlined how seafarers negotiate differences in faith on board by largely confining displays and expressions of faith to private domains (usually cabins), limiting public discussion of beliefs and values, and by embracing an occupational culture that may be at odds with ideas of piety. For these reasons, a casual observer joining a multinational vessel may fail to appreciate how significant faith is to some, but not all, seafarers. Many seafarers described how, at times in their careers, their faith has acted as a lifeline, offering them solace, comfort, and a feeling of protection. Such 'support' is controversial inasmuch as there is a longstanding argument, by those influenced by the work of Marx, that faith should not be encouraged or fostered at the expense of necessary improvements to living and working conditions; that faith should not be used as a 'sticking plaster' to cover up the wounds associated with exploitative employment; that it should not be 'the opium of the people' (Marx, quoted in McKinnon 2005).

At sea, however, there is little doubt that many seafarers taking part in our research relied on their faith to help them cope with extremely challenging and difficult living and working conditions. The times when seafarers described their faith as most strongly supportive of their well-being on board were largely when they were new to their career, when they were new to a specific vessel, when they experienced challenging relationships or situations of high stress on board, when they were bored, when they were anxious about their families, and when they feared for the safety and viability of their vessel. In these situations, seafarers who had a faith described engaging in behaviours that they had been taught to prac-tice at such times by their religious teachers ashore.

The Role of Faith in Maintaining Emotional Stability, Staving Off Boredom, and Counteracting Loneliness

From a superficial standpoint, religious practices and the support they offered differed between seafarers of different faiths. For Buddhists, for example, medita-tion proved helpful in relieving stress, maintaining self-control, or staying calm in challenging interactions. One seafarer explained,

> We seafarers, too much worry, all the time, so Buddha says be calm and don't stress, so that is why we have meditation. It helps.
>
> (*New China*, Junior Officer, Chinese, Buddhist)

He also described how he believed that his faith had allowed him to become more 'cool' and even-tempered, which, in turn, had allowed him to get on with col-leagues on board who might otherwise have riled him. He gave the example of some of his Filipino colleagues 'teasing' him with regard to the contested sover-eignty of specific islands. He described how

> I think you need religion ... [in] any kind of job, Buddhist strong point maybe you become this good man, good people. [...] I understand people, I become good, you know. [...] Anywhere. [...] like when joking, you know, Filipinos love to joke, I just laugh, not angry. I know it's for fun and that's good. I am very cool now. And then they tell sometimes, 'Oh, Chinese, they get our islands.' I tell them, 'No, not me, maybe our government', and we just laugh.
>
> (*New China*, Junior Officer, Chinese, Buddhist)

A fellow officer and Buddhist on the same ship also described how his faith allowed him to remain calm. He began describing how he felt that it was not wise to get upset and agitated about things breaking in the engine room (he was an engineer) and went on to explain how Buddhism encourages followers to practice acceptance, which he considered to be of great importance. He said,

> If something happen, finish, then we start from here. [...] My religion helps. Helps a lot. Should be calm. I keep calm. No need too much worrying. [...] You have a lifetime, this one, have life and death. Even in Buddha words, everything there is a depreciation. Everything. But the period is different. For the sun, for the earth. The appreciation period create and appear and again finish. We have to think like that. We cannot expect everything to go the way we want. That's why we have calm—not to cry...even if somebody die, it is not actual Buddhist people should not cry. We should know how to practice the art of letting go. People that we love, beautiful things, all things [...] Yeah, we know already born here, live here, die. That's how life is.
>
> (*New China*, Senior Officer, Sri Lankan, Buddhist)

The role of religion in helping seafarers to remain calm was not specific to Buddhism, however. Seafarers of other faiths also drew on their religions, and related rituals and practices, to maintain a level of equanimity in the face of adversity. A Roman Catholic seafarer, for example, also reflected on how his religious beliefs had helped him to stay calm when dealing with difficult interactions and relationships on board. He described how, on one of his ships, he found the captain extremely difficult, to the extent that he very much wanted to sign off the vessel before completing his contract. He explained that

> Our captain was a genuine pain in the ass. That time I really wanted to sign off at once. [...] When that happened, I was on my own and God was just there, and he's the only one you could talk to. You could ask for help from him. Yes, God and family and you tell yourself, 'If I pay attention to the person causing my hardship, what will happen to me?'
>
> (*New China*, Junior Officer, Filipino, Roman Catholic)

This seafarer was not alone, and one of our interviewees went into some detail in explaining how, despite not being a very 'religious' man, he had found that religion and a religious colleague had helped him when he was a cadet. Cadets are frequently subjected to harsh treatment on board cargo vessels, which is often understood by senior officers to be part of an initiation into 'sea life'. In some cases, rather blatant bullying is justified on the grounds that it is simply a test of a young seafarers' 'mettle'. Such experiences can be very disheartening. In the context of a confined, strongly hierarchical, institutional environment from which there is no escape, even researchers who have boarded vessels where captains are unfriendly and abrasive have described finding these kinds of behaviours demoralizing and difficult to tolerate (Turgo and Sampson 2021). In the case of the aforementioned seafarer, the captain's behaviour rendered him increasingly mute and downhearted. Fortunately, a junior officer had noticed the change in him and endeavoured to offer him help and advice. Part of this related to drawing on his faith for support. When he signed off, the seafarer decided to have a rosary tattooed on his hand to remind him of what had happened. He explained that

This is a tattoo of a rosary, so basically a rosary is tattooed on my right hand. I am not really a religious person, like going to the church every Sunday, that kind of thing. So, with my second vessel, we had a Latvian captain, and he was not particularly good to me. Regardless of my efforts to do my best, he was always finding fault. So, I really had a terrible time with this captain. But I was still lucky because, at that time, we had a second mate who was a born-again Christian, and when this was going on (maybe it was a form of bullying, I don't know), he already noticed that my demeanour had changed from a cheerful cadet to a very quiet one. Before, he said, I looked very enthusiastic about things and all, and then later on, I became taciturn and withdrawn. He said that I lost my jolliness, and my efforts at work were reduced to minimum, something like that. And he said I looked exhausted all the time. Then when we were together on the bridge, he would tell me stories from the bible about not losing hope, and he would say some words of encouragement. He said that discouraging people is the easiest thing to do, and that some people find fulfilment in bringing people down, and that I should not be discouraged, no matter what. Then he said something like all the insults that I got from the captain, I should use them to fertilize my dreams? He was very helpful to me. He really helped me get back to my old footing. He told me to pray every day and remember that trials are part of Christian life. Because of him I was able to finish my contract without any problem and then when I was back home, I got this tattoo as a reminder that God will always be with me in my life. So, in a way, this tattoo is my weapon, and my show of promise to God that I will never be put down by anyone.

(*Caribbean Dream*, Junior Officer, Filipino, Roman Catholic)

The idea that turning to the practices associated with different faiths, whether meditation or prayer, was helpful in alleviating stress was expressed on multiple occasions during our interviews. Seafarers often feel very isolated and lonely while away at sea (Sampson and Ellis 2019), and this can impact negatively on their mental well-being. In this context, seafarers with a faith appeared to have access to a means of calming their anxieties and, as one seafarer put it, unburdening themselves of worries. He told us,

There are times that you are not feeling well, and your mind is full of worries, all you have to do is to whisper all your burdens to Him, pray to Him.

(*New China*, Chief Cook, Filipino, Roman Catholic)

However, in the context a of a highly monotonous life on board, seafarers also talked of the ways in which faith could go further in offering them support. One seafarer suggested that turning to God had a refreshing effect on him. He felt that

> Religion, in a way, gives me strength; praying calms you down; you think that God is there to help you and that you'll weather everything. So yes, religion has a role to play in making life on board bearable in many ways. When you are bored to death of life on board, you are fed up with what you're doing in the lounge, like watching the television, you go to your cabin and pray, you talk to God, and then when you are done, you feel refreshed. I don't know for others, but that's what I feel.
>
> (*New China*, Deck Cadet, Filipino, Roman Catholic)

A colleague on the same ship similarly explained that faith helped seafarers stave off some of the negative elements of life on board, such as loneliness and boredom. He implied that this was particularly important to less experienced seafarers, who were less inured to these unwelcome aspects of life at sea:

> I think religion, one's faith, helps you fight off stress and boredom, and loneliness. But in a way, you get used to them on board. But because you are a Catholic, you ask for help from God.
>
> (*New China*, Rating, Filipino, Roman Catholic)

An experienced captain reflected on how he felt that seafarers who had faith, any kind of faith, had 'someone' to turn to, however alone they were or how lonely they might feel. He explained that

> It's a basic human need to have someone, some beliefs, whatsoever. If it's our God or another God, it's never mind. Any human, anywhere. And, of course, at sea, we've special demanding situations that, depending on your personality, but yes, I believe it's a good help. If you have at least belief in something, that will help you. You have something to cling on to in times of need. You don't feel alone.
>
> (*Caribbean Dream*, Captain, Swedish, Lutheran)

Thus, in relation to maintaining emotional stability, staving off boredom, and counteracting loneliness, it seems that religion has an important part to play in some seafarers' lives.

Faith as both comfort and a source of unease

Seafaring is recognized as being amongst the most dangerous occupations (Hansen 1996; Nielsen and Roberts 1999; Roberts and Marlow 2005; Zevallos et al. 2014). Ships are out at sea in challenging weather conditions; they may be subject to equipment malfunction and structural failure; and, in normal circumstances, the daily work of seafarers entails operating heavy machinery and working in a potentially hazardous,[1] mobile, and noisy environment. Consequently, there are times in some seafarers' careers where they face experiences that are so dangerous that they fear for their lives. In 2015, a journalist used transcripts from the black box of a stricken vessel to reconstruct the events that led to its demise—it was ultimately lost with all hands to a hurricane at sea (Slade 2015). The book makes sobering reading, but the original transcripts bring home the degree to which seafarers are ultimately very alone, despite serving as part of a crew, and how, on occasion, this means that they experience facing a terrifying death, far from home, from help, and from loved ones. In such situations, seafarers with faith may find some solace in their beliefs and rituals. In her account of reviewing the transcripts, Slade notes that

> In the twenty-six hours of recording, there were hours and hours of silence while the two people on the bridge—officer and helmsman—drove the ship and watched for hazards steeped in their own thoughts.
>
> (Slade 2015, p. 337)

In this case, the sense of isolation and the helplessness of the crew in the face of the elements, along with their inability to avoid the fate that eventually overcame them, were haunting realities conveyed by their sparse conversations picked up on the bridge recordings of El Faro. In their last twenty-four hours, it is possible that those with faith fared better than those without it as, according to our interviewees, faith often did provide them with a sense of solace when they were very afraid on board. One seafarer explained how, like the crew of El Faro, he found himself and his colleagues caught up in extreme weather. He explained that, in this situation, he felt in serious need of his God to hold on to:

> There was one time when, for one week, the weather was very rough. That was the time when I felt I really needed God because I had nothing to hold on to. Our safety was in the balance. [...] You would not wish to be on board. It's total chaos. I wish I could describe it to you properly. Your cabin looks like it has been ransacked, with your things strewn all over the floor. Then there was a time when we had a hole in the bow because when the waves hit the anchor, it smashed against the bow and it created a hole there. The pump room became flooded as a result of that. We were in the middle of the ocean. Nobody was working any more aside from those on the bridge and those in the engine room doing some necessary monitoring of the equipment. We just waited for the

---

[1] Noxious fumes accumulating in enclosed spaces can be particularly lethal, for example.

weather to calm down. Some of the crew were already not feeling well, throwing up most of the time. All of us were already instructed to wear life vest, just in case. I was already prepared for the worst. If there was a call of abandon ship, then I should be ready for it. [...] That was the time when I felt that I really needed God in my life [laughs].

(*Caribbean Dream*, Motorman, Filipino, Roman Catholic)

Another seafarer was surprised that, on one occasion, when he believed he was facing death, his thoughts did not turn to his family at all, but instead, he found himself pleading with God for an 'easy death'. He said,

Going back to the bad weather, when I experienced it once in Biscay Bay, that was the time when I realized that when you think you're going to die, you don't think about your family already; no, I was not thinking about my family any more, I was thinking of myself, what kind of death I would have. That time I already gave up, in fact, when we were on our fifth day, and I was so unwell, I just asked God for an easy death.

(*Caribbean Dream*, Rating, Filipino, Roman Catholic)

Many of the Roman Catholic seafarers who were involved in our study drew on their belief in God in an almost superstitious way. They told us that they had established private rituals and practices on board that they considered offered them protection from harm. One practice related to carrying artefacts such as paper copies of prayers and rosaries for protection. These items were often ignored in relation to their original purpose—in the case of the rosary, prayer counting—but were carried to afford the individual safety in much the way that a superstitious person might carry something for 'luck'. One seafarer explained how he did not use his rosary during prayer but sometimes carried it with him to protect him from accidents. He explained,

They act like my protection. I feel like I am away from any potential accident when I have them with me. They are just in my cabin, actually, and I don't use them.

(*Caribbean Dream*, Messman, Filipino, Roman Catholic)

On a different vessel, a seafarer described keeping his rosary in his locker so that he could touch it before going to work. He explained,

I also keep a rosary in my locker. [...] I placed it there, sir, then I touch it before I go to work.

[...] I do it so that I would be protected every day because our work is danger-ous. I feel that I get protection from harm.

(*New China*, Rating, Filipino, Roman Catholic)

Another seafarer described how

> Though you could not be using the rosary, it is just there close by, which you could touch before going to sleep. I think that's the reason why I always bring some with me. [...] You know what, when I lie on my bed and see the figurine and my rosary, I feel settled; there is peace of mind. I think that is what the feeling they give me. There is this sense of security.
>
> (*Caribbean Dream*, Rating, Filipino, Roman Catholic)

There was evidence that some of these practices were passed on to seafarers, directly and indirectly, by other seafarers. One seafarer explained that he started to carry something like a novena in his wallet. He described how

> I have some like the one in my wallet; it's a small, slim pocketbook. In Roman Catholicism, it is called...[interviewer interjects with 'novena'?] [...] No, ahhh, yes, something like that. [...] in my wallet. [...] do you remember the ones they sell in Quiapo,[2] small librettos, that's what I carry with me. [...] It has been with me for a very long time already, since I started working as a seafarer it has been with me. [...] I read in a news article that a survivor from a shipwreck was carrying it when the tragedy happened. [...] He was the only survivor. [...]. The one I carry with me it's given by my wife.
>
> (*New China*, Bosun, Filipino, Iglesia Filipina Independiente)

Superstitions that were unrelated to religious icons or paraphernalia also influenced the practices of some seafarers. These seemed to be simultaneously practiced (out of habit or on a 'just-in-case' basis) and dismissed as irrational in some cases. One seafarer told us,

> There are certain things or items that you never ever speak of, or bring on board, you know. That is from many many years ago and has been with us. But those younger ones, I am not sure if they have even heard about it, and they do not know about this. So, for them, I don't think. Not that I believe them! But I do them out of habit.
>
> (*Caribbean Dream*, Chief Engineer, Norwegian, Lutheran)

While another similarly explained that he didn't believe the superstitions he practiced, but he followed them as there was no harm in doing so. He said,

> It's not that I believe in them but because I have become accustomed to following them, so I don't question anymore. For example, I avoid sweeping the floor

---

[2] Quiapo is a district in downtown Manila famous for street shopping and the Minor Basilica of the Black Nazarene. Around the church are stalls that sell religious items and amulets.

at night as it would drive luck away from the home. I follow that because there is no harm in doing it.

(*Caribbean Dream*, Able Seaman (AB), Filipino, Roman Catholic)

However, there were a couple of examples of seafarers who strongly believed in superstitions and carefully observed them at sea and at home. One explained that

Because I grew up in the province, I have become accustomed to believing in superstitions, like not sweeping the floor at night. I learned them from the old people in our place [...] I believe in them, also in witchcraft [...] There were events in my place that strengthened my belief in them. My grandfather was a traditional healer, and he told me stories of battles against witches and monsters.

(*Caribbean Dream*, Wiper, Filipino, Roman Catholic)

Superstitions were both rooted in the traditions of seafarers' homelands and (sometimes) passed on between people with different cultural backgrounds. However they were acquired, observing them served to make seafarers feel a little safer in their hostile environments. In this way, they served a similar function to faith but were usually supplemental to religious beliefs and less strongly held and observed. Their relatively superficial nature meant that they did not tend to be a great source of inner conflict or disquiet among seafarers. This contrasted with religious beliefs, which, as touched on in Chapter 4, were not only a source of comfort to seafarers but could also be a source of unease. One seafarer described how he felt that he had assumed two different identities, a mischievous shipboard persona that involved knowingly acting against the teachings of his faith and a more devout personality ashore. This was personally difficult for him. He described finding it challenging to reconcile the demands of his religion with the need to fit in with his colleagues on board. He explained,

It is something like this: I have become two, in a way. On board I act like a mischievous child. I like the feeling of being able to make the people around me happy with my antics, even if what I do are contrary to the teachings of my religion. Ashore, the things that I do on board are not good. But on board I make many people happy, and I feel really happy that I am making everyone happy. [...] I don't know how to reconcile these things, how to avoid sinful things and do the right ones and, at the same time, feel happy and make other people happy. It's very difficult.

(*New China*, Rating, Filipino, Jesus Is Lord)

Another seafarer talked of how he felt obliged to take part in drinking sessions even though he considered it a sin. This was something that had concerned him when he contemplated a life at sea as he understood there to be a shipboard 'culture of drinking'. Although he seemed reconciled to this to an extent, he had earlier described how his religion was the 'basis of' his 'being', and he stated that 'regardless of requests and enticements I should be saying 'No''. In this context, his regular drinking appeared to trouble his conscience, and he periodically attempted to sidestep the demands, with varying degrees of success. He described how

> Before I do something which is in contradiction to my beliefs as a Baptist Christian, like drinking, I ask forgiveness from God. I say, 'Lord, here we go again, I will be drinking with my mates and you know why I will do this.' So if it is Saturday night, I know that I will have to sin again because there will be drinking and all, and I ask for God's forgiveness. But sometimes, after dinner, I go straight to my cabin to avoid committing a sin. However, of course, I am not always successful. On my way up, I will meet somebody who will drag me to the lounge and that's it. I must drink. Or if I am already in my cabin, I will get a call, and if I don't answer the phone, somebody will be sent to fetch me. In a way, everybody is asked to join the fun. I can't say no to them.
>
> (*Caribbean Dream*, Rating, Filipino, Baptist)

Where seafarers did not conform, or where they did not keep their religious views private, they could find themselves in conflicts with others and at risk of ostracization. One seafarer described how, on board one of his ships, a relatively inexperienced seafarer made the mistake of being very vocal about his religious beliefs. Initially, the seafarer was politely tolerated by his colleagues, but at some stage, their patience ran out. Not only did he find himself at odds with a senior officer and in trouble with the captain as a result of his vociferous proclamations, but he also came to be avoided by many of his colleagues, who were weary of his views but reluctant to become embroiled in an argument. In this instance, the seafarer did not seem to be fully aware of the way in which his beliefs were alienating him from his colleagues on board, but this does not mean that he was unaffected by being shunned. The participant described how

> So, this AB was fairly new on board, and he was very vocal in letting everyone know about his religious beliefs. He was even preaching to us during break, though we were just very polite; we would just nod and smile. He was saying that their religion was the true religion, and that their bible was the true bible and that their leader, Brother Eli, was the new prophet sent by God. So, all the while, the AB was preaching to all about his religious beliefs. But this officer, our third officer had a different belief. For him, though he believed in God, he believed that the bible was written by people like us, though they were inspired by God. So, one day after dinner, whilst we were in the lounge, the AB went on his usual way of saying that Brother Eli was sent by God and that the bible they were using was the true bible of Christianity. Our third mate, tired and

exasperated of hearing the same crap from the AB, stood up and told him to shut up, and then there was a really heated argument afterwards. They only ended their debate when the captain came in because he heard the noise from the crew mess, which was right next to the lounge. [...] Actually, the two of them had no direct dealing with one another, but the third mate was really pissed off with the AB. I think the AB was advised by the bosun after that to refrain from talking about his religious beliefs in the presence of other seafarers so that there would no problem like what happened with the third mate. [Interviewer asks, 'Did the AB follow the advice of the bosun'?] Yes, and no [laughs]. Yes, because he stopped his preaching for maybe a month but after that he started again sharing his religious beliefs with us, but we were not paying attention to him any longer and many were in fact avoiding him.

(*Caribbean Dream*, Junior Officer, Filipino, Roman Catholic)

It is self-evidently not just at sea that some individuals run into problems in balancing their need to evangelize with a need to avoid conflict at work. In her book about the lives of a group of conservative evangelicals living in London, Anna Strhan recounts a tale told to her by one of her participants. The thirty-six-year-old man told her that when he was working in the city, he set up a Christian prayer group in his company and helped organize carol services. He explained his frustration that only around 200 of the 1,500 people in his office ever attended a carol service, and he decided to try to take 'the gospel to all my colleagues' (Strhan 2015, p. 83). His method was to give out a pamphlet he had written himself, with an invitation to a follow-up talk with a guest speaker, to every individual in his office. Within fifteen minutes of completing the distribution, he was summoned to see the company's head of human resources, who was absolutely furious and told him that what he had done 'is no different from giving people an invitation to join a Nazi rally, or an invitation to join a jihad' (Strhan 2015, p. 840). He explained to Strhan that his intention had not been to offend. Strhan observes that, at this time, and in an affirmatory kind of way, he gained support from members of his evangelical group, which operated beyond the workplace. This allowed him to feel part of a bounded moral community outside the workplace with whom he had access on a daily basis. In that sense, his situation was radically different to those seafarers who feel a need to evangelize at sea. For them, evangelism carries with it greater risks and fewer protections, and it remains relatively unusual to come across seafarers who engage in the long-term practice of any kind of evangelism on board.

It was abundantly evident in our research that community support was central to many seafarers in observing their religious obligations. For some seafarers, religious practices and rituals were so intimately bound up with their feelings of community and family that they found it painful on board to engage in religious meetings or discussions. One rating explained that despite checking with his wife that his family had attended church every Sunday, he did not personally wish to engage in group religious activities on board. He suggested that these would merely serve to encourage homesickness and sadness and that it was better to simply regard time on board as a hiatus from 'real life'. He explained,

> When I chat with my wife on Facebook, I still ask them if they went to church on Sunday, I check on them. It is like a routine for me. I should add that I am at sea to support my family, so this is not my real life. My real life is ashore. I am here to earn money for my family so what I do here is plainly about earning money. And you see, if we do prayer meeting on board, soon we will miss our family because we will talk about homesickness, our love for our family, all those things, and then we will be emotional until we all cry. So, it is much better if we just talk about funny things or do some other things to forget that we are thousands of miles away from our families. So, after work, we drink a bit. Then when feeling tipsy go straight to the cabin and sleep. Then wake up in the morning and work. You know, if there is a regular prayer meeting, I think, people will start missing their families because they will be forced to talk about what they feel, their innermost thoughts, those things. Then as a result, many will request to shorten their stay on board. Believe me, that is true!
>
> (*Caribbean Dream*, Messman, Filipino, Roman Catholic)

Thus, although drawing upon religion while on board was a source of comfort, support, and solace for many seafarers, it could also be a source of inner turmoil, conflict with others, and emotional pain. In this context, it was not surprising, perhaps, to discover the multitude of ways in which many seafarers simply seemed to shed their religious identities as they came up the gangway and only reclaimed them once they returned home to their 'real lives'.

The Significance of Chaplains

Port chaplains are usually, but not exclusively, Christians serving Christian faith-based charities. They do not only support Christian seafarers on board, however, but also visit ships with, and offer their services to, seafarers of various nationalities and faiths and to those with none. In the context of the remote, institutionalized, and work-orientated lives of seafarers, shipboard visits from chaplains and volunteers have the potential to make a considerable difference. For our participants, this seemed to be the case. Seafarers were overwhelmingly positive about the visits they received from chaplains and the practical support they offered. One captain talked with admiration of the selflessness of chaplains and how he admired them, telling us that

I admire this spirit of voluntarism, whatsoever. Whatever they do. That's a very good...very good, er...I lost the word. Very good human, er...way to be a human. Giving of yourself without requiring of anything.

(*Caribbean Dream*, Captain, Swedish, Lutheran)

In the case of this particular captain, he described having no need of any particular service or assistance from chaplains and suggested that the mere demonstration that seafarers are being thought of by someone, somewhere, was sufficient to make him feel content and pleased to receive chaplains on board. This general sentiment was described in different ways by several seafarers, who emphasized how a visit from a chaplain could make them feel valued. One, who had noted the aged nature of some chaplains, told us,

I think all of them are very good, very helpful always; I can't say anything negative about them because what they do is very difficult, especially for old chaplains. I really appreciate what they do. They are nice to talk to, you feel relaxed and valued.

(*Caribbean Dream*, Electrician, Filipino, Iglesia Filipina Independiente)

While chaplains were always open to chatting and hoped to provide a listening ear to shipboard workers, for some seafarers, their value lay in the practical assistance that chaplains gave them. One described how chaplains had played a long-standing role in facilitating communication between seafarers and their families. He said that prior to the internet, chaplains had helped seafarers by posting letters for them, while, in the current context, they sell SIM cards and phone credits. He seemed as surprised as our research team had been that chaplains in many ports were willing to provide a kind of free personal shopping service for seafarers who regularly called into their port. The seafarer explained how

I think their presence on board is always good. I should say that when they come on board you know that you could have SIM card if you need one and phone credits, too. And they are there to listen if you have problems or concerns. I remember also many years ago, before we had internet on board and when phone calls were expensive, we would ask the chaplain we would meet to help us send letters to the Philippines. So, we would leave him our letters and some money, and he would be the one to send them to post. They were really very helpful. And if you visit the port regularly, you could ask the chaplain to buy some items for you. So, you give him money and then when you come back, he will give to you the item that you asked him to buy with no extra charge! But in my case, I would give some money, say 10 dollars, my donation to the seaman's club; I would tell him.

(*Caribbean Dream*, Messman, Filipino, Roman Catholic)

In an environment where many seafarers had lost confidence in the shore-based personnel working for their own companies (Sampson et al. 2019), trust was uniquely embedded in the relationships between seafarers and chaplains (Cadge et al. 2022). Many seafarers regarded chaplains as people they could talk to confidentially. In some cases, they would turn to a visiting chaplain to report a problem that the crew was experiencing on board. Sometimes, these problems would be passed on to the International Transport Workers' Federation (ITF) or to a Maritime Authority if they were serious in nature, for example about unpaid wages or health and safety. In other cases, chaplains would make use of their networks to request that a chaplain in the next port of call visit the ship and check on the situation. Increasingly, social media is playing a role in keeping seafarers in touch with chaplains, and this allows for closer connections and better follow-up services. Beyond this, seafarers also trusted chaplains with their own money, which was given to them for future purchases, which the seafarer would receive next time the vessel came to the port, or to be sent 'home' on the seafarer's behalf. Furthermore, in a strange country where they did not know anyone, could not find their own way around, and had limited time, many seafarers valued chaplains as 'friends' in a foreign land. One explained,

> I think, sir, we still need them. Not all ports are close to a mall, and sometimes ships do not have internet on board. Or, sir, remember chaplains provide us with free transport, so they are a very good help to us. And with chaplains, you feel like you have a friend in a foreign country and with seaman's club, I don't know, I feel safe when I am there. So, it is good to have them. We still need them.
> (*Caribbean Dream*, Motorman, Filipino, Roman Catholic)

Another suggested that

> They are very helpful to us. I can't speak for everyone, but I think chaplains are always a great help to seafarers. You could trust them with your money, say, sending money back home or if advice for the cheapest place to buy gadgets, that kind of thing.
> (*Caribbean Dream*, Motorman, Filipino, Roman Catholic)

Beyond this, for a small number of seafarers, chaplains become of great significance when they find themselves ashore in the midst of some kind of crisis. This could be following an accident or illness, as we witnessed in the course of our fieldwork, when a chaplain made several hospital visits to a seafarer who had been disembarked for emergency medical treatment. The seafarer concerned was immensely grateful for, and touched by, the initial visit, in the course of which the chaplain facilitated a phone call home to the seafarer's wife. A field note recorded how the seafarer told his wife that, because of his visitors, he no longer felt alone, and it goes on to describe his expression of gratitude to the chaplain and researcher. Beginning with the seafarer's words, the researcher's note states:

'See the people who are visiting me', he said to his wife, 'the chaplain and his friend. I don't feel alone any more.' Then the seafarer cried. [...] Before we left, the seafarer thanked [name]. 'I will not forget you', he said. 'You were here when I was not expecting you. You did not know me but you found time to see me.'

(Porton field notes)

Hospital admission is a relatively routine reason for chaplains to visit seafarers who have been forced to disembark their vessel but who have been unable to immediately return home. Another situation involving the disembarkation of seafarers and the prevention of their immediate return home arises when seafarers run into trouble with the authorities ashore following a perceived/actual breach of regulations. These situations are less commonly experienced by chaplains and seafarers, but when they do arise, seafarers may find themselves stranded with limited resources for a long period of time. On their website, one charity providing port-based chaplaincy and welfare services for seafarers describes a case in which they had become involved. They recount how

Stella Maris has been called upon by the local representative of the International Transport Workers' Federation (ITF) to assist seafarers who are sometimes held as material witnesses in pollution cases by the Coast Guard. A couple of years ago one such case involved six seafarers who were put up into two apartments in a nearby suburb of New Orleans. The ITF representative made us aware of their circumstances and we at Stella Maris provided communion services and visits to the seafarers where they stayed. Stella Maris arranged for a local Filipino group active with Stella Maris to pick up the seafarers who were mostly Catholic and took them to church. This volunteer group also fixed meals for them. Stella Maris staff would bring them to the centre so the seafarers could use email and just have a change of scenery. This situation lasted for approximately four to six months as they awaited the trial.

(United States Conference of Catholic Bishops, 'Reflections from an AoS Chaplain in the Port of Houston', https://www.usccb.org/committees/pastoral-care-migrants-refugees-travelers/aos-featured-stories-faith-filled-life-sea, accessed 18 November 2021)

In the account by Stella Maris, some emphasis is placed on the faith-based support that they provided to the seafarers who were awaiting trial in New Orleans, and mention is made of providing communion and transport to church for services. On board ships, some seafarers also described the faith that underpins the work of chaplains as significant to them. In some cases, the presence of a chaplain on board reminded them of their faith and of their religious obligations. This seemed welcome in a context where seafarers commonly described a sense of separation from their religion and associated practices while on board. One seafarer explained how

The presence of chaplains on board reminds seafarers of the need to communicate with God regularly. In a way, when they come on board, we become conscious of our obligations to God. You see, seafarers are very busy on board and tend to focus on their work and, in the process, forget God. So, when chaplains come on board, it feels like, yes, they are here to remind us of the importance of God in our lives.

(*Caribbean Dream*, Electrician, Filipino, Iglesia Filipina Independiente)

Participants in our study who were in the habit of receiving Mass at home also described how they welcomed the increasingly rare occasions when a Mass might be arranged on board. Occasionally, they had experience of requesting the Mass via the captain on board. One seafarer explained how decisions arise with regard to requesting a Mass and then recalled a particular shipboard experience when he and colleagues wanted a Mass in order for a priest to bless the ship:

Most of the time, the crew would have a discussion amongst themselves about the need for a Mass to be held on board. We would say, 'Let's have Mass on board.' 'Okay, then, that's a good idea.' Then we would call the mission and request for a priest to come on board to hold a Mass. In our case, there was really no special reason. We just agreed amongst ourselves that a priest was needed to bless the ship.

(*New China*, Rating, Filipino, Roman Catholic)

Sometimes, a Mass was requested for a specific reason. Most often, this was when a particularly unfortunate event had befallen the ship or a seafarer. Understandably, suicides, accidents, and sudden, unexpected deaths have a major impact on most seafarers. Crews on cargo vessels are generally relatively small, and as a result, they feel closely connected to such events. There is no member of the crew that a seafarer will not have had contact with after some time on board. In some cases, they will know their colleagues well, as a fellow member of a work group, as a manager/supervisor, or as a provider of services such as food. In the engine department, seafarers will all work in the relatively confined space of the engine room and will frequently engage in tasks jointly as a team—receiving stores or pulling pistons, for example. On the 'deck' side of the ship, officers of the watch hand over to one another at the beginning and end of their watches and may be on the bridge together during pilotages or on the aft or fore decks while mooring. Deck ratings all work together under the supervision of a bosun, who takes instructions from the chief officer, and all seafarers come into contact with the galley staff on a daily basis. In this way, on a professional level, ships' crews normally operate as interconnected and closely coupled units. Any untoward events impact on how they feel about being on board and about the spaces they frequent. One seafarer explained how, on board his ship, an AB had a heart attack and died. He did not describe this as a personal emotional loss but explained how it unsettled him and his colleagues for a significant period of time. In this context, the captain at the time decided to request a Mass, perhaps to honour the seafarer appropriately or to soothe the remaining seafarers and alleviate their distress. The seafarer told us,

> An AB died; he had a cardiac arrest. So, the captain arranged for a Mass to be held on board. That happened in 2005. [...] They were on shore leave, and it was very hot outside. So, they went to a seaman's club and had a round of drinks. Then suddenly he lost consciousness. People were saying that maybe because it was very hot outside and then he was drinking cold drinks, so they said, his system had a shock. I don't know. So when we left the port after that and docked in Houston, the captain, who was Filipino, asked for a chaplain to hold Mass on board. [...] It's weird, it felt different. We had this feeling that he was just around. We were sensing his presence. So there was a bit of unease. Then maybe for a month, we were scared of being alone. But I thought it was only in our minds. Then, I had a workmate there who would always ask me to come with him for his visit to the engine room every night. It was funny, but I understood him. So I kept on advising him that the fear was only imagined, but regardless, the fear was still there and that continued for a month or so. [...] in a way, that [the Mass] helped us to calm down. That lessened our anxieties.
>
> (*Caribbean Dream*, Rating, Filipino, Roman Catholic)

Amongst the small number of seafarers who, across the length of their careers, had experienced a Mass being held on board, we found one seafarer who acknowledged that he had not willingly attended the Mass that he had experienced but had attended because he felt obliged to by the captain. He reflected that he would not do this again but would hope to feel able to tell the captain that he did not want to attend a religious service which was unrelated to his own faith. He explained that

> I attended a Mass on board because the captain required us to attend. You can't really say no. Now, I think I can argue my way; I can say no, since I am on board not for this. When I attended this Mass, I was just there, I did not do what they were doing. My presence was enough. I was just there because I wanted our captain to see that I was there. But I think next time I would decline. I would tell the captain that it's not my religion. I hope he would not mind.
>
> (*New China*, Rating, Filipino, Jesus Is Lord)

This example illustrates some of the potential difficulties that may arise when religious services are held on board multinational/multi-ethnic ships. It is possible that the increasing rarity of such service provision relates to an awareness of the sensitivities involved.

Conclusion

Left to their own devices, seafarers generally confine religion to the private shipboard domain. This serves to avoid the emergence of conflict, accusations of hypocrisy, and the emotional overload that might accompany the kinds of discussions and soul searching that can be associated with spiritual group discussions. This renders faith largely invisible on board, and some seafarers only learned of the faiths observed by others through gossip or as a consequence of behaviours relating to diet and alcohol. This public behaviour did not diminish the importance of faith to most seafarers on board. However, it was apparent from seafarers' accounts that, on board, many felt relatively free of the faith-related strictures that they faced ashore. In some cases, this did not trouble seafarers, who felt that they had no option but to embrace the shipboard occupational culture and also felt that their lives of privation were such that they had an entitlement to prohibited activities such as the engagement of sex workers. However, there were some seafarers who found that the double identities they constructed, as 'salty seafarers' on board and 'pious respectable citizens' ashore, created some personal tensions and inner conflict. Overall, despite frequently neglecting their faith-based practices on board, faith did remain important to most religious seafarers when they found themselves in difficult conditions—facing adversity. Similarly, they valued the visits from port chaplains—not always in their role as religious figures but overwhelmingly as 'friends' and welfare service providers. However, the provision of these services requires more than the presence of willing personnel who are motivated to visit ships and provide assistance to seafarers; it requires organization and resource that is located within wider community structures. In the next chapters, we focus on the relationship between chaplains, seafarers' centres, and local communities; on the ways that charities have come together to provide services to seafarers; and on the similarities and differences that are found between port chaplaincy and other kinds of chaplaincy in the United Kingdom.

Chaplaincy and Seafarers: Faith at Work. Helen Sampson, Nelson Turgo, Wendy Cadge, and Sophie Gilliat-Ray, Oxford University Press. © Helen Sampson, Nelson Turgo, Wendy Cadge, and Sophie Gilliat-Ray 2024.
DOI: 10.1093/9780198913290.003.0006

PART III
CONTEXTUALIZING PORT CHAPLAINCY

6

Port Chaplaincy and the Wider Community

Introduction

In providing for seafarers' faith and welfare needs, there has been a long tradition in the United Kingdom of charities, the government, companies, and local communities working together to support seafarers calling at British ports and, beyond this, ensuring that British seafarers calling at overseas ports also have their needs catered for.

In 1942, a report on the welfare of seafarers and factory workers was presented to Parliament (HMSO 1942). At this time, the Seaman's Welfare Board had already been established to advise ministers on 'all questions concerning the welfare of British, Allied and Foreign seamen in British ports and of the crews of British ships in overseas ports' (HMSO 1942, p. 8). Furthermore, Seaman's Welfare Officers were already in place covering most major ports, and in Teesside, Aberdeen, Southampton, and Hartlepool, welfare work was supported by the establishment of Port Welfare Committees. A welfare fund financed activities or developments approved by the Seaman's Welfare Board, and funds for this purpose were donated by private individuals, the shipping federation (representing British shipowners), and the Royal Seaman's pension fund.

In relation to hostel accommodation, recreational facilities, waiting rooms at recruitment centres, and support to hospitalized seafarers (donated toiletries, stamped envelopes, reading materials), the 1942 government report reveals the way in which the voluntary sector was incorporated into the network of welfare providers that came together to meet seafarers' needs under the auspices of the Seaman's Welfare Board. Prior to 1940, the provisions made for seafarers' welfare were wholly made on the initiative of charities, and a 1945 government report notes that 'In general, only the voluntary organisations played any effective role in the field of temporal welfare in the years before the outbreak of war. Neither the government nor the shipping industry came into the field to any extent until 1940' (HMSO 1945, p. 8) While voluntary organizations were often supported by large donations made by ship operators, and owners, the report suggests that 'the work done by the voluntary organisations made it unnecessary for the industry (or the Government) to take any special steps to deal with the problem' (HMSO 1945, p. 9). It is also clear from the report that by this time (1945), the focus of voluntary organizations was on the provision of welfare to all seafarers, regardless of their faith or background. The report went on to recommend that a shipping levy be applied to ship operators and seafarers, along similar lines to National Health Insurance contributions, in order to meet the costs of seafarers' welfare. It noted, however, that there was some 'evidence which leads us to expect that it will not be possible to maintain a full club system' (providing seafarers' welfare) 'without a continued loss on running expenses' (HMSO 1945, p. 37).

It is extraordinary that the situation has changed so little in the intervening years. There are still calls to introduce a ship levy made in some quarters, and there is no doubt that the provision of seafarers' centres (replacing seaman's clubs) places considerable strain on charity resources and is reliant on voluntary donations, including both goods and services. Moreover, in many international ports, there is no welfare provision for seafarers whatsoever (Sampson et al. 2022).

In the twenty-first century, the funding of seafarers' centres and port chaplaincy services has been shown to be even more challenging, as ship operators have become somewhat removed from seafarers (Sampson 2013). Family businesses where ship owners once had personal contact with the seafarers operating their ships (and therefore some personal commitment to them) have become few and far between (Sampson 2024), and it is far more common for ships to be run by third-party ship management companies and shareholder-owned corporations. In addition, more that 70 per cent of the world fleet is now flagged with what are termed 'open registers' (UNCTAD 2021). located in states such as Panama and Liberia, and crewing is organized by third-party crew agencies recruiting labour in countries such as the Philippines, China, and India. In this context, the link between local ship owners and local seafarers has been effectively severed, and today, seafarers' centres are fortunate if they receive direct support from local shipping businesses.

The international maritime community is conscious of the need to provide seafarers with better welfare support, and in order to address the problem of inadequate provision, the Maritime Labour Convention 2006, required all members states to 'promote the development of welfare facilities in appropriate ports following consultation with shipowners and seafarers' organisations' (ILO 2006). It also went beyond this, however, to address financing thus:

> In accordance with national conditions and practice, financial support for port welfare facilities should be made available through one or more of the following: (a) grants from public funds; (b) levies or other special dues from shipping sources; (c) voluntary contributions from shipowners, seafarers, or their organizations; and (d) voluntary contributions from other sources. 2. Where welfare taxes, levies and special dues are imposed, they should be used only for the purposes for which they are raised.
>
> (ILO 2006, Guideline B4.4.4)

This clause has encouraged the belief, in some quarters, that in the future, much-needed financial support will be raised from public funds or industry bodies (including shipping companies) in support of international port-based welfare services. As we will describe, however, the evidence from this research indicates that such financial support has yet to substantially materialize, and there are those who believe that it never will.

The consequences of a lack of shoreside facilities for seafarers and shortfalls in funding for the facilities that do exist cast a long shadow. There are very many ports that lack centre facilities for seafarers of any kind at all, and in our research, we encountered one benevolent individual attempting to meet seafarers' welfare needs quite alone from the back of a vehicle that he owned himself. A directory published to support global seafarers (https://www.seafarerhelp.org/en/seafarers-directory accessed 1 March 2024) indicates that Europe is the region with the largest number of seafarers' centres overall. There are 158 seafarers' centres identified in Europe, 125 in North America, 51 in Asia-Pacific, 38 in Australia and New Zealand, 17 in the Middle East, 19 in Africa, and 10 in South America. This amounts to a total of 418 seafarers' centres across the globe. In line with these figures, it is worth highlighting that published ethnographic accounts indicate that seafarers' centres and welfare services are infrequently encountered by seafarers (Sampson 2013) and that in providing 121 seafarers' centres of the 418 that exist worldwide, the Mission to Seafarers is one of the major providers of seafarers' centres globally (see also Chapter 1).

Where centres do exist, or where chaplains maintain a 'presence', there are considerable efforts made locally to try to redress the funding imbalance. This involves chaplains in the organization, and conduct, of fund-raising activities, and we have discussed these extensively in Chapter 3. What we have yet to consider, however, is how the fundraising activities of local chaplains and the national organizations by which they are employed connect with, and are embedded within, local community networks and organizations. In this chapter, we consider the local connections between seafarers' centres and their adjacent communities as well as the connections between seafarers' centres and associated national organizations and community groups.

Local Connections between Port Chaplains, Seafarers' Centres, and Community Groups

In the course of our port-based fieldwork, we were struck by the support for the centres and for seafarers that came from the local community. The Riverside centre seemed to be particularly closely connected to the community and received a huge amount of local support. Most commonly, this took the form of donations. Often, local people would simply show up at the seafarers' centre with arms full of donated goods. These largely consisted of a combination of home-made and second-hand items. Local 'knit-and-natter' groups regularly donated woolly hats, for example. On receiving some of these gifts on behalf of the centre, Nelson felt struck by the generosity of the public towards seafarers, and he wrote in his field notes that

> A woman came to the centre to bring a bag of donations—knitted beanies and gloves. She said that she comes to the centre once a month to hand in her donation, some she made herself, and others given to her by her friends. Whenever people like her come to the centre, I feel a sense of wonder, how some people would spend time to do things for the benefit of others, just very heart-warming. I told her that many seafarers would surely thank her for her time and generosity.
>
> (Riverside field notes)

Such was the generosity of the public that organizers found it difficult to manage the workload associated with receiving, sorting, and distributing items brought by volunteers. Nelson was surprised at the level of donations whenever he was left in charge of taking telephone calls. On one routine occasion, he noted that, in just an hour, he received two calls about bringing donated goods to the centre. He commented in a fieldwork that

> As there were only two of us left in the centre, myself and the volunteer, I played the role of a telephone receptionist again. In an hour, I must have answered five calls, three from seafarers wanting a lift and two from people living close to the centre wanting to leave donations of clothes and toys.
>
> (Riverside field notes)

Indeed, such was the supply that sometimes, receiving donated goods seemed overwhelming, and Nelson was given cause to speculate about how it could all be managed. He wrote in a field note that

> Whilst [name] was away, somebody came in bringing a donation of used clothes and shoes to the centre. It's raining donations in the centre! Oftentimes, I wonder where they put all the donations that they received. The centre was overflowing with bric-a-brac of almost anything and everything. I even spotted some lingerie on a side table!
>
> (Riverside field notes)

A peek into a storage room at one seafarers' centre confirmed to him that his instincts in suspecting that the centre must be overwhelmed with donated goods were correct. In a field note, he recorded that

The door to the storage room was a ar so I had a peek. It was overflowing with donations of all types and sizes. Bags and bags of clothes were piled on top of one another. There were also huge pieces of luggage. I saw toys and even carpentry tools. The storage room was a veritable Aladdin's cave.

(Riverside field notes)

Curiously, it seemed that more items were always welcome, despite the fact that the centre seemed to be awash with donated clothes and goods of every kind, shape, and size. The centre manager spent a good deal of time cultivating networks in the city and educating people about seafarers' welfare and needs, and his efforts were often rewarded with action. On learning about seafarers and their needs, members of the community responded in a variety of ways. Some switched from donating to charity shops in the city and instead brought clothes to the seafarers' centre, while others found themselves thinking of the seafarers' centre when faced with leftover food and snacks following work functions. In a field note, Nelson recorded that

Today, two ladies visited the centre and left two bags of clothes. They said that they attended one of [name of centre manager]'s talks and decided to donate their husbands' used clothes to the centre instead of leaving them in charity shops. Some minutes after they left the centre, a man in a suit arrived bringing sandwiches and packs of crisps. He said that his office had a meeting, and there was some left-over food which he thought would be better off left to the centre for the staff to enjoy, or maybe for the seafarers.

(Riverside field notes)

The Riverside centre manager seemed particularly adept at raising awareness, and with it, practical support from the local community beyond his port. He gave the impression of never being truly off duty in relation to promoting the image of the centre and in drumming up support for his cause. Standing in for him, one day, Nelson experienced at first hand how exhausting the emotional labour associated with putting on your 'best face' for the public could be. In a field note, he reflected that

I think it is also entertaining visitors in the centre, I mean people who come to the centre on a regular basis to either make a donation or inquire about what they could provide to the centre, which at times, for me, is exhausting.[1] And the thing is, I would only do it when the staff were away. For instance, some days ago, with the staff away, I happened to entertain two visitors. They said they heard [name of centre manager] talk at an event a month ago, and they wanted to inquire about

---

[1] Riverside was located just outside the port limits, and visitors did not have to clear port security in order to visit the centre. This increased accessibility was a factor in the relatively high number of 'visits' from local members of the public.

the possibility of helping in the centre. As the centre manager was temporarily out and about, I told them to wait for him, but at the same time, as we were the only people in the centre, I wanted to play a good host to them, so I explained to them what I do and what I experienced in my fieldwork at sea. I thought that would, in some ways, inspire them even more to help in whatever way they can the centre. After half an hour of discussion, which I enjoyed tremendously, the centre manager arrived, and I introduced him to the visitors. Whilst they were having a chat, and I was in my chair, sipping my tea, it dawned on me how exhausted I was. And I realized that it was the intense focus that I had to exert whilst listening to their questions, and answering them, because I wanted to put my best foot forward, and I felt like I owed it to the centre to help them gather more supporters. And come to think of it, in some days, aside from looking after the seafarers visiting the centre, the staff, it was [name of manager] who had to sit down with these people and explain to them why their help is most needed in the centre.

(Riverside field notes)

In Porton, one chaplain spent less time with unaffiliated community members (people in schools, for example) and more time with people who were connected to the parish church. When the opportunity arose, he would take seafarers out to religious services, where they could meet, and be seen by, local parishioners. This was beneficial for seafarers, who had an opportunity to practice their English and meet new people, and educational for parishioners, who had the opportunity to meet seafarers face to face and to directly find out more about their lives, work, and welfare needs. An occasion such as this was captured in a field note describing how

After the Mass, we lingered for a while and had tea with the rest of the congregation. As [name] knew the vicar and many of those who attended the service personally, the seafarers were welcomed warmly by everyone. The seafarers noted how special they were, the centre of everyone's attention. They were also toured in the church by one of the parishioners.

(Porton field notes)

Parishioners would often knit woolly hats and gloves for seafarers, supplementing these with gifts of other warm clothing and treats such as chocolates. This was also common practice elsewhere in the United Kingdom, and a stakeholder told us,

We also get on a day-to-day basis support from parishes who will collect gifts; we take a lot of gifts in the form of things like knitted woollen hats, and Toblerone, and chocolates, and warm clothing, and the parishes will collect that, and that's a really, really good thing to take with you on a trip. It's a good way of establishing, I think, a good friendship.

(Stakeholder from the United Kingdom)

The popularity of donations of woolly hats has lent them an emblematic status, and seafarers readily associate gifts of woolly hats with the visits of port chaplains. The Mission to Seafarers (MtS) accounts for 2019/2020 showed that, in 2019, the MtS received 1.6 tons of woolly hats intended for disbursement to seafarers across the globe! That amounts to an awful lot of hats!

In Porton, there was some cross-over between the parish and the centre, which was embodied by the curate, who was also a centre volunteer. He acted as a regular conduit of information and gifts, which flowed to and from the centre and visiting seafarers. In assisting him, Nelson was struck by the quantity and weight of goods that he took on board and the physical labour that was associated with climbing on board vessels loaded down with goodies. He wrote that

> I decided to do ship visiting with Father [name], a curate and a volunteer in the centre. He comes to the port every Thursday and does ship visiting. He used to be a port chaplain, but when he was asked to work as full-time curate in a local parish, he has asked that he devote a day each week for ship visiting. Father [name] was by all means ready with ship visiting. He had packed his ruck sack with bookmarks, small square papers with printed bible quotes (all laminated), all done in the parish by some of his parishioners. As I was his assistant, I carried the bag of chocolates for him. It was very heavy. Father [name] was in his early sixties. And he was also carrying a heavy ruck sack.
>
> (Porton field notes)

The curate had established a way of encouraging members of his parish to think regularly about, and donate to, seafarers and the mission. As a result, he often had chocolates with him to take on board for seafarers. Nelson discussed with him the gifts that he was given for seafarers, and he discovered that the curate had established some staple mechanisms for prompting parishioners to donate to seafarers. These include setting up a box for donations located within the church. Nelson noted that

> On our drive to the small ports along [place], Father [name] said that the chocolates came from his congregation, numbering around thirty. He said there is a box in the church where his parishioners drop their donations. From time to time, he also uses his own money to buy chocolates. In other times, people would come up to him to give money. He has also a family that volunteers to make all the small gifts (bookmarks, prayer cards, etc.) for seafarers. The gifts are delivered to him on a weekly basis. He said that he is oftentimes overwhelmed by the generosity of people, giving gifts to people that they have not met in person.
>
> (Porton field notes)

The curate was not the only member of the Porton team with a close connection to local parishioners. The port chaplain had adopted a volunteer role in his local church, which allowed him to lead morning prayers once a month and to encourage parishioners to support fundraising and gifting drives such as Christmas collections, for example. Nelson described how

> Before going to the port, [name] conducted a morning prayer in [name] Church. [Name] serves as a volunteer lay leader in the parish and leads a morning prayer once a month, usually the second Wednesday of the month. Aside from the training that he gets from this volunteer work, he also gets to connect the parish to the work that he does in the port. For instance, parishioners get to donate goods to the centre [...] every Christmas for distribution to seafarers. [Name] also said that some women parishioners would knit woolly hats for seafarers. Others would donate used clothing. Some would even give him money. In a number of cases, he said, after every Mass, he would be approached by some parishioners to donate small amounts of money. 'For your ministry to the seafarers', they would tell him. So, devoting some of his work time outside the port allows him to access more resources for the benefit of seafarers. For [name], this is another way of 'fund-raising' because he can't always rely on the office in London to provide for all the seafarers' needs. Through this work with the church in [place], he was also able to bring seafarers there to attend church services if they wanted to.
>
> (Porton field notes)

Churches could be a very important source of assistance to chaplains. Where they welcomed healthy congregations on a regular basis, chaplains and seafarers' centres could rely on them to generate a significant level of consistent support for centres and for seafarers. However, even smaller congregations were recognized by chaplains as being valuable sources of donations.[2] One participant described to us how small churches constituted important sources of help and how appeals linked to significant religious festivals or dates could be useful in mobilizing supporters as well as themed days such as 'woolly hat' day. They told us,

> Sometimes, I go and give talks in small churches and I'll get a small donation. So, we all have to be aware of it... even if we're just based in the office and it's not our work. We have to be aware of it, but then we have individuals who have particular expertise. So, we have upstairs our Development Director; we also have a Senior Community Fund-raiser and he's very good at engaging—he knows how to engage churches. He will actually go out and speak to local

---

[2] Port chaplaincy may be relatively unique in its collection of donated goods both because of the need/demand for goods amongst seafarers and the less restrictive context. (Donations in medical settings may pose health risks, for example, making them less welcome.)

centres and advise them about different things they can do. Then we have different appeals—we have the woolly hat day, the Lent appeal, the Christmas appeal.

(Stakeholder from the United Kingdom)

Another participant talked about a small group of Catholics who met regularly and had taken up seafarers' welfare as a good cause and provided regular donations to the centre. They explained that

> Say, for example, I gave a talk to a school in November and then we'd go back, give them a list of the things that they need and then they'd come in and then we have parishes that one or two of my volunteers are parishioners in and they are very generous and give us things, and then there's a group at [parish] who meet regularly, an elderly group, housebound; they donate a lot of stuff to us. It comes from predominantly Catholic schools and Catholic parishes, yeah.

(Chaplain from the United Kingdom)

No matter what form they took, donations from the public were welcomed and valued by the chaplains and volunteers working in seafarers' centres. In Riverside, where a rudimentary scan of the centre revealed a cornucopia of free gifts, to which seafarers could help themselves, it seemed impossible that they could find any use for further donations, and yet they kept up the pressure in the community to generate more. It transpired that they had found ways of transforming donations of unwanted clothing into cash, which could contribute to the running costs of the centre. As such, a couple of times each month, a van would be loaded up with clothing and taken to a company that would pay small sums of money for each kilogram that was delivered.

In the face of rising costs and a challenging financial climate, both Porton and Riverside endeavoured to capitalize on every asset and advantage at their disposal when raising much-needed cash. In both cases, when the opportunity arose, they rented out space in the centre to facilitate meetings of civic and hobby/society groups. These strategies, aimed at raising much-needed funds, enabled the centre to offer more free services, such as free tea and coffee to seafarers. A stakeholder explained,

> So, if you're getting lots of charitable donations, then you can provide more services for free. If you're not getting enough charitable donations, then you will start to look at what you can charge for. But then you have to look at something that is commercially successful. So, I know in [place] they have a lot of dock workers who will use the centre. So, they're the people who buy the drinks, and they'll buy the food. And it works. So, the seafarers will have their free wi-fi because the dock workers are buying everything. And the dock workers at least then are getting lunch. So that kind of works well there. In other places, they'd

have to look at other ways of doing things. So, this is a question we're looking at with my centre; we have a new chaplain there. And hopefully, this time next year, we'll have some lessons that we can share with the rest of the mission.

(Stakeholder from the United Kingdom)

Notwithstanding the importance of cash and donations, there were other ways in which volunteer members of the community could help out. Those willing to attend the centre regularly made very welcome volunteers, sharing in the burden of ship visiting, bus driving, and centre operations. One participant explained to Nelson that

I'd rather have volunteers than donations if I'm honest. I think somebody's afternoon is far more valuable than a few hundred quid in the bank. Because it's another person that's out there potentially helping people. Don't get me wrong, I know they need money in order to provide PPE [personal protective equipment] and all the rest of it.

(Porton volunteer)

As we became more familiar with the work of port chaplains and of seafarers' centres, the extent to which welfare services for seafarers are reliant on the voluntary sector became increasingly apparent. Riverside and Porton relied heavily on volunteers, with the employee-to-volunteer ratio at Riverside running at about 1:5. A volunteer elaborated as follows:

This centre, at the moment, got twenty-two volunteers, and we only got one, two, three, four employees it's mainly run by, so we are very dependent on volunteers. And a lot of the volunteers here at the moment are ex-seafarers; as you know, most of them are ex-captains, ex-chief engineers.

(Riverside volunteer)

The recruitment of volunteers was understood across the sector as vitally important in providing a decent service to seafarers. However, in some locations, recruitment proved challenging, especially when it came to recruiting younger people. In Porton, it was not terribly easy to recruit volunteers, and this was understood to be a significant problem, as the following interview extract described:

I think it's recruiting young people to volunteer in the organization. That's certainly a challenge; how you'd resolve it I don't know because any voluntary work is, or most voluntary work is, very difficult to resource with younger people and I could accept that. [...] you really need people from this local area. In an ideal world, yes, you can have lots more people of a younger age, but I can't see it happening unless it became some kind of paid opportunity for them.

(Porton volunteer)

Given its dependence on volunteers, it was unsurprising to find that, in his talks to community groups, the enterprising manager of the Riverside seafarers' centre placed an emphasis on donating time as well as goods and cash. A field note recorded that

> I think [name] is doing a fantastic job of drumming up support for the centre and raising awareness about the centre and the work that it does for seafarers. Once a week at least, he is invited to give a talk to organizations in the area and in the city wherein he discusses life at sea and the welfare work that the centre does for visiting seafarers. In the months that I have been in the centre, people would drop in to leave donations like used clothes and toys. Some people would give money. Others would enquire about volunteer work. For instance, today, a woman in her fifties came in and had a chat with him. She said she attended one of his talks, and she thought she now had the time to do volunteer work for the centre.
>
> (Riverside field notes)

The Riverside manager's concerted and consistent approach yielded dividends over the long term, keeping the idea of volunteering at the centre alive in the community. This was seen to attract volunteers who might otherwise be a little hesitant or timid in making an approach. One member of the Riverside staff explained that attracting volunteers was down to the sharing of information between members of the community. He said,

> Word of mouth, just word of mouth all the time or someone who themselves has known about us and has maybe, there was a new volunteer come in last night she comes in this evening, she passed here many times and she always thought to herself 'I must call in.' I don't know what happened, but she did, bit the bullet and called in the other day and is now, I'm not saying committed, but she's showing an interest that she'd like to do this on a more regular basis so that's going to work well.
>
> (Riverside staff)

The seafarers' welfare services provided in Riverside and Porton, and in the United Kingdom overall, are not unique in their (over-)reliance on volunteer workers. A recent report by *Human Rights at Sea* estimated the value of volunteer work in relation to the provision of port-based welfare services for seafarers in New Zealand at NZ$ 600,000 (Shepherd and Hammond 2020). There is no doubt that in the United Kingdom, as in New Zealand, these volunteers constitute a vitally important element of the provision of welfare to seafarers. However, their contributions can be erratic, their hours limited, and the tasks they are willing, or able, to engage in can be restricted. This means they can only ever be a part of the solution in bridging the gap between seafarers' needs and centre and chaplain resources, and they should not be taken for granted when it comes to the provision of port-based welfare services to seafarers.

Beyond volunteers, therefore, other solutions have to be explored in considering how to deliver services to seafarers. In this context, one member of the Riverside team talked about the importance of sharing the burden of work across a variety of faith leaders, a move that they felt was long overdue. They explained,

> I'm opening it up, and I should've done this a long time ago, to other denominations; I don't want anyone to think that the Church of England or Roman Catholics have a monopoly of seafarers' welfare. So, I'm inviting the Methodists and the United Reformed and the Baptists initially to see if there's any interest that they could bring to the table and then, beyond that, go and open up to other religions and denominations. I mean, we have contact with the Chinese pastor in town, we have contact with the Greek Orthodox, with the Imam and others, and the Jewish gentlemen in town; there are two, so we have contact with them, and we're not really on first-name terms, but they know that we're here, and if we call them up or take someone to their place of worship, they will look after them.
>
> (Riverside staff)

This aspiration is one that is shared by others in the field of port-based welfare, but it is yet to be realized and may bring with it challenges of its own.

Connections between Seafarers' Centres, National Organizations, and National Community Groups

Our research clearly indicated the ways in which successful seafarers' centres had close and strong connections with local community members and parishioners. However, centres also relied upon connections with national and international organizations and community groups. These included national and international charities, governmental and non-governmental organizations, and members of the business community.

In the United Kingdom, seafarers' centres are generally financed by charities rather than private or corporate concerns. A recent annual report for one centre demonstrated that it received a grant from the local Apostleship of the Sea of £121,250, which was a reduction of just over £11,000 on the previous year. It received an equal amount of income from a second, locally based, religious charity. In addition, it raised £13,274 from a voluntary port levy and £8,480 from hiring out rooms. The centre was also in receipt of a Merchant Navy Welfare Board grant of £3,715.

The Mission to Seafarers, Stella Maris (also referred to as AoS) and the Sailors' Society all supported the seafarers' centres located in the hinterland of one particular port that was familiar to us.[3] A specific charity had been set up to financially support and manage the provision for seafarers in the area, and this entity posted accounts showing operating costs of £115,077 for the financial year to March 2020. Voluntary shipping levies of £52,722 contributed to the payment of these costs; the bar, café, and shop located at the staffed seafarers' centre and used by port personnel, as well as seafarers, generated £21,323 in income, and there was £22,507 received in donations. These funds were supplemented by a £20,000 grant, the source of which was not specified. This left the charity with a slight surplus for the year concerned. This was added to its reserves of £95,031.

As with these examples, seafarers' centres generally depend on larger maritime-related charitable bodies. They also receive support from other charities and sometimes from the Merchant Navy Welfare Board (MNWB) and the International Transport Workers' Federation's Seafarers' Trust (ITF-ST). However, the financial situation for the largest UK seafarers' welfare charities—the MtS and Stella Maris—has become more challenging over recent years. The MtS posted a deficit operating budget for the five years from 2015–2019, and as a result, they have engaged in a cost-cutting strategy that has incorporated centre closures in some cases (such as Southampton seafarers' centre in 2018, for example) and the sale of associated assets/land. In their 2019 accounts, Stella Maris noted an increase in income arising from donations and grants compared with 2018 but what is described as a significant decrease in legacy income (from £256,125 in 2018 to £99,997 in 2019). They also experienced a fall in 'Sea Sunday' income, which generated £554,647 in 2018 but £514,405 in 2019. In the case of both charities, steps are being taken to ensure that the substantial levels of reserves that they manage are maintained. These steps should leave the long-term future of the charities relatively secure, but they demand short-term savings at the local level and create a more challenging financial context for the operation of local centres. In the course of our research, we often learned of chaplains having to try to engage in fund-raising to fill the gaps in funding that their centres faced. One stakeholder from a large charity explained both the context for these activities and the skills and effort that port chaplains are drawing upon to raise funds and the profile of their work and centres. She described how

As with other charities, the work becomes more challenging or becomes different. And the number of legacies are falling away because…I think it's an impact of sea blindness. Because people are no longer really conscious of the sea, not conscious of the maritime organizations, so we're seeing the legacies are falling. Trustees have concerns about that. But I think it's just about engaging a new

---

[3] One of which was staffed and one of which was accessible twenty-four hours a day but was unstaffed.

generation. So, my chaplain in [place], last year—he has a fundraising committee—last year, he raised £30,000. I don't even know how he did it. He does a lot of talking. Big team of volunteers, so he has about five volunteers that help him do ship visits. With him and his volunteers, they do around eighty ship visits a month. Then he has five or six volunteers with links to different churches that will do fund-raising, and they just have lots of events, and they keep the work of [name of charity] in the public eye. That makes the job of a chaplain a lot more challenging because you're not just doing spiritual care, you're also doing volunteer management and recruitment, admin and fund-raising. But it keeps [name of charity] in the public eye.

(Stakeholder from United Kingdom)

While they were usually dependent on larger charitable bodies for grants and resources to cover operating costs, local centres were themselves often well established and historically well-funded concerns, which had previously benefited from a considerable number of legacies and donations. As one stakeholder explained,

Our funding comes from donations over the years—over many, many years. Seafarers, very often you'll find the funding comes from families of seafarers, through donations, or from ex-seafarers, or from charities. So, in the UK, there are a number of charities that are funding organizations [names three charities] . . . they're international—they all fund certain things, but then, historically, because Britain is a maritime nation, we've been fortunate, we just had lots of funding. And these have come through donations. Through individuals, through the church. We don't get money from the church but from church congregations we get money, so we do Sea Sunday every year to help raise our profile. So, we have people who will give regularly. This organization has benefited from legacies. So, people who have gone to sea, or their relatives gone to sea, want to say thank you to [name of charity]. And they'll leave [name of charity] quite a lot of money, and then that money's been invested. So, in terms of contemporary charities, I would say [name of charity] is quite well-resourced.

(Stakeholder from the United Kingdom)

As the United Kingdom has declined as a major seafaring and ship-owning nation, however, so too have legacies to seafarers' centres and/or the charities that support them. In this context, the introduction of voluntary port levies has the potential to be a lifeline for some centres. In our research, Porton had established a voluntary levy that was delivering a significant amount of income to the charity running local seafarers' welfare services. However, Riverside had only recently introduced the levy and was struggling to win the support of the captains calling at the local ports. One participant shared the challenges at Riverside with us as follows:

We're not a particularly attractive charity, we're not a children's charity, we're not a cancer charity, we're not particularly emotive, we're not—dare I use the expression—a sexy charity. It doesn't appeal to everyone, so we have to pick and choose who we would, where we direct our fund-raising to, so we ask for support from some charitable foundations. We have [organization], we have [organization], [organization], organizations like that where, if we have a particular project, we can put it to them, and hopefully they'll fund it. For example, the vehicles; 70 per cent of the vehicle, the outright cost of the vehicle, is funded through the vehicle replacement programme whereby [name of organization] make a contribution, and from that contribution then there is a pot which we can dip into so we can have a vehicle. So that's up to 70 per cent of the cost of vehicles. We then have to fund the 30 per cent and, of course, all the running costs and the maintenance of the vehicle, so that helps. Yes, constantly looking for avenues to raise funds, what we have now set up is a voluntary port levy, and this is really on the back of MLC 2006 [Maritime Labour Convention 2006], where there is this recommendation that states ship owners and/or charterers have a responsibility to seafarers' welfare. So, we've taken that recommendation from that and used that to our advantage to try and raise some funding through the port levy. And the means of doing that is when a vessel departs the port, we send a request for payment. That's only as good as it takes, when we do it the right time and people are feeling in the right frame of mind that they will fund it; a lot of those who're responsible for paying, 'That's voluntary', they say, 'we don't have to pay it', so they won't. Even though it might only be minimal, maybe even 0.1 per cent of the overall expenditure, the maximum a ship will pay will be £50. On average, it'll work out about £15–20 per ship, and that's if everyone was to contribute, that would give us about £100,000 a year and that would really offset some of the expenses. So that would allow us to engage some more personnel, which would then put people back into the port because our area of responsibility is really quite large. It's not just the Port of Riverside, it's [place], which is a bit of a distance away, it's [place], but like I say, if everyone was to contribute, that would be very helpful, which would then offset some of the operational costs.

(Riverside staff)

Not only were ship-owning/operating companies asked to donate to some seafarers' centres via a voluntary levy paid by their vessels, but in areas where some traditional ship-owning and operating companies survived, there were also initiatives and events aimed in their direction, and in the direction of the commercial port operators and the wider maritime cluster,[4] in order to extract financial support. One participant described how

[4] For example, vessel insurers known as P&I clubs and classification societies.

Yes, I mean shipping companies do support, they have, I mean for example in [city], there is a very big dinner called the Sea Pie Supper, which will attract maybe 600 people associated with seafaring companies, and that raised something like £3,000, which was divided to the seafarers' charities, so we do need charitable support in that way. The Association of British Ports will support some of our activities; they'll give us facilities for free, so we get help.

(Stakeholder from the United Kingdom)

The need for chaplains to build support in the wider maritime sector was common across the globe, and a chaplain in North America described how she was trying to build up relations with the ports, the harbour masters, and the port authorities in order to garner future financial support for her centres. She described how she was:

[...] trying to build relationships between the organizations and the people in the port, the port harbours. The harbour masters, the port authorities. We did work as a welfare committee through the Merchant Navy Welfare Board in England. That's been a struggle to maintain. I'm further down the road with [place], so I have a very good working relationship with the harbour master in [place], who has also just come on our board. I am a member of the port security committee for [place]. And we're working on a wellness project for all the people in [place], including seafarers domestic and foreign, and the port partners and this kind of thing. Like a crisis plan at a crisis intervention. Management system for them. Which is terrific. I am acknowledged as the port chaplain in [place]. We are acknowledged as port chaplains in [place] as well.

(Chaplain from Canada)

Perhaps the most natural wellspring of support for seafarers' centres and port chaplains is their own parish or the parish in which their centre is located, if different. As described earlier in the chapter, many found their parish leaders, and the local parishioners themselves, highly supportive. However, this was not always the case, and support often faded at the higher management levels of the institutions involved. When asked if they felt supported and understood by their church, one chaplain openly described some of the difficulties he had with individuals serving in the higher management roles of the church. He explained that

[significant pause] No. [I don't feel supported.] Not by the Church. By the [name of charity], yes. But by the Church, not necessarily always. I'm lucky—I've got a very supportive Bishop in [place], [name], she's lovely, very supportive. But trying to get Church support can be quite difficult. Of course, the churches have got so many demands on them. So actually, getting that church support, you don't always feel you have it. [...] the Vicar in [...], she's very good, she's very support-ive, she'll do services for me. But in terms of wider support, in terms of parishes that will donate regularly or collect things for you—I think once I start doing more church engagement, my answer will change because I think a certain amount of it's based on the fact that we've not really had contact with some of them, but...some of the ones which we have had it's been...some support's been fantastic, but from some parishes it's been quite lousy. Sometimes from the top it's not been very good.

(Chaplain from the United Kingdom)

Despite the fact that the Church as a national institution was not universally regarded as supportive to local seafarers' centres, national churches (Anglican and Roman Catholic in the United Kingdom) were significant in raising funds and awareness in support of seafarers' welfare. Sometimes, this could be via national communication such as newsletters to parishioners across the country. The Anglican newspaper, the *Church Times*, regularly features articles about sea-farers and port chaplains, for example, and has a 'paid-for' circulation of approximately 23,000. This figure obscures the fact that the likely readership is much higher, with copies of the *Church Times* being made freely available to the public.

Alongside communications and publicity, there are also specific events organ-ized by UK churches in support of seafarers. The best known of these is probably 'Sea Sunday'. On the second Sunday of July, Anglican, Roman Catholic, and Methodist churches, among others, hold services and supporting activities aimed at raising awareness of the work and life of seafarers and the welfare support pro-vided to them by port chaplains and seafarers' centres. In this modern, digital age, events are supported with online materials and videos posted on YouTube as part of a concerted drive to raise funds for Stella Maris and MtS. A major part of these initiatives is simply awareness-raising, as one of the barriers encountered by chaplains and their organizations when it comes to fund-raising is a general lack of awareness among the British public of what a seafarer does and why it matters locally, on the ground. A chaplain told us,

We do hold some events, some annual events. We also go around to churches, for example, on [event] sharing our ministry, but apart from raising funding...in fact, we are more concerned how we can raise awareness to the general public about the existence of the seafarers and their contribution, they contributed to our daily lives and the economy.

(Chaplain from Asia)

Awareness-raising was seen as particularly important in a context where seafarers were felt to be afforded little consideration by those shipping goods, producing goods, and consuming goods. One chaplain was perplexed and frustrated by this apparent blindness to the contribution of seafarers to the global economy and to trade. They reflected,

> If you have a big manufacturer in the world that is transporting goods by sea, why are they not supporting seafarers? So, this kind of things gets me thinking, 'If I rely on the sea to ship all my goods, it was my money and all my...I have more to lose if the crew is not happy, whatever shipping company I may have. I may ship with Maersk, or with MOL, or with Evergreen or whatever, but why am I not contributing to ensure that the crew is [looked after]...There must be reason!'
>
> (Chaplain from Australia)

Conclusion

In many ways, seafarers and chaplains share a strong sense of invisibility in the global world. In this context, where they might otherwise feel cast adrift from land-based society, it is even more important than it would be otherwise for chaplains to foster and maintain both national and local connections with small and large-scale groups and with appropriate networks. It is also important for them to find the most efficient and viable ways of working, which are likely to involve working with other organizations and individuals engaged in delivering welfare services to seafarers. It is these ways of working, and the challenges that accompany them, to which we turn in Chapter 7.

Chaplaincy and Seafarers: Faith at Work. Helen Sampson, Nelson Turgo, Wendy Cadge, and Sophie Gilliat-Ray, Oxford University Press. © Helen Sampson, Nelson Turgo, Wendy Cadge, and Sophie Gilliat-Ray 2024.
DOI: 10.1093/9780198913290.003.0007

7

Practical Ecumenical Cooperation amongst Organizations Providing Port Chaplaincy

Introduction

Caring for seafarers is a global collaborative effort between individuals working for organizations affiliated to secular and religious charities. Seafarers often move between organizations and receive support across geographic locations. A leader with the International Seafarers Welfare and Assistance Network (ISWAN) in the Philippines described their 'good working relationship with ICMA [International Christian Maritime Association]' in the region as well as referrals they make to Stella Maris, which has a dormitory and can subsidize costs. Other organizations do the same: 'if they [other organizations that serve seafarers] have a problem, they will ask us...we help each other out in that way' (stakeholder from the Philippines). Organizational leaders also told stories of working with specific seafarers and ships as they moved between ports to ensure that a problem that had been identified in one port continued to be addressed at the next.

This capacity for, and commitment to, collaboration across organizations and across national borders is a distinct feature of international port welfare work. This approach—in both religious and secular organizations—is nurtured locally and globally in training, at conferences, and via formal events. 'We did a session on collaborative work amongst the Christian maritime associations', an organizational leader explained, 'and it was quite interesting to try and get people to collaborate and work together' (stakeholder from the United Kingdom). These kinds of gatherings regularly include leaders from port welfare committees as well as the Sailor's Society, ISWAN, and other organizations.

This chapter describes the collaboration or practical ecumenical cooperation that is a hallmark of seafarers' welfare today. We briefly describe the history of the International Christian Maritime Association (ICMA) and the North American Maritime Association (NAMMA)—two key religious umbrella organizations—before outlining how these collaborations function. We focus both on the ways in which ecumenical collaborations enhance service provision for seafarers and on the occasions when religious groups experience tensions, most commonly around personalities and sharing space, religious ritual, and arguments over the appropriateness of proselytizing (or not) in port contexts.

The International Christian Maritime Association (ICMA) and the North American Maritime Ministry Association (NAMMA)

The ICMA is the central, overarching, religious organization in seafarers' welfare today. While smaller religious umbrella organizations worked together nationally and regionally in the past, global ecumenical efforts were formalized with the creation of ICMA. This creation resulted from an initial consultation in 1967, which included the International Council of Seamen's Agencies and the World Council of Churches. At a gathering in Rotterdam in 1969 that included more than 100 delegates from 52 Christian-based volunteer organizations, historian Paul Mooney explains, 'Those who came together...felt a pervasive sense of God's providence at work among them. Their eyes were opened to their common calling, and they were moved to found a common organisation for working together and representing Christian maritime ministry in the shipping industry and the world' (Mooney 2019). In this 2019 history of the ICMA, Mooney further explains, 'In a short time, this sense of collegiality would spread across Christian maritime missions and into port ministries, as people in maritime ministry realised that their common concerns and shared objectives in working among seafarers were better served by collaboration' (Mooney 2019, p. 2).

The ICMA was founded in order to foster 'collaboration and mutual aid amongst constituent bodies'. It aimed to be the 'collective and respected voice of the association within the industry and outside of it; which can offer counsel and be heard within the councils of those bodies whose deliberations in any way affect or influence the lives and welfare of seafarers' (Mooney 2019). The ICMA lobbied to become an observer at the International Labour Organization (ILO), a status that was granted in the late 1970s. In 2002, it was granted observer status at the International Maritime Organization (IMO). ICMA member organizations have worked hard together, over time, in response to the challenges of multi-religious and multi-ethnic environments, flags of convenience, and other security/access issues. They have supported training for port chaplains, advocated for seafarers, built relationships with international bodies, and supported each other in their work for multi-faith and multi-national seafarers around the globe. The ICMA holds regular 'plenary conferences' where member organizations come together, and regional groups work together around specific challenges.[1]

The ICMA currently has twenty-seven member organizations. When it was founded, only the Houston International Seamen's Center chaplaincy team was working ecumenically. By the 1980s, most ports had an established ecumenical network—usually with Protestants and Catholics. Paul Mooney argues,

---

[1] The 2019 plenary conference was held in Taiwan and attended by Turgo.

ICMA's task going forward [...] is to provide space for those who work in ministry among seafarers, fishers, and their families to come from their different churches and agencies to meet, discuss, share, learn, grow and be stronger people. ICMA is also asked to be the collective and representative voice of those who come together as Christians in the service of seafarers and to stand for seafarers and fishers, especially when their rights are denied, or they are in danger.

(Mooney 2019)

Since 2017, the ICMA's General Secretary has been Jason Zuidema, who also serves as the Executive Director of the NAMMA, a dual role that has enabled chaplaincy groups to work even more collaboratively. The NAMMA emerged from the lineage of maritime groups in North America that have worked together in support of seafarers since the mid-nineteenth century. This lineage includes the American Seamen's Friend Society (ASFS), the United Seamen's Service to the National Council of Seamen's Agencies (NCOSA) started in 1951, and the International Council of Seamen's Agencies (ICOSA), a name change from NCOSA in 1967. This group changed its name to the North American Maritime Ministry Association (NAMMA) in 1991. The vision or 'why' of both the NAMMA and ICMA is to be 'for the benefit of seafarers and fishers and their families' (Mooney 2019). Because relatively few seafarers live in North America, the NAMMA focuses more on port chaplaincy work than the ICMA, which also aims to support the families of seafarers (stakeholder 4).

Both the ICMA and NAMMA include people and organizations from a wide variety of Christian backgrounds. It has been argued that 'it's a pretty incredible ecumenical mix where people practically can work together, serving seafarers, in ways that's probably not found in many other ministries' (Mooney 2019). Members include more conservative and more liberal Christians and tend to avoid the questions that would separate them. One interviewee told us that

We have [...] members who are pre-church Evangelicals, Southern Baptists, Catholics of all kinds, Lutherans...all sorts of different church groups, that have figured out ways to work together, and they're usually fairly forgiving with one another, and sometimes they avoid the tougher theological questions that separate them from amongst each other.

(Stakeholder from Canada)

Today, the ICMA tends to work more with organizations that serve seafarers. In one interviewee's words, 'the Mission to Seafarers, the Apostleship of the Sea, the Sailors' Society, the German Seamans' Mission, the Nordic Seamans' Missions, and then there's a smattering of smaller missions...ICMA, at this time, is sort of more of an organization of organizations: an association of associations'.

The NAMMA works more with port chaplains as local service providers. Both groups partner with multiple organizations that serve seafarers.

Local Experiences of Ecumenicism

The successes of ecumenicalism have helped welfare services to continue and thrive in ports all over the world and have paved the way for the creation of more cooperative endeavours between faith organizations. While seafarers have benefited from the sharing of resources between welfare organizations (with better-resourced seafarers' centres and more support on the ground), port chaplains and other maritime welfare charity stakeholders have, nonetheless, viewed and experienced ecumenicalism in various ways. Being in the driving seat of ecumenicalism in ports, these people's daily experience of ecumenicalism, and their views of it, provide us with a better understanding of what ecumenicalism means from the point of view of those who enact it on a daily basis.

Most port chaplains who were interviewed for the study described ecumenicalism in positive terms. One chaplain, for instance, said that working with others from varying faith traditions had helped her personally in leveraging tolerance for others, which is very important in port welfare services as seafarers come from different backgrounds. The diversity of faiths and ethnicities of the people that they work with makes for a workplace that thrives on coming together regardless of differences:

> It helps me also to have like all these ecumenical colleagues from different backgrounds and different like denominations as well because that helps me to have that mind set of like I'm culturally…I'm tolerant. Like I have a German colleague, a Polish colleague, an Indonesian colleague, and a few British colleagues as well and then there's me from [place] so we reflect, in our ministry, our different cultures and our different backgrounds. So we have a Lutheran, a Presbyterian, a Catholic, like Irish-raised Baptist working for the Anglican, it's like, you know, there's already that mix, which helps us to approach the job in a more open way.
>
> (Chaplain from the United Kingdom)

Ecumenicalism also makes possible the inclusion and participation, in seafarers' welfare, of the wider faith community, and groups who profess none. In this way, the welfare of seafarers becomes the concern of many, not just a select few:

> I think you can serve seafarers in a wellness sense like going on board ships and bringing practical, meeting practical needs like driving around seafarers. So, like we have volunteers with MtS [Mission to Seafarers] that wouldn't say they were religious necessarily but do have a heart for service, for people, for just for the

wellness essentially of seafarers and helping them have a better life. I don't see an issue with that as long as you're in it for the fact that you want to serve. I think why not let an atheist or include like Muslims, Buddhists, anybody who has a different faith as long as they're willing to come together for the cause.

(Chaplain from the United Kingdom)

We have interviewed port chaplains who were very receptive to, and had plans for, involving and recruiting more people from various faith backgrounds aside from Christianity. In many ways, ecumenicalism has both planted the seed of openness and inclusivity to welfare work with seafarers and also grown from it. One port chaplain explained why the involvement of other faiths is important to port chaplaincy:

It was something that's been on my mind, and something for the [place] I want to do. Again, having the time to do it. I want to try and build an inter-faith chaplaincy or network—not necessarily a team, but a network of people we can call on ship, we need it, because...let's say a Turkish ship rocks up,...and there's a death. [...] I can do a certain amount to minister to them, and support. But wouldn't it be nice of somebody from their own faith could come with me? Because...my own personal point of view, if my Gran died, I wouldn't particularly want the local Imam popping round and saying...I'd want a Christian minister to come round because actually I'm Christian. Not that I wouldn't want the Imam to—you know, if he was a nice chap he could pop round for coffee—but if I'm looking at mourning and grieving and looking at funerals and last rites and so on, for me the Imam's not gonna be much use. Just as the local Christian chaplain...might be appreciated, but wouldn't it be good if we could offer—hang on guys, would you like us to take or you know, bring the Imam down with us, or the Rabbi or whoever?

(Chaplain from the United Kingdom)

Another expressed a similar sentiment, saying,

I'm working very close together with people I very much respect and enjoy working with who are not Christians. [...] we both see the need for seafarers to get the support they need, so basically what unites us is actually the need we're seeing, but actually working together actually we come closer to each other as well.

(Stakeholder from Belgium)

In most cases, local groups come together to support educational campaigns and service provision to seafarers. 'In this industry of helping, we are all connected', a leader reflected (stakeholder from the Philippines).

Despite much good will and substantial success arising from ecumenicalism, it is not always problem-free for people who have to deal with the nitty gritty of ecumenicalism on the ground. Translating ecumenicalism into actual policies and daily practices was a challenge for some of our participants, especially those who had previously worked in a different sector prior to coming to maritime welfare services. One official of a maritime charity observed,

> When I first started and I felt that some of the relationships were a bit fraught locally—there was all kinds of conflict—I went to meet [name], and I said to him, 'I don't really understand how ecumenism works in the maritime sector. Because in the HIV sector you just respond to the people.' And I did say to him that when things were crucial in the HIV pandemic in the early days when people were dying, if the religious people involved had not worked ecumenically, then a lot more people would've died. [...] I've worked alongside Roman Catholics. We've written books, we've campaigned, we've done all kinds of things [...] it was very ecumenical because it was focused on people living with HIV. So, I sometimes think that we need to re-orient ourselves in a way—we need to remind ourselves constantly that it is the seafarer who counts.
>
> (Stakeholder from the United Kingdom)

In addition, as dialogues between and amongst maritime welfare charities continue in relation to bridging differences, there is a view shared by many that, in the current context, ecumenicalism's tendency is more towards words and less towards action on the ground:

> If it doesn't too much, if it doesn't involve too much talk. So, you know, quite often ecumenical things can be very wordy and there's lots of meetings but not much happens, and that is one cartoon of ecumenism.
>
> (Stakeholder from Belgium)

Based on our interviews with both port chaplains and maritime welfare charity officials, one aspect of ecumenicalism has continued to be a source of tension and disagreement amongst welfare providers. It concerns theological differences between faith organizations. These differences impact on both the perceptions and experiences of ecumenicalism:

> That's where I find it so frustrating sometimes when some [...] chaplains are so protective of their own brand, like whether they're AoS [Apostleship of the Sea] or Mission to Seafarers. You know, they're so protective of their own society or they're like 'the Catholic way is the only way' or 'the evangelical is the only way', you know, when the whole plinth of your job is that you're ministering to all these people who don't believe the same thing as you.
>
> (Chaplain from the United Kingdom)

In this environment, rather than promoting religious tolerance and the ability to go beyond one's theological biases, we found that ecumenicalism could, in fact, spur people to become more assertive about their beliefs, impacting negatively on the delivery of welfare provision to seafarers. Highlighting what is happening in airport chaplaincy as a contrast to the maritime field, and to describe a very positive and effective example of ecumenical working, a maritime welfare stakeholder said,

> I mean also I see the same in [place] airport; you have basically a mission all the churches can agree on, but actually not everybody, you know, but we have to do this together so, for example, in [place] airport, you have a Roman Catholic airport chaplain, you have a Protestant airport chaplain, and you have an Anglican/Old Catholic airport chaplain. Basically, the three of them, they work closely together as a team to provide ministry to everybody. So for most of the people they encounter there (and the same is true for seafarers), let's say a Roman Catholic Filipino, in most cases is not going to object that an Anglican chaplain prays with him.
>
> (Stakeholder from Belgium)

It is around the issue of differences in theology, primarily in relation to the provision of religious services to seafarers, that many maritime welfare charities struggle. As a way to work around their challenges, port chaplains are often clear about their expectations of each other regarding the delivery of religious rituals to seafarers:

> I think there needs to be a respect of other people's traditions, and I think that you need to understand that if you're serving the needs of Catholic seafarers, that's different to say another kind of seafarer. So say, for example, somebody's dealing with a Catholic seafarer; I would expect that person to tell me so that we could then arrange for them to receive the sacraments because, obviously, we know all the people in that location...and we'd be able to do that, so I think there does need to be a respect of the traditions, and if that isn't there, then that's quite difficult to operate because we do serve everybody practically, but when it comes to different Mass and stuff like that, there is a difference, and I think that needs to be respected, and I think if that's respected, everything else will follow.
>
> (Chaplain from the United Kingdom)

Although tensions occur and, at times, can result in antagonism between port chaplains, there have been efforts to bridge theological gaps and differences. A welfare charity official, for example, explained how, through high-level meetings, they dealt with the issue of providing religious services to mainly Catholic Filipino seafarers:

So, we came up with an agreement, and the agreement was simply that when we hold our services, we will say who we are, which is what we were already doing. And we will let people know if they want to receive—if we're having a Eucharist service, they don't have to take holy communion, they can come up for a blessing. Which is what we say—anyone in our parish churches. And then we also said if they want to see a Catholic priest, we can arrange that, or we'll help facilitate that. Which is basically what we were saying anyway. But this time, what we did say was that if the AoS gives us the details, phone number contact, then we can hand it to the seafarer, we can facilitate that. But we were doing this anyway, that's my argument. And if we weren't doing it anywhere, we should've been doing it because that is best practice. And that responds to the needs of the seafarer.

(Stakeholder from the United Kingdom)

However, it is not just theological differences between major faith organizations that sometimes fracture the landscape of welfare services to seafarers. As more and more faith organizations stake their claim to welfare provision, another aspect of faith-related services has become a sticking point for the otherwise smooth relations between maritime welfare organizations. For instance, both the Mission to Seafarers and Stella Maris are united in their stand that the religious conversion of seafarers belongs to the past and is not on the cards when providing welfare services to seafarers. Nonetheless, some other religious organizations take a different view and are actively engaged in proselytization in the ports. Long-established seafarers' welfare providers often consider such practice to be a threat to their work and to the well-being of seafarers. This is because seafarers do not readily distinguish between welfare charities and often perceive all welfare providers as belonging to the same organization. The act of one becomes the act of all. Concerned individuals noted that the impact of proselytization can be traumatic for seafarers, and most welfare providers considered this to be unacceptable. For example, a chaplain described a negative experience relating to proselytization that had taken place in a port:

We went on board a ship once and a gentleman had been baptised—he was Hindu—and somehow, he found himself being baptised. And he was distressed to the max. And his shipmate said, 'Can you please talk to him? Because he is really scared that he has done something that will anger his Gods.' So, our folks had to go in and assure him that this was not the case. And they prayed with him, for him, and assured him, through their particular means, that he was gonna be okay, that this was not something he had to worry about. Because he'd been sort of bamboozled into this. And he was frightened, he was really truly frightened. We're not allowed to go on board ships and proselytise—we are not. We have to respect that there are many other faiths on board ships now. It's not the British Navy any more, it's not the British merchant marines. It's ... we have our issues when those people refuse to accept our rules around how to treat the seafarers. And they're only going on board for their own single-minded purposes, and we do not.

(Chaplain from Canada)

As port chaplains and maritime stakeholders translate ecumenical ambitions into actual practices on the ground, they are also the ones who experience its many opportunities and challenges. While ecumenicalism allows for continued cooperation between welfare organizations, it also brings forth the possibility of fractious relations and contested interpretations of shared goals and the Christian ethos.

When the Sharing of Centres and Services Works Well

In recent years, maritime welfare charities have shared resources, such as the buildings that house seafarers' centres. This practice is based on a commonly held belief that it is beneficial for both maritime welfare charities and for seafarers. On the part of welfare charities, shared centres translate into better management of resources and the provision of more, and better, welfare services to seafarers. For seafarers, on the other hand, they mean that, in ports that they visit, they have access to more people to look after them, as well as better-resourced centres.

One example of a successful shared seafarers' centre that we came across in our research was a centre in the Far East, which, as one of its chaplains explained, was a real enterprise being jointly owned and maintained by four different maritime welfare charities. The pulling together of resources has enabled the centre to establish a satellite centre within the vicinity of the port providing a place for seafarers to relax when they have limited time and are unable to travel to the main centre. It was described to us as follows:

It's owned by, I think, if I'm not wrong, it's kind of owned by the Marinas [place] as a registered charity in [place]. But it's kind of formed with the four organizations. The Mission to the Seafarers is kind of the lead organization taking care of most of the work there. Our second site is in the container port, which is just outside the gate, if I can put it that way. So, there's a place for the seafarer to come in, to relax, especially those who are coming on shore for a short period of time to buy themselves a beer or some other drink. We provide free coffee, tea, and some other drinks.

(Chaplain from Hong Kong)

The same sharing of resources happened in another port, and the involvement of other organizations helped the centre with fund-raising to cover its running costs, spreading the load across a number of individuals and organizations:

> I mean [port] we work close together with the old Catholics, the old Catholic church in the Netherlands, so for example, on the board there is a person from the Dutch Protestant church, the Reform church, there's a person from the old Catholic church, and there's a person from the Anglican church. And then there's some people who are not linked with any churches, so they're sort of on the board level. But then in terms of finances, quite often there can be a bit of support from the Protestant, local Protestant churches, there can be support from let's say the national old Catholic church.
>
> (Stakeholder from the United Kingdom)

One oft-cited benefit of sharing resources is the proper coordination of ship visits by port chaplains. In ports where buildings are shared, our interviewees highlighted how port chaplains sometimes divided ports into zones and allocated different organizations to each zone in relation to responsibility for ship visits. This avoided repetition of visits and allowed welfare organizations to cover as many ships as possible:

> In [city], port chaplaincy is quite often organized, well in a way ecumenically, but basically all the port chaplains and all the volunteers from the different missions and from the different churches basically all come together and basically says, 'Right, well, two of you go to harbour one, and two of you go to harbour two', etc. etc. etc. But basically, instead of everybody trying to visit the same ship, to basically be pragmatic and say, 'Right, well, you know, all of us are doing the same thing, so basically let's just play it smart and basically divide how we take care of the port', that's what's happening in [name of port city] and in [name of port city].
>
> (Stakeholder from Belgium)

The interviewees also argued that the sharing of resources could translate into the provision of more varied activities and welfare services to seafarers as more people could contribute ideas of how best to serve seafarers' needs. One port chaplain, for example, cited how they were able to hold more social activities and incorporate more facilities into their centre because of the involvement and input of fellow port chaplains. This clearly benefited the seafarers who visited the port and the centre:

> There was a new initiative for giving out some goodies or presents during the Chinese New Year. This was proposed by me, and my Senior Chaplain, here, happily accepted this suggestion. I said, 'Because, since we are in [place] I appreciate we're giving out Christmas presents every year, but as an organization

based in [place], which pretty much is of the Oriental cultural society, we said it probably would be nice if we could provide this kind of a...'. 'Yeah', he said, 'Yeah, that's nice. That's good.' So, yeah, so far, not that I'm aware of because, as I say, we have a very strong and good team spirit...like the other Chaplain, he proposed to have a...we call it a 'prayer booth'. He identified a spot in our centre where we can set up a prayer corner (we call it a 'prayer booth') where the seeker could write down their prayer request.

(Chaplain from Asia)

Financial constraints are one of the most significant challenges for many seafarer centres as they experience cuts in grants and declining donations and other forms of assistance both from the public and private spheres. In our study, we found that many port chaplains were spending more time fund-raising for their welfare services than they had previously and than they liked to do (see Chapter 3). In this context, the financial benefits that were said to accrue as a result of the concerted efforts of chaplains from a variety of organizations working together were greatly valued:

It's an ecumenical effort in [place] because we are four organizations there. So yes, we're doing it. Having said that, because we are also four unique organizations, we're doing this individually, so each one of us they also have their own events raising their funding or supporting their own staff.

(Chaplain from Asia)

Beyond financial considerations, there are more mundane aspects of welfare work in the port that benefit from ecumenicism. There have been cases when working alongside other port chaplains has helped individual welfare providers to navigate awkward situations, as with the example of this chaplain, who was refused admission to a ship because of her gender. She told us,

I don't wear a collar when I go on board ships. For some people, it's very disturbing to see a woman in a collar. I got...um...rather unceremoniously ejected from a ship once because they're talking to me and one guy says, 'Wait—are you a pastor?' And I said 'Yes'. 'No, no, no, no, no, no', he says. 'You have to go now. We don't do women pastors. My country, no women are pastors. You have to go right now.' I said, 'Really, where are you from?' He says, 'Croatia. We're Catholics. No women, no women.' I said, 'Okay'. He said, 'You send us a man.' No problem. So I call my Roman Catholic buddies up from the AoS: 'Do me a favour. Go on this ship.'

(Chaplain from Canada)

In cases when specific religious services are required and the attending port chaplain does not fit the bill as their religious affiliation is different to that of the person needing assistance, working alongside others translates to more readily available resources, which can be tapped on demand. This happened to a chaplain who was called in to minister to seafarers following a traumatic fatal incident on board:

> And I got up there and I understood just before I left that an accident had happened in [place] where a chap had fallen off the ship. And unbeknownst to anybody. He had not been seen or heard, but he tripped on—something was happening, and he fell. And he landed on the dock and if they'd gotten to him earlier...but they didn't, and he died. And so the [place] chaplain constituency was called, the AoS chaplain was called. So he took a priest with him, and the two of them drove like a bat out of hell up to [place] to do a service of a Requiem Mass of the guy who died because they were devastated.
>
> (Chaplain from Canada)

Providing welfare services to seafarers, far from the public eye and at great physical and emotional cost, can sustain a community spirit, both amongst the welfare providers themselves and the wider public that supports their efforts. In contrast to working on their own on a daily basis, working together and sharing resources strengthened team spirit, as described by the following chaplain:

> We have our weekly chaplaincy team prayer meeting and coffee time together. Vocationally, we have a social gathering together, having a meal at one's home or going out together. We love to sing. Doing things as what a human being should do, social, friendship. That's very important for us, and, of course, then other organizations, say, for example, Christmas. We have a Christmas party, Christmas presents, and words of encouragement to each other or helping each other out. If one say, for example, might have a certain thing...he or she, caught up in certain things, then we'll try to step in to help so that they don't have to call in for the duty. Someone will cover them. I think we have a very good team spirit.
>
> (Chaplain from Asia)

The sharing of resources between maritime welfare organizations, often in the form of running seafarer centres together, helps to address many of the challenges that are faced by the seafarers' welfare support sector. From maximizing resources to building community spirit, the coming together of welfare charities forms part of the bedrock of strength that underpins the contemporary maritime welfare sector. However, instances of cooperation would also appear to come with their own set of challenges. While, indeed, there were success stories, and many of them, we were also told about a variety of differences and disagreements.

Sharing Resources and the Flaws That May Emerge in Ecumenical Solidarity

In the preceding section, we enumerated the various ways that the sharing of resources between maritime charities and organizations has benefited both welfare organizations and seafarers. Successes in sharing resources were described by many of the port chaplains that we interviewed. They spoke positively of such arrangements in the centres where they worked. However, other interviews and the fieldwork that we did in seafarers' centres revealed that ecumenicalism could present another 'face'. There were undoubtedly downsides to the practice of sharing centres and resources. In most cases, such difficulties could be attributed to individual/personal differences between chaplains and/or the faith traditions that they belonged to, which permeated their daily dealings with each other.

In some cases, differences emerged in the opinions of chaplains about what their work should consist of. We were told of a case where a deacon was completely opposed to the standard practice, amongst chaplains, of selling SIM cards to seafarers on board. He considered that his task was one that was primarily associated with Christian ministry and, for him, this did not encompass SIM sales work. However, the participant who provided the example to us held a different view. He felt that SIM card sales were important in establishing good relations with seafarers and provided good grounds for accessing vessels. He explained that

One of our deacons in the US was very much against selling SIM cards. He was a Roman Catholic deacon. He wouldn't sell them. His idea was that he was there to minister to the seafarers. 'Yes, you are.' 'Well, I'm not going to sell SIM cards.' I said, 'But that's what they need.' 'No, no, no, no—I wasn't ordained to sell SIM cards.' And I was thinking, I never joined the mission to sell SIM cards, I joined the mission…well initially to experience a different sort of ministry before offering myself for ordination. Then I stayed because I loved it, and I believed in what I did. But I didn't join to sell SIM cards, otherwise I would've gone to O$_2$ and got a commission at least for it. But his theology that he'd been taught that there was no issue with, and he was a very bright man. But the way he was applying his theological education was…well, 'I wasn't ordained to sell SIM cards.' Well none of us have joined to sell SIM cards. But the way I looked at it was that a practical ministry is a gateway to a pastoral or spiritual ministry. By selling the SIM cards, that's an excuse to be on the ship. Then you start talking, and they might tell you there's an issue and 'I've been sent home and unfairly dismissed' or 'We've not been paid.'

(Chaplain from the United Kingdom)

Where they arose, major differences in standpoints most often related to the role of chaplains with regard to proselytization and the differences between proselytising and discipleship. Another flashpoint for conflict related to the sacraments and ordination. Different views emerged about whether Protestants or non-liturgicals should deliver the sacraments to seafarers. Beyond this, we were told that

> [T]he third one is about the question you asked about service models. Should chaplains do just chaplaincy (or whatever they consider to be just chaplaincy, just sort of spiritual stuff, do the sacraments, that sort of thing) or should they be driving vans, and selling phonecards, and cleaning toilets, and doing other things? And there's actually quite a range of opinion, but many port chaplains do a lot more things than chaplains in other domains might do. Many of our chaplains get deeply involved in administering the seafarers' centre, dealing with volunteers, driving vans, answering telephone calls, learning lots of things about SIM cards and the internet and whatnot, and I would suggest that our chaplains might be more hands on, like doing practical things, than chaplains in other areas. That we do less of the sacramental, theological stuff perhaps, and more of the hands-on, practical work than chaplains in other areas. And then, the last thing I'll say is, in talking in the maritime industry, sometimes there's a way of talking about it, it's like learning a new language. There's a way of talking about chaplaincy that is very theological, but then there's also a way of talking about our work that can be translated; it's like coding in a different way. You're saying the same thing, but you're saying it in a way that shipping companies and government officials can understand. And this is a really important thing: new chaplains and people who lead organizations, that's incredibly important for them to understand. That they can talk about seafarer ministry and they can talk about seafarers' welfare, and they're talking about the same thing, but they need to learn how to say the same thing with different words without speaking... Without, not lying, but misrepresenting themselves. That there are ways of saying to two different groups the same thing without misrepresenting, but you have to learn how to talk the lingo in both ways.
>
> (Stakeholder from Canada)

An additional source of difficulty between chaplains could be attributed to the personalities of the parties concerned and/or to their underlying theological differences, especially relating to proselytizing. Such frictions were often described as minor and were therefore not treated as an existential threat to the spirit of ecumenicalism between welfare organizations. The interview extract below provides an example of this:

> Not that kind of... I mean we're all humans. We do have... we're not perfect. We do have tension sometimes, of course, but I would say they are not the kind of

major issues. Occasionally...so we might have like, for example, one incident, someone came to me and said, 'Your chaplain visited my ship. This is my ship.' Oh, okay [...] I said, 'Oh, sorry for that but to prevent such things happening in the future how about you provide me with a list so we can avoid this kind of thing?' [...] sometimes, because each one of us we have our own pastoral meetings, correct our mistakes, we do things different.

(Chaplain from Asia)

The case of one seafarers' centre where we did fieldwork further underlined these difficulties. While continued cooperation was, indeed, affected throughout our stay, some problems that beset working relationships in the centre pointed to conflict coalescing around specific areas of self-interest. Many of the difficulties and differences cited have been echoed by other chaplains we interviewed in the project, to varying degrees.

In our fieldwork, we found that some port chaplains felt entitled to make critical judgements about the work and practices of peers working alongside them but working for other organizations. This took place in a context where port chaplains were used to working with a high degree of autonomy. The criticisms, therefore, had the potential to be highly sensitive and there was always a risk that they would get back to the port chaplains concerned. The following field note highlights the example of a worker who was critical of another chaplain's habit of driving the 'company' car between home and work and, in doing so, underlines the day-to-day challenges of closely working together:

Whilst in the car with [name], I asked them how far was their place from the port in [place], and they told me that, without traffic congestion, it would normally take an hour on the road. They then added that they drive their own car to the port rather than use the mission's car for the daily commute. When they said this, it struck me as odd. Why would they stress their non-use of the mission car for the daily commute to the port? Then I remembered that [another chaplain] in fact had the use of the mission car from their place to the port. The car that they were using to do ship visiting was also the same car used in the daily run from their place to other places that they needed to visit. I thought that [person's name] was making a dig at this arrangement.

(Porton field notes)

We also observed how port chaplains whose organization maintained and ran a centre would comment on the amount of time they devoted to cleaning the place (there was no employed cleaner) themselves. In a sense, as other port chaplains and their volunteers were sharing the same centre with them, there was an implicit expectation that all parties using the centre should share in the responsibility of tidying up the centre and a certain unspoken resentment about the fact that they were not 'pulling their weight':

> I did ship visiting with [name] today. I was supposed to see her in the centre at 10.30 a.m., but I arrived early. By 9.45 [name] was already in the centre. She then told me that she spends close to an hour cleaning the centre before going ship visiting. In my interview with her some days ago, she said this with a shrug, almost like I think a dig at [name] because she is the only one doing the cleaning, whereas [name] could also share with the burden of cleaning the place.
>
> (Porton field notes)

While some differences and disagreements are swept under the carpet, and remain unarticulated, others come to the fore, and when they do, the tension may spill over to other parties as well. One long field note bears this out:

> In February, as we were driving back to [place] from Porton, [Karl] showed me an email sent to him by [Sheila], a volunteer, who does the admin work for him [...]. In the email that Sheila sent to Karl, the former was venting her frustrations at [Jenny's] intrusive manners. The charities have their own respective offices in the centre, and as the layout of the building goes, anyone of them is no bother to anyone when they are in the centre as they do their work in separate offices anyway. But apparently, one time, as Sheila was in the shared kitchen, Jenny talked to her and asked about the work that she does for Karl. So Sheila explained to Jenny that she was doing the paperwork side in the centre. Jenny then made a comment that they would not do that with their volunteers because of confidentiality. In a way, Jenny was saying that the volunteer should not be doing what she was doing! But the thing is, Jenny had no business saying it because Karl was running a different organization altogether.
>
> (Porton field notes)

Such intrusion into the affairs of other organizations inevitably led to irritation and woe. The volunteer who was at the receiving end of the chaplain's remark had no way to answer back and instead communicated her displeasure to the chaplain she was working for.

Sharing the same centre with others, especially when one runs it while the other just shares space, also resulted in the monopolization of the use of space, which frustrated affected port chaplains. restricting them from performing certain activities or proposing changes to how the centre is organized. The 'ownership' of the centre becomes the sole domain of one organization, and the others are pushed to the margins. This was the impression we got in the course of our fieldwork, and it was recorded in field notes as follows:

As the [organization] holds the lease to the centre, [name] does not waste time to let [name] and his volunteers know this. They are the boss of the centre, that's what they wanted everyone to know. So, for instance, they decorate the centre with so much of the organization's stuff that it is at the point of over-saturation. They also demand [via email] that they should be informed of all people that [name] brings to the centre (that includes me) and the kind of work that they do. [Name] only brings to the centre volunteers and some occasional guests (like me and personnel from the central office in London, who occasionally visit) […] One good example of [name's] fixation with 'owning' the centre is by telling [name] that they will use the centre with other people so [name] (by implication) should not come to the centre on that particular date.

(Porton field notes)

We also witnessed tensions over the development of projects that were planned as single-organization initiatives. This occurred in the course of our fieldwork in connection with the establishment of an unstaffed centre at a river port that fell within the geographic region covered by two port chaplains from different organizations. A field note describes how

There are ports along the river [place], and seafarers have no place to stay for internet and some snacks when they go ashore on that long stretch of the river. So [name] negotiated with the port authorities to donate a place for a centre to be run by his organization. The plan was for a twenty-four-hour unmanned centre with free wi-fi and a vending machine where seafarers could unwind whilst on shore leave. When the other chaplain [working for the sister organization] heard about it, they asked someone in [name's] organization to send an email to him to demand that they be involved in the project.

(Porton field notes)

It was not just personality quirks or personality differences that were exposed in sharing resources and centres but rather, differences in theology as well. These tended to surface when organizations were required to work in close cooperation. In our interviews, we found that differences in religious practices which were borne out of distinctive faith traditions were being cited by port chaplains as one of the major problems they faced when working alongside other welfare providers.

It transpired that despite religious ministry being one of least significant provisions made by chaplains to seafarers, from the seafarers' perspective, chaplains themselves and the organizations they represented had become quite wrapped up in discussions and arguments over the organization and delivery of religious services for seafarers. There were concerns from Catholics about women delivering services and about services being termed 'Mass'. One female interviewee described how

Obviously, I'm Church of England because the Roman Catholic Church doesn't ordain women. I think the [...] leadership let's say—had some concerns. I don't know where these concerns emerged from. And I think everything came to a head when we appointed our Filipino chaplain.

(Stakeholder from the United Kingdom)

It emerged in the course of the study that a furore had been generated by the appointment and subsequent practice of a specific chaplain who was originally from the Philippines. The chaplain had the remit to minister to the Filipino community in a large city, and he also came to act as visiting port chaplain at the port concerned. As part of his duties, he liked to offer religious services to seafarers, and as a Anglican from the Philippines, he referred to these as Mass. However, his use of the term outraged some of the Catholic chaplains in the local area, who complained to their leadership in strong terms. This resulted in an email exchange followed by a prolonged, high-level discussion between the organizations providing welfare at the port. An interviewee explained how, initially,

We got a very peculiar email from the leadership of the [organization] saying that we shouldn't use the word 'Mass'; basically we shouldn't mislead the seafarers. So, I took the time to respond and tell him that actually, we have many traditions within the Church of England—some of us use the word 'Mass', some of us use 'Holy Communion', some of us use 'Eucharist'. So, we will work in the tradition in which we are accustomed. But we will obviously announce that we are Anglican.

(Stakeholder from the United Kingdom)

This exchange mushroomed into a major point of discussion, which led to the involvement of the ecumenical secretary general of the Church of England, who was brought into the conversation in a bid to resolve the difficulties that had emerged. For some individuals, it also caused them to reflect on broader faith differences between seafarers and how these could, and should, be met. Our interviewee continued, telling us that

It caused a big debate—there was all this to and fro-ing between [person's name]—I think they stopped communicating with me because I was just saying, 'This is what we'll do—we'll announce who we are',...which is what chaplains are doing anyway. So there was all this to-ing and fro-ing, so I said to the secretary general, 'Let's speak to the ecumenical secretary of the Church of England.' So the ecumenical secretary came in. He's the person who manages ecumenical relationships for the Church of England as a whole. So basically, what we did...because if you're responding to these issues from your organizational boundaries, you may lose sight of the fact you are actually part of a church. And the Roman Catholic Church and the Church of England and all the other churches have ecumenical dialogue in various different ways. They work ecumenically in various different ways. Sometimes, they even share church buildings. So there's this whole ecumenical movement that is being led from the centre of the church. Coordinated by the ecumenical secretary. So he came and spoke to us, and he took it away and had some conversations with his opposite number in the Roman Catholic Church. So we had all this—and then the two secretary generals met; the leadership met. So we came up with an agreement, and the agreement was simply that when we hold our services, we will say who we are, which is what we were already doing. And we will let people know if they want to receive—if we're having a Eucharist service, they don't have to take Holy Communion, they can come up for a blessing. Which is what we say—to anyone in our parish churches. And then we also said if they want to see a Catholic priest, we can arrange that or we'll help facilitate that. [...] By having this debate, here, I think it's good because we've cleared the air. We've now got formal agreement, this is what we're going to do. And it's interesting, because this has come from the UK. [...] But outside the UK, people tend to negotiate these things locally. We have all these big debates, but the other side of that is the issue around other faiths. Not every seafarer is Christian; some of them are Muslim. So we're having that debate in the mission. I haven't done any work on it, but we have people in the Church of England who lead on interfaith.

(Stakeholder from the United Kingdom)

Despite the formal agreement that had been arrived at by the leaders of the respective organizations providing chaplaincy at this port, and others, it was evident that tensions on the ground remained. In one port, the Anglican chaplain believed that the Roman Catholic chaplain used these as an excuse to try to exert control over his activities and maintain overall charge of all port chaplaincy services in the port. He resisted this at every opportunity as he had limited patience with the chaplain and resented the efforts to attempt to control him, believing that they were inappropriately stepping over an invisible, metaphorical line between them. The Roman Catholic chaplain implied, in their interview, that they were frustrated at not being given full reports by the Anglican chaplain on both the seafarers who he had visited and the volunteers who he was expecting. The chaplain believed that this impacted negatively on the service that they were able to provide to seafarers, and this was an ongoing point of friction between the individuals concerned. The Roman Catholic chaplain explained their point of view as follows:

It's difficult to work in the situation, for example, now because I don't know when these, when volunteers are coming in. I've got to manage my volunteers with my expectations, so for me, it would be ideal if we could have a set system where I knew who was coming in each day.

(Chaplain from the United Kingdom)

Underlying differences in theology could underpin differences in chaplains' understandings of how welfare, as opposed to religious services, were delivered to seafarers. Practical support to seafarers (e.g. the sale of SIM cards) was dismissed by some individuals as not part of their remit in providing chaplaincy to seafarers. Occasionally differences such as these, generated strong feelings as chaplains exchanged their ideas about appropriate and inappropriate ways of reaching out to seafarers. However, some participants felt that debates about the delivery of religious services and the language used to describe these were misplaced. They considered that they were somewhat inconsequential to seafarers, who rarely enquired about religious denomination and who were often disinterested in the provision of religious services altogether. At interview, one participant observed that

I sometimes think that we need to re-orient ourselves in a way—we need to remind ourselves constantly that it is the seafarer who counts. It's interesting because seafarers—when they come into the centres, they will call anybody and everybody Father—particularly the centre manager, they'll just call them Father. Because they're so used to people coming in the name of Christ, they're not interested in your denomination. Unless they want a particular...they want to see a Roman Catholic priest, then they will probably be asked. But otherwise they always speak to their family. They might not even want to go to chapel. Maybe they all want to go to [...] do some shopping.

(Stakeholder from the United Kingdom)

Placing seafarers centre stage was a valuable exercise for some of those who provided port chaplaincy services. However, others did not consider that their service should be determined by the wants of seafarers. These differences of view were a reminder that individual chaplains and the religious organizations providing chaplaincy services, or seeking to provide them, sometimes had fundamentally different philosophies about what they were doing and why they were doing it. This was seen within organizations (as the previously cited example of the chaplain who would not sell SIM cards, even though his colleagues in the same organization did so, demonstrates), but it was also a very clear division between different faith organizations. The organizations with clearance, from the Merchant Navy Welfare Board, to visit ships in UK ports and offer chaplaincy services were, however, united in a view that their brief did not include proselytization. However, some organizations that wished to send ship visitors to vessels held a very different view. For them, proselytization was the only objective, and this was not seen as appropriate by others, given the needs of seafarers and the fact that the ships serve as their homes as well as their workplaces. Uninvited proselytization was seen by many UK welfare charities ministering to seafarers as overly intrusive and an abuse of their privileged access to ships.

These are complex issues, and, as one interviewee pointed out to us, what one chaplain considered to be proselytization might be regarded quite differently by another. He explained,

> The question of proselytism, that is a challenging one, because this gets us into the denominational diversity. One person's proselytism is for another person just discipleship, and the question of what does that look like … is giving a bible to someone immediately proselytism? Or can that be framed in different ways? And these are tough questions that NAMMA and ICMA chaplains ask and debate and have been long-standing questions of asking and debating. How does that look? But usually, the answer to that comes in practice, this would be my argument. That usually, proselytism is more clearly seen when the chaplain—and those are groups that usually don't want to become part of NAMMA or ICMA—when Chaplains don't wanna give practical help. They want to go on board and give bibles and do their thing, but they don't have any interest, or are even antithetical to things like giving rides, and helping people go to Walmart, and getting toothpaste, and helping with wi-fi, and operating a seafarers' centre.
>
> (Stakeholder from Canada)

This difference of approach could be useful as a way of differentiating between the services that were offered by organizations running seafarers' centres in the United Kingdom and the outreach provided by some other organizations, most notably Jehovah's Witnesses. Our interviewee continued, saying

> The biggest, most common example would be those from the Jehovah's Witness group who do ship visiting. They have clearly said they don't want to be involved in seafarers' centres, they don't want to give rides and do the other diaconate work, and so then they would—by their own choice, but it would also probably be very problematic in NAMMA and ICMA, but mostly by their own choice—they haven't approached us to be part of our network at all.
>
> (Stakeholder from Canada)

Although, they had not approached the NAMMA or ICMA, Jehovah's Witnesses were frequently identified by port chaplains as having visited vessels, leaving behind religious materials and sometimes disgruntled seafarers. In the course of our fieldwork, we also encountered vessels where Jehovah's Witnesses had been on board and left materials and where they had irritated the seafarers, who had felt obliged to host them. One field note recorded how

In the crew mess, we saw some religious literature left by the Jehovah's Witnesses who had been on board in the morning. When I met the OS [Ordinary Seaman] from my home town, I asked him about the visit of the Jehovah's Witnesses, and he told me that they had learned from their previous experience with them that they usually visit to talk about the bible and, in some instances, encourage them to try joining their religion. So when they came on board, and when they discovered that they were Jehovah's Witnesses, many of them, including him, excused themselves by saying that they were busy with work. But they stayed long enough to even have lunch with the crew to the annoyance of the chief cook and the messman, who had to listen to their biblical exegesis thereafter.

(Porton field notes)

These activities, by Jehovah's Witnesses in particular, were regarded with considerable antagonism by chaplains and volunteers delivering services to seafarers in Porton and Riverside. They felt that the practices of Jehovah's Witnesses could be mildly aggressive and were inappropriate in a context where 'captive' seafarers lived and worked on board. As one put it,

Yes, I'm a Christian, but if someone came into my home and my workplace and is going 'You're not a good Christian, you need to read your bible more', like I don't want that, you know. It's not appropriate in the workplace, it's not appropriate in your home, and seafarers are not in a position where they can walk away, and often, at times, their culture causes them that they want to respect visitors and be respectful to them and open so they're not going to walk away or they're not going to be so brash as to say, 'Listen, I don't want to hear that right now.'

(Chaplain from the United Kingdom)

There was a very strong shared sense amongst our interviewees that Jehovah's Witnesses and others who boarded vessels solely to proselytize jeopardized their ability to continue to minister to seafarers' welfare needs in the future. One chaplain described how

We're not in it to proselytize. So, we don't believe in telling somebody they should become a Christian, but there are ship visitors out there who do believe that. I think that really hinders your work, and there's plenty of reasons why it's not a good idea to do that. [...] and it hurts our reputation because seafarers don't care what badge you wear, they don't understand the difference between them I think.

(Chaplain from the United Kingdom)

This sense that the actions of others could threaten the activities of their staff in providing welfare services to seafarers strongly united our interviewees, in different parts of the world, who expressed frustration that the port authorities continued to let ship visitors from the Jehovah's Witnesses and other similar organizations visit ships even though some seafarers felt harmed and aggrieved by their activities. As one chaplain explained,

> We've spoken with the harbour master and they say, 'Well, really, we can't refuse to give them access.' I say, 'But you won't let us go on board and proselytise.' And these people, we find their literature everywhere…these people came, 'What is all this about?' And it's overt. And it's distressing. I'm distressed for the seafarers who are distressed. I'm not distressed for me. I don't care. I only care about them. They are my concern. These people are not truthful about why they're going on board the vessels.
>
> (Chaplain from Canada)

This concern about the harm that Jehovah's Witnesses caused, both to seafarers and to the reputation of other welfare providers, had led to a clear policy in some organizations that they would not cooperate with Jehovah's Witnesses in providing port welfare services. As one interviewee explained,

> In terms of organizations that we don't want to work with, I think one that keeps popping up everywhere is the Jehovah's Witnesses. That's because they're not a maritime organization. They're not there for maritime welfare. They're there to give people their magazines and to recruit members. That's not the same thing. They're not there to respond to justice and welfare issues. So we've had occasions where Jehovah's Witnesses have gone on ships and pretended to be us. We had that recently in Dunkirk. So my chaplain spoke to the harbour master or the port authority and I said to him, 'Also you need to go and write to the Jehovah's Witnesses. And warn them not to use our name.' In this country you can't do that, it's illegal. But they're not going on there to ask the seafarer if there's anything they need. They're going on there to give the seafarer their magazine. Because they want to recruit more members. And I don't know why they think seafarers are going to make good members. It's not about recruiting people, it's about serving people. So we don't do anything with the Jehovah's Witnesses. […] So all the maritime sector is a bit worried about Jehovah's Witnesses.
>
> (Stakeholder from the United Kingdom)

Conclusions

The sharing of resources between welfare charities in ports has helped cash-strapped organizations to systematically coordinate their work with one another in order to cover more ships and provide better services to seafarers.[2]

---

[2] This degree to collaboration is one of several aspects of chaplaincy in ports that is unique to that sector, as considered further in Chapter 8.

However, working from the same centre and in the same geographic space has sometimes given rise to tensions between members of different welfare charities, which may be associated with individual personalities and also differing theologies. In the main, such problems have been overcome, at least to the extent that operations on the ground can continue unimpeded. There are, however, some views and some organizations that are not tolerated by the main providers of port welfare services in the United Kingdom. These are organizations which do not see their work as associated with the provision of practical assistance to seafarers at all but, instead, seek to convert crews to their faith and increase their congregations.

Chaplaincy and Seafarers: Faith at Work. Helen Sampson, Nelson Turgo, Wendy Cadge, and Sophie Gilliat-Ray, Oxford University Press. © Helen Sampson, Nelson Turgo, Wendy Cadge, and Sophie Gilliat-Ray 2024.
DOI: 10.1093/9780198913290.003.0008

8

Port Chaplaincy

What Makes It Distinctive?

Introduction

This chapter situates the work of port chaplains within the wider field of chaplaincy, illuminating some of the ways in which it is both similar to, but also different from, the work of chaplains in other sectors. We are quite simply asking: what makes port chaplaincy unique? By evaluating it through various analytical lenses related to structural arrangements, the constituencies that chaplains work with, the sector-specific tasks they perform, and the economic models that sustain their work, it becomes more possible to isolate the distinctive aspects of port chaplaincy. What becomes apparent in this chapter is the degree to which, relative to many other types of chaplaincy, the work of those who provide pastoral care in ports is international in its reach, operation, and 'client base'.

Furthermore, compared to chaplains in many other sectors, who typically work with a wide range of clients, staff, and other stakeholders, port chaplains exercise virtually no ministry towards permanent port staff. Their work is more or less entirely directed towards seafarers alone. This has implications for the extent to which they act as 'religious advisors' to their institutions or settings, something that is increasingly common in many sectors of chaplaincy. These are just some of the ways in which, as we will see, port chaplaincy is a very distinctive form of religious ministry and one that, compared to many, is still almost entirely undertaken by the Christian churches. It is yet to fully embrace the multi-faith ethos and approach that has been prevalent in many other sectors for at least the last two or three decades, although there are important indicators of future change.

Defining and Mapping Chaplaincy: An Overview

It is noticeable that definitions of 'chaplaincy' and/or 'chaplain' have changed over time to reflect the way in which this form of religious activity has adapted to new social realities. A definition from the Oxford Reference Dictionary in 1986 defined a chaplain as: 'a clergyman attached to a private chapel, institution, regiment, ship, etc.' (cited by Ryan 2014, p. 10). Some chaplaincy positions were (and still are) attached to offices of state, such as monarchs, bishops, and other dignitaries. Today, another more up to date definition of a chaplain has been proposed, which reflects a changed societal landscape:

> A chaplain is an individual who provides religious and spiritual care within an organisational setting. Although this role has evolved from within the Christian churches, the term 'chaplain' is now increasingly associated with other faith traditions. Chaplains may be qualified religious professionals, or lay people, and while religious and pastoral care may be central to their role, the increasing complexity of many large public organisations has led to an expansion in the range of their activities.
>
> (Gilliat-Ray et al. 2013, p. 5)

By 2013, chaplaincy had evolved to become a versatile, multi-faith endeavour, no longer reliant on male religious professionals. However, just a year after this definition was offered, the authors of a report published by the respected Christian think tank 'Theos' on the scope and significance of chaplaincy in the United Kingdom noted the limits of the definition, with particular reference to port (and other transportation) chaplaincy work (Ryan 2014). They noted that 'port chaplains who support seafarers...may operate *with* organisations, but tend not themselves to sit *within* an organisation' (Ryan 2014, p. 10).

Although there has been an overall decline in association with organized religion (at least in the United Kingdom), the sphere of chaplaincy has grown, especially in relation to the work of chaplains who work *with* rather than *within* institutions. As Pattison notes,

> the words 'chaplain' and 'chaplaincy' have been released from beneath the carapace of professional restriction to become a loosely designated role allowing all manner of people with a sense of concern, married with variable competence and intense commitment, to enter highly restricted arenas.
>
> (Pattison 2015, p. 15)

Where chaplains were once associated with a fairly narrow range of institutions, they can now be found in more or less any sphere of public life, and their numbers are growing. The Theos report offered a comprehensive mapping of the scope of chaplaincy in the United Kingdom and identified chaplains associated with the following: *culture* (community art, sport, theatre); *education* (school, further education, and university); *emergency services* (ambulance, fire and rescue, police, Beachy Head (suicide prevention)); *family and support* (residential homes, Mother's Union); *health care* (hospital, hospice, AIDS/HIV, primary care); *justice* (prison, community/ex-offenders, courts, immigration and removal centres); *localized/geographically situated* (port/seafarer, waterways, town centres, street pastors); *military and related* (army, navy, Royal Air Force, cadets, scouts and guides); *transport* (bus, train, trucker, taxi); *vulnerability and minority groups* (deaf, blind, national groups, e.g. for Poles, gypsies/travellers); *workplace* (media, oil and gas, industrial, Canary Wharf/finance, construction, retail); *other* (Bishops' chaplains, politics, e.g. Speaker's Chaplain at Westminster) (Ryan 2014, pp. 14–16). To this comprehensive list we can add chaplains to leisure facilities and showgrounds (Gilliat-Ray 2005), agriculture/rural communities, homeless people, and local authorities. It has even been known for chaplains to work in exhibition centres and casinos, and they are being recruited in increasing numbers to large business/corporate organizations, particularly in the United States (Miller et al. 2018).

Chaplaincy originated to provide religious and pastoral care to those whose circumstances limited them from participation in regular parish or church life. Although many chaplains still work 'behind closed doors' in restricted institutions and settings and with those unable to access their normal religious communities, the growth of chaplaincy in recent decades appears to be in those areas of social life that are more accessible to the general public and within plain sight. In the Foreword to the Theos report, it was claimed that 'the proverbial man on the street seems as—perhaps more—likely to meet a chaplain in his daily life as he is to meet any other formal, religious figure' (Nick Spencer, cited in Ryan 2014, p. 6). However, contrary to this view, and given that port chaplains work in highly secure and regulated environments away from urban centres (Montemaggi 2018), we suggest it is unlikely that the 'proverbial man on the street' is likely to meet one, let alone have very much understanding of what one does. So, before thinking about the unique aspects of their chaplaincy, we offer an overview of the kind of ministry port chaplains provide.

The Work of Port Chaplains: Going on Board

Before meeting any seafarer, chaplains undergo in-depth security training and screening in order for them to work safely within the port environment. Having successfully completed these preliminaries and obtained visitor permits, they must pass through security control. This may be easier said than done and is dependent upon the vagaries of local arrangements; at least one chaplain in our study worked in a privately owned (rather than government-owned) port. His only means of meeting seafarers was for them to call him in order to meet outside the port gate. In this case, his car was his 'office'. But more usually, and once inside the port, chaplains must navigate a vast geographic area, avoiding all the machinery and potential dangers associated with the industry, such as cranes, forklift trucks, shipping containers, and lorries. Within such an inhospitable environment and subject to prevalent weather conditions, preserving their own physical safety (and that of others) places considerable demands upon them in terms of being aware of moving metal and vehicles. These demands are over and above the distances they must then travel around the port (either on foot or by car) to access ships and seafarers. Contravening security regulations can have serious consequences for the future work of port chaplains, with infringements potentially leading to the denial of future access.

Port chaplains may or may not have a seafarers' 'centre' or other premises to use as their base. If they have such a facility, it may be little more than a portacabin, but at least it provides a space from which to organize and facilitate their work. Prior to visiting ships, chaplains will need to equip themselves with some key material resources, such as top-up phone/SIM cards and portable wi-fi, perhaps some snack foods to share with seafarers, any donated gifts (such as warm clothing/woolly hats), or religious materials such as prayer cards, leaflets, or rosaries. Chaplains may plan to visit particular ships (some are 'regulars'), but more often than not, they will simply climb the ship's gangway and seek permission to board. This isn't always granted, of course (perhaps due to the dangerous nature of the cargo they are loading/unloading), but their ministry is often welcomed on account of the welfare and support services that they (alone) provide. However, they have to be prepared to meet a potentially lukewarm response resulting in disappointment and low spirits. As one told us,

> The port won't offer you transport and just feel like you went through all these hoops just to try to get to that ship and then you go on board and they're like 'We don't need you.' So, yes, that kind of stuff is frustrating, and sometimes it can make you be like 'Oh, why am I even doing this?'
>
> (Chaplain from the United Kingdom)

Chaplains may have to be quite dogged in their efforts to overcome the physical and bureaucratic challenges of boarding ships, but their persistence seems to be driven by their recognition of the extreme loneliness and isolation of seafarers and the fact that there are no other personnel or organizations who can offer a similar service. Once on board, chaplains will usually be taken to the crew's mess, where they might meet seafarers who are preparing meals or enjoying a break. They will often try to meet with the captain and the cook (two of the more lonely roles on board) and generally 'loiter with intent' (Pattison 1994; Miller 2007; Johnston and McFarland 2010) in the hope of meeting seafarers who may need their support. Timing is everything, however, as seafarers work long hours (typically between 8.00 a.m. and 6.00 p.m. and only have two fifteen-minute coffee breaks and one lunch break), and chaplains will be lucky if they manage to speak with many of them during working hours.

As well as the material and practical services they offer via the sale of SIM cards and the distribution of donated clothing, snack foods, or religious material, they will also try to discern what, if any, the pastoral needs of the crew might be. On rare occasions, these may be explicitly religious, and they might be asked to conduct a religious service (most often by advanced request via the captain). Usually, this would be held in the mess, but not always, as this rather exceptional extract illustrates:

I remember doing the communion from the reserved sacrament of the ship, and they did the service in the officer's lounge. Then the captain said, 'Can you go down to the engine room, because the engineers can't come up?' I said, "Yeah, no problem', and so we went down, and I remember standing in the engine control room. You know, the noise of the engine, the alarms going off…the engineers covered in oil because something had gone wrong and they were having to pull apart part of the engine. Full of oil, the stink of the stuff. But I was standing there in my cassock with the sacraments.

(Chaplain from the United Kingdom)

Such explicit religious ministry is unusual and most likely to be requested as a result of a particular incident or occasion. It nevertheless illustrates the potential demands and professional flexibility that the role may require.

In our research, chaplains spoke about the emotional burden that crew sometimes want to offload during their time in the port. The issues are unsurprising—homesickness, relationship breakdowns with kin at home, absence from rites of passage, bullying and abuse on board the ship, as well as the deprivations and working conditions that are an inherent part of life at sea. Indeed, it appears to be the case that when things are going wrong—seriously wrong—on board, seafarers will hope for a chaplain to visit in order that they can share their concerns in confidence. Implicit here is an understanding that the chaplain may be able to take appropriate action on behalf of the seafarer by alerting port inspectors or other agencies. However, this potential advocacy role played by chaplains can be one of the reasons why their access to ships is prohibited, by some captains and companies, and chaplains must steer a careful course. In practice, conversations about sensitive professional or personal issues usually emerge once the more immediate and practical services of port chaplains have been secured and when seafarers feel that they can trust the individual chaplain concerned. In most cases, seafarers' initial priority is to establish contact with their families. The SIM cards that chaplains have available for sale—usually more cheaply than other providers—are a vital first step in creating the conditions where more pastorally focused conversations can follow.

Port chaplains inevitably encounter seafarers from many different parts of the world, and consequently, they have the scope to become skilled intercultural communicators. Many chaplains will try to learn a few phrases in the languages associated with the main nationalities engaged in the seafaring industry, such as Russian, Tagalog, Mandarin, Ukrainian, and so on. Similarly, port chaplains are likely to encounter mixed-faith crews and may find themselves acting as 'brokers' for the religious and spiritual care of those who are not Christian. We heard accounts of chaplains facilitating the breaking of Ramadan fasts, and enabling some Sikh seafarers to access a gurdwara while their ship was in the port. Nevertheless, some chaplains were painfully aware of the limits of their provision. One told us,

I mean we've got the contact numbers. If we meet a Muslim seafarer who would want to go to a mosque or something, we can give them an address and things like that. But when you look at, I guess in our seafarer centre, well we're sat in a chapel aren't we? So it's not really, it's not a multi-faith kind of room.

(Chaplain from the United Kingdom)

Others had yet to consider the possibilities in relation to support for people of other faiths:

INTERVIEWER: Have you ever thought of, say, getting a Muslim as a volunteer or a Sikh, whatever, or a Hindu as a volunteer in the port?
RESPONDENT: No, I haven't thought about that actually.

(Chaplain from the United Kingdom)

Although a more multi-faith approach to port chaplaincy work is yet to become fully embedded, it was clear from our data that chaplains regard the provision of accessible welfare services to seafarers of all faiths (and none) as their paramount responsibility—with religious ministry coming second.

The nature of seafaring means that tragic loss of life occurs from time to time. Sometimes, deaths at sea are accidental, but of course, there are also times when a death might be regarded as suspicious. Regardless of the circumstances, coast-guards will sometimes contact a port chaplain to help with the pastoral and religious needs of the crew:

Like one time we had a ship coming into [place] and we already knew that one of the seafarers on board was missing, like before they showed up something had happened. Nobody knows the truth even to this day if maybe he committed suicide, maybe it was a medical emergency, maybe something went wrong with equipment, I don't know, but the seafarer was gone.

(Chaplain from the United Kingdom)

So, port chaplains, like their counterparts in many other sectors of chaplaincy, often have to act in emergency situations, and the nature of their role makes them one of the vital 24/7 'emergency services' following a tragedy.

The Work of Port Chaplains: Beyond the Ship

The operational norms of ports are variable. Bulk handling of cargo in some remote ports is not always highly mechanized, and not all ports operate on a 24/7 basis. However, the processing of cargo on and off ships is becoming increasingly automated, with the consequence that vessels might only be in port for a matter of hours (Sampson 2024). The rapidity with which ships arrive and depart means that chaplains compete for the limited time and attention of crew. If seafarers are permitted to leave their ships, port chaplains who have access to suitable vehicles are able to take them either to seafarers' centres in the port or, potentially, to shopping malls in nearby towns and cities. If there is a seafarers' centre, these spaces provide a welcoming environment for crews to make their phone calls, buy souvenirs and snacks, relax, and, if necessary, speak to a chaplain. Some centres have a small chapel where religious services can be held and where private worship can occur, but generally speaking, such spaces are rarely used by seafarers. Regardless of destination, the transportation of seafarers can provide a good opportunity for chaplains to engage in relationship-building and pastoral conversation 'on the move'.

As well as enabling seafarers to contact their families directly via SIM cards or portable wi-fi, chaplains can also play an important (if indirect) role in communications between seafarers and their families. One chaplain told us about a vessel where the satellite phone on board had broken down, and families were becoming worried:

> The satellite had broken and...so everyone on the ship wanted internet SIM cards. Everybody. Because they had no satellite phone or anything. And so we put a post on Facebook—we were there hours sorting it all out—and then afterwards we put a post on Facebook that we visited that ship and what had happened on board. And then the wife of the Chief Officer commented. Well she hasn't heard from her husband for two weeks. And that was very unusual for him. So the families were starting to worry, has the ship sunk, been taken by pirates? And so we put this post on and she'd just been searching the name of the ship and our post came up. And we got a reply saying to us, 'Thank you so much for this' and, you know, really thanking us because now the families know that they're okay, they don't need to worry.
>
> (Chaplain from the United Kingdom)

Away from ships, chaplains may also have a vital role in visiting seafarers who have been injured on board and have to be hospitalized once the ship has arrived in the port. Chaplains are probably the only people who would know of such an incident and have the capacity to provide pastoral support. One described the significance of such visits:

> That could have been a situation where you thought, 'He doesn't really want me there' [in the hospital] but I kept going back, [...] So sometimes you think that you're not making any impact at all, but I've always said to my volunteers as well you need to persevere, [...] Sometimes [...] you just know that you have made somebody's life a bit better.
>
> (Chaplain from the United Kingdom)

Given the significance of the practical and pastoral services that chaplains pro-vide and the extent to which they support the welfare of seafarers, it was surpris-ing to hear how much their work is restricted by limited resources of time, voluntary support, and finances. Such constraints mean that some chaplains spend as much time engaged in straightforward fund-raising as they do in pas-toral work. The financial vulnerability of some port chaplaincy operations is described in the following poignant extract:

> I don't have enough money—it's just strictly a matter of economics. We have ah...our funding is...it's not sustainable at this point. We're working very hard to try to create ways to raise money. But it's getting to the point where it feels like we're all about the fund-raising and not about the work. Which is when I start getting very angry with my board, and say to them, 'You guys need to remember that we do the work for which you raise the funds.' That's how this job divides itself out.
> (Chaplain from Canada)

Some of the chaplains in our study were undertaking their work as an extension of a parish-based role. In these cases, they were often able to draw upon the sup-port of their congregations in terms of the donation of material things that are highly valued by seafarers. Others, who were not formally associated with a par-ish, nonetheless made a point of relationship-building with churches located proximate to ports, thereby extending their potential volunteer base.[1]

Regardless of institutional arrangements, most chaplains have considerable autonomy, which allows them to shape their working lives, and there are some distinctive principles that they all seem to abide by. This includes things such as a 'respectful attitude towards the secular authority and values that structure its con-text' (Pattison 2015, p. 21). To this we might add that 'in the UK chaplains exist in public institutions because of the public good that they profess to serve and their ability to address the sacred without recourse to an uncompromising religious ideology' (Todd et al. 2015, p. 333). They tend to share a commitment to being non-judgemental and a clear understanding that chaplaincy is not a platform for proselytism.

The preceding paragraphs offer a picture of the kind of activities that port chaplains engage in. Their primary services of practical and pastoral support for seafarers is situated alongside their facilitative and communicative work within and beyond the port and the pressures upon them to secure financial and mater-ial resources. But to what extent is their work unique? What kind of analytic lenses enable us to discern the way in which port chaplaincy is both similar to and also different from other sectors of chaplaincy?

---

[1] As mentioned previously, port chaplains are relatively unique in processing the donation of many goods, and also, worked with lots of volunteers.

So What Makes Port Chaplaincy Distinctive?

In their conclusion to the *Handbook of Chaplaincy Studies*, Todd, Cobb, and Swift suggested ways in which the study of chaplaincy might be developed in future. One of their recommendations was the need for a 'nuanced, critically reflective map of the phenomenon of chaplaincy and of the way it is constructed and understood' (Todd et al. 2015, p. 332). What follows in this section isn't so much a 'map' but rather an effort to identify some analytical frameworks through which we can begin to discern and appreciate the distinctive work of chaplains in a range of sectors. We begin by considering the bureaucratic and institutional context in which the work of a chaplain is performed and the way in which this can shape the role.

Structural and organizational arrangements

'Chaplaincy is a highly contingent practice because of where it is situated and what it serves' (Todd et al. 2015, p. 334). In this section, we are not so much concerned with the physical 'where' (though that comes into it) but rather the organizational 'where' of chaplaincy. The Theos report, cited at the beginning of this chapter, distinguished between chaplaincy *with*, and chaplaincy *within*, organizations. Chaplains who work *within* are typically recruited and funded by the institution, and thus more subject to its overarching ethos and aims, for example justice or military effectiveness (Kevern and McSherry 2015). Consequently, chaplains working *within* an organization are potentially more likely to feel the tensions of being 'between two worlds'—the institution in which they work (e.g. the 'host' or 'employer' prison or hospital) and the institution with which they identify (their religious organization) (Holst 1982; Cadge 2012; Sullivan 2014). They are more likely to be embedded within a hierarchical structure with line management and accountability arrangements that are framed by clear operating standards or 'codes of conduct'. A good example of this would be the HM Prison Service Instructions and Prison Service Orders, which outline the operational rules and guidelines for the running of prisons. Chaplains working *within* large hierarchical organizations may find more opportunities for promotion or specialization, an ability to shape the policies of the organization by serving on committees and working groups, and scope to play an educational role in relation to religious matters more broadly (Woodhead 2015). One of the reasons institutional chaplaincy has been able to flourish in recent decades has been the willingness of chaplains to become 'educational and knowledge resources on which various professional groups—from mental health professionals to lawyers and prison governors—draw in their professional practice' (Woodhead 2015).

Chaplains working *within* an institution are more likely to be part of multidisciplinary teams involving other professionals. This is most especially evident within health care (Cadge 2012), where chaplains may play a crucial role in supporting decision-making about treatment and end-of-life arrangements. Chaplains who work *within* an institution—thereby encompassed by bureaucratic and contextual structures that most likely reflect total or partial state funding—have more scope to be influenced by the professionals with whom they must work. As a consequence, some have collectively sought some degree of organized professionalization in order to legitimate and promote their own sphere of operation. By now, there are well-established formal bodies to support the work of chaplains in sectors such as health care, prisons, education, the military, and so on. Despite its relative infancy, Muslim prison, education, university, and hospital chaplains in Britain have formed professional associations that mirror those of Christian colleagues and have established educational programmes that can give them credence and authority both within and outside their communities and institutions (Gilliat-Ray et al. 2013).

Those entering chaplaincy *within* an institution will typically undergo rigorous and systematic internal 'vetting' in relation to their credentials, whereas chaplains working *with* an organization may be subject to less rigorous scrutiny. This has become particularly relevant in those sectors where chaplains have to take some account of policies associated with the prevention of terrorism and radicalization (in the United Kingdom, known as PREVENT). Chaplains working *with* an organization may be far less encumbered by the need to attend to such policies, although, of course, they may be subject to other kinds of security issues.

As a sector that works *with* an organization, rather than *within* it, port chaplains share with others in the same bureaucratic and institutional arrangement, the challenge of working within a flat organizational structure, with relatively little (if any) opportunity to contribute to the wider institution or setting. It is difficult to envisage ways in which a port chaplain could be 'promoted' within any hierarchy, and there are currently no sector-specific formally accredited training programmes they can join. They typically work in isolation from other professionals and thus lack the same opportunity to develop their knowledge and skills in relation to them or to work as part of a larger 'team'. In this way, the character of their work—from an institutional and bureaucratic perspective—is no different from other chaplains who work *with* organizations.

Regardless of sector or organizational arrangements, most chaplains have scope to work right across an institution or setting, from the most senior office-holder, to the most junior member of staff. Hospital chaplains support staff, just as much as they support patients and their families. Similarly, chaplains in educational settings are there for the pupils *and* the staff. A court chaplain can minister to those attending court as well as to court officials. The capacity of chaplains to act as 'connectors' in an increasingly differentiated and fragmented society and within large organizations is often considered a particular strength of their work (Woodhead 2015). However, the spatial 'where' of port chaplaincy means that chaplains have little opportunity to exercise such an organization-wide role. So, for example, in comparison to airports or railway stations, where there are large public areas that are under cover from the weather, there are no such spaces in ports. For their own safety, and given local rules and regulations, chaplains cannot 'loiter with intent' in the port environment in the hope of picking up 'passing trade'.

Because chaplaincy originated *within* organizations, chaplaincy within organizations typically has a much longer history compared to many of the sectors with which chaplaincy *with* organizations has emerged in recent decades. As a result, there is a substantial body of literature and interdisciplinary research underpinning chaplaincy to the military, to prisons, to educational establishments, and so on. On account of its historicity, port chaplaincy has been similarly well documented, certainly relative to the newer forms of chaplaincy *with* organizations. Port chaplains are members of historic Christian maritime organizations, such as the Mission to Seafarers and Apostleship of the Sea (now known as Stella Maris). Although there are some well-established bodies associated with chaplaincy *with* organizations (such as Theatre Chaplaincy UK, formerly known as the Actors' Church Union, established 1899), port chaplains can, in comparison, lay claim to a far longer international history and associated supporting corpus of literature compared to almost all other sectors that work *with* organizations.

Who Do Chaplains Work With?

We have already noted that port chaplains have a highly focused ministry directed towards seafarers alone…and towards an occupational group whose work is largely 'invisible to society' (Montemaggi 2018, p. 502). But port chaplains also work with a distinctive demographic. The nature of the employment market means that the vast majority of seafarers are healthy, fit, men of working age and the personal circumstances where they can be away from their dependents for weeks or months at a time. In terms of age and gender, the obvious similarity is with prisoners, the overwhelming majority of whom are relatively young men.[2] Port chaplaincy is undertaken by both genders, and exactly half the chaplains in our sample were women.

---

[2] Of the UK prison population, 68.1 per cent is aged between twenty-five and forty-nine, and only 4.1 per cent of the prison population in the United Kingdom is female: UK Gov Justice Data, 'Prisons Data', https://data.justice.gov.uk/prisons (accessed 2 August 2022).

Chaplains in nearly all sectors work *within* or *with* institutions characterized by religious, linguistic, and cultural diversity, but the extent to which port chaplains must work with such diversity and across international borders makes their work decidedly 'global' in character. It is hard to imagine chaplains in other sectors acquiring a basic vocabulary in Russian, Tagalog, or Mandarin in order to do their day-to-day work. But there is another characteristic of seafarers that port chaplains must take account of, namely the religious (or non-religious) character and culture of the countries from which seafarers originate. For example, Filipinos come from a society where some 86 per cent of the population is Roman Catholic, with a further 6 per cent from other Christian denominations (Miller 2020). As a Communist society, China has no official religion, and over half the population claims no formal religious affiliation (https://www.pewresearch.org/religion/2023/08/30/measuring-religion-in-china/. Accessed 12 March 24). Over 70 per cent of Russians claim membership of the Russian Orthodox Church, while in Latvia, there are strong Lutheran influences alongside Roman Catholicism. Seafarers bring the religious 'cultures' of their societies with them, and in some cases, these societies will be far less influenced by currents of secularism or discourses around 'spirituality' than others. This reality makes port chaplains knowledgeable about aspects of global religion, and Christianity in particular, in a way that would not be typical for chaplains in other sectors.

Associated with the highly multicultural, multilingual, and multi-faith character of port chaplaincy, and the origins of this form of sector ministry, is the extent of the global networks that port chaplains can access both within and beyond the maritime sector. For a seafarer facing bad news from home, a chaplain is well placed to arrange immediate action through their worldwide networks with fellow chaplains (Down 1999). Although other sectors of chaplaincy have international networks (e.g. the International Prison Chaplains Association), these are typically orientated towards professional support and training rather than advocacy for those whom chaplains serve. Over time, port chaplaincy organizations have become adept at using their own sponsoring/sending religious networks and organizations in support of seafarers: 'In 1985 the ICMA [International Christian Maritime Association] held a plenary conference in the Philippines and focussed attention on the plight of Filipino seafarers working on board overseas-registered ships; the Cardinal Archbishop of the Philippines himself presented the conference's concerns to the government of the Philippines' (Down 1999, p. 130). The extent to which port chaplains undertake such networking makes them a distinctive group of religious professionals within the world of sector ministry.

Since the 1990s, there has been a drive towards multi-faith approaches to religious and pastoral care in public institutions in sectors of chaplaincy that work both *within* and *with* organizations. For example, the Patient's Charter, introduced in the United Kingdom in 1991, set out the rights of patients receiving care within the National Health Service. The first of these specifies 'respect for privacy and religious and cultural beliefs' (Gilliat-Ray 2003), with no distinction made between Christians and those of other faiths. Over the years, structural arrangements and appointments have been made to enable (at least in theory) the religious and pastoral care of patients from a wide range of traditions. HM Prison Service made a similar commitment to more multi-faith provision in the 1990s and 2000s (Beckford and Gilliat 1998), as did the military when chaplains from other faiths were appointed in 2005 (Hafiz 2015). Outside these state-funded institutions, there are chaplains of other faiths associated with the police, airports, courts, leisure facilities, and so on (Gilliat-Ray 2005). Broadly speaking, therefore, chaplaincy in the United Kingdom is now a multi-faith endeavour both in terms of its ethos and with respect to the religious identity of those involved. However, port chaplaincy continues to be a largely Christian undertaking; we found no chaplains of other faiths during the course of our research (although we were told of some by interviewees). Furthermore, chaplains themselves (as we noted in the quotation above) seem not to have adopted an approach to working with seafarers of other faiths beyond simply 'facilitating' or brokering access to personnel or facilities. This situation may be starting to change. From 2019/2020 onwards, there has been a clear commitment by the Mission to Seafarers to use a donation from Seafarers UK to increase the diversity of its personnel and to meet the needs of seafarers from other faiths (MtS 2019). However, the point remains that such a development—to the extent that it occurs—is considerably behind most, if not all, other sectors of chaplaincy.

The Economic Model Underpinning Port Chaplaincy

Chaplains who work *within* organizations can typically rely on a relatively stable financial model supporting their work, usually in the form of taxation. However, chaplains working *with* organizations are more reliant upon sponsorship, charitable donations, or receipt of benefits associated with providing free (or subsidized) chaplaincy services, such as access to facilities with little or free rent or, perhaps, a car-parking space. Port chaplaincy is heavily reliant on donations from seafarer organizations (such as Seafarers UK, cited above) and corporate business partnerships, as well as fundraising undertaken by, or from, private individuals (such as in relation to legacies). Although funding is a significant challenge for the chaplaincy organizations through which port chaplains are employed, they have adopted a professional and entrepreneurial approach. For example, there are few chaplaincy bodies working *with* organizations (or even *within* organizations) that have things on sale via a website, but the Mission to Seafarers has an online shop for the purchase of merchandise that supports the organization (such as books, and charity Christmas cards).

Being so reliant on donations and sponsorship, there is a particular need to 'evidence' their work to potential donors, and so both the Stella Maris and Mission to Seafarers websites contain extensive information about impact. Port chaplains have clearly become adept at providing regular and detailed information documenting ship visits, encounters with any seafarers, and every visit made by a seafarer to a centre. Trustee reports provide detailed analysis of the kinds of issue that chaplains encounter, from a need for pastoral and religious advice to a requirement for health support and legal assistance. The following extract from the 2019 Mission to Seafarers' Annual Report is illustrative of the kind of detail that port chaplains have become accustomed to providing about their work, such that every vehicle journey undertaken by a chaplain to facilitate their work is documented:

All of our employed and grant-funded chaplaincies provide monthly reports of their activities as follows:

- 28,660 ship visits (2018: 23,524) meeting more than 143,300 seafarers (2018: 117,600) on board;
- 188,245 visits made to our seafarers' centres (2018: 91,931) (29 of our grant-funded or employed stations have centres);
- 130,600 seafarers transported (2018: 60,385);
- 3,308 seafarers registered with he Mission to Seafarers' Philippines Family Network (2018: 12,842) and through our network:
  - ¬ 656 sought pastoral support and counselling
  - ¬ 3 sought access to legal advice
  - ¬ 10 sought access to medical advice;
- 1.6 tons of volunteer-knitted items (hats, gloves, and scarves) were sent to our ports around thE WORLD.

The above outputs, when joined with our global family network, amounted to:

- 75,220 ship visits (2018:70,600), encountering approximately 376,000 seafarers (2018: 353,000) on board their ships;
- 435,000 visits (2018: 673,000) made to our 121 (2018: 121) seafarers' centres;
- 400,000 seafarers transported (2018: 439,000).

(Mission to Seafarers, 'Trustees' Annual Report and Accounts for the Year Ended December 2019', https://register-of-charities.charitycommission.gov.uk/charity-search?p_p_id=uk_gov_ccew_onereg_charitydetails_web_portlet_CharityDetailsPortlet&p_p_lifecycle=2&p_p_state=maximized&p_p_mode=view&p_p_resource_id=%2Faccounts-resource&p_p_cacheability=cache accessed 18 February 2022)

The extent of reporting and recording documented here—especially in a sector that works *with* organizations rather than *within them*—is not typical in the chaplaincy sector as a whole.

Pastoral and Religious Duties

Perhaps with the exception of chaplains working with prisoners serving life sentences, chaplains generally work with people who are 'in transit' through an institution or who are associated with it as a result of their engagement with other organizations or settings. They 'normalize' religious faith in otherwise secular environments, and chaplains have to learn how to 'get in', 'get on', and 'get out' of their encounters. In this respect, port chaplains have much in common with their counterparts in other sectors, who also need to be skilled at rapid relationship-building. Regardless of setting or institution, chaplains tend to be engaged in the same kind of religious and pastoral activities, such as counselling, bereavement support, arranging worship, brokering and facilitating relationships, crisis/emergency ministry, and so on. They may also have some involvement in sacraments and rites of passage or the marking of ceremonial/festive occasions. The nature and extent of engagement in these is likely to reflect their context so that, for example, hospital chaplains might well perform more baptisms than prison chaplains (or port chaplains, for that matter). As a result of our research, we found little evidence of port chaplains marking any rites of passage on a regular basis, and this would not be unusual in many other sectors of chaplaincy either. They were, nevertheless, involved in ceremonial occasions associated with seafaring, such as 'Sea Sunday'.

However, chaplains also acquire sector-specific skills and knowledge that signal their varying arenas of expertise. Prison chaplains tend to acquire a deep understanding of issues around law and security; health-care chaplains become knowledgeable about aspects of illness and medical care; sports chaplains will likely acquire familiarity with the rules and discourses of the sports team they support, and so on. In a similar way, port chaplains can also lay claim to their own specialist knowledge of issues associated with seafaring and shipping, including the dangers and impact of piracy, ship and port security practices, justice and welfare issues associated with shipping, health and safety in ports, international communications (including SIM cards and portable wi-fi), intercultural relations, and global Christianity, to name the most significant.

Chaplains as Advocates

Associated with this sector-specific knowledge is the scope for chaplains to acquire an important role as advocates for, and defenders of, the rights of those they serve. Their capacity to act as intermediaries in situations where there is an imbalance of power, knowledge, or other form of capital means that chaplains often have a well-established understanding of their advocacy role that is an integral part of their identity as chaplains (Foster 1975; Morgan 2010). Minimally, in the case of health-care chaplains, this may simply be a reminder to nursing staff to contact a patient's family or provide more painkillers, but there are instances of chaplains undertaking significant advocacy roles that challenge the policies or norms of an institution. For example, Muslim chaplains in some British hospitals have been successful in enabling families to have their loved one subject to a non-invasive post-mortem using an MRI scanner (as opposed to an autopsy) in order to maintain the integrity of the deceased body in accordance with Islamic norms (Ali and Gilliat-Ray 2012). In relation to mental health, Kinghorn suggests:

> It is not unthinkable—or, at least, *should* not be unthinkable that a well-equipped chaplain might challenge a psychiatrist's core formulation of a particular patient's mental health problem. Chaplains might argue, for example, that what a psychiatrist labels 'depression' in a particular patient is best understood as unresolved shame, or that what a psychiatrist labels 'paranoia' in a particular patient is a contextually appropriate response to racism and neighbourhood violence.
>
> (Kinghorn 2015, p. 187)

Exactly this kind of intercultural advocacy, in relation to what could be misunderstood as a mental health issue, was reported in research with a Muslim chaplain in the north of England:

> One day the Chronic Pain Consultant rang me and she said, 'we have a Pakistani patient in the hospital, and we think this patient has got a mental health issue. He's fastened his legs and won't walk and he doesn't want to talk to us and he's saying his pain is too much... we are referring him to the Mental Health Institute.' I said, 'it could be a form of him managing his pain... back in India and Pakistan, when people are working in the fields, when they are in pain they will fasten something tight around the legs or arms or wherever they have pain. That is the way they look at it because they can't afford to get treatment.' That was very eye-opening for them...the cultural aspect of how people manage their pain.
>
> (Ali and Gilliat-Ray 2012)

In many institutional settings, chaplains have an important advocacy role in helping their clients to navigate bureaucratic structures and regulations that can appear overwhelming and obscure. For example, a student who is unsatisfied with their treatment by a university administration, who exhausts the support offered by personal tutors, head of department, student services, or counselling may find that chaplains are well placed to offer not only support but also practical strategies to resolve such difficulties due to their knowledge of university hierarchies ('the right word in the right ears and at the right time'). Being embedded within the fabric of an institution—or at least being an 'insider' to some degree—gives chaplains an opportunity to play an important mediating role because they are 'not like' any other official or officer. In our data, it was clear that port chaplains are potentially the only people to whom seafarers can turn to confidentially report issues of concern that can then be reported to port authorities or other agencies. This advocacy role is also evident in the Mission to Seafarer's 2019 'Trustee's Annual Report' cited earlier, which notes the role that port chaplains have played in helping seafarers to access legal and other forms of advice relative to their employers. In this way, their advocacy role mirrors the scope that chaplains have in other sectors to defend the interests of hospital patients, prisoners, military personnel, university students, and so on. There is, however, an important difference. Port chaplains are not trained to provide legal advice in cases of labour disputes, and so referral to other agencies (rather than taking up individual cases themselves) is their best form of advocacy. Some industry stakeholders (like crewing agencies) are critical of welfare organizations where they are perceived to be trying to do 'lawyering' for seafarers. Port chaplains need to avoid being perceived in such a way because they need the help of the industry in order to secure funding and to continue to access seafarers. In many other sectors of chaplaincy, both *within* and *with* organizations, there are usually more opportunities for 'clients' (whoever they may be) to seek support from a range of other welfare services in addition to, or as an alternative to, those provided by the chaplaincy. However, port chaplaincy is one of the rare forms of pastoral ministry where there simply are very few alternative, trusted, representatives of organizations that seafarers can turn to during their brief sojourn in ports. This was noted in the Theos report cited earlier. It states:

> There are fields and organisations in which very few, or any, welfare or pastoral support structures exist other than that provided by chaplaincy. A good example of this is the work done by port chaplains and organisations such as the Apostleship of the Sea [also known as Stella Maris] which are exceptional in seeking to help and support seafarers in a huge range of pastoral ways. Seafaring is a relentlessly tough industry and one in which the rights of workers and the support available to them are extremely limited. In such a context, the pastoral work done by chaplains is invaluable—there simply aren't other people available or willing to do it. It includes a huge amount of very practical work—such as helping with money transfers abroad, providing phone SIM cards and internet at a fair price, helping with transport around the ports, and bringing clothes and toothbrushes to seafarers stuck in hospital.
>
> (Ryan 2014, p. 35)

Conclusion

Despite the potential loneliness of their day-to-day work and their clear focus on ministry to seafarers (alone), port chaplains may intermittently maintain a complex web of institutional relationships, including with port authorities, shipping companies, their sponsoring religious organizations, and the network of Christian bodies that serve maritime industries around the globe. Their scope for relationship-building is extensive and international, making them human sign-posts who can facilitate and enable information-sharing for a wide range of stake-holders. Both individual port chaplains and their sponsoring organizations have the capacity for entrepreneurialism and a particular kind of knowledge about communications technology. One of our interviewees had ideas about the poten-tial for 'virtual' seafarers' centres, and some chaplains make good use of social media to broker a wide range of relationships with, and on behalf of, seafarers. Although chaplaincy has always been, and is likely to remain, dominated by face-to-face relationships, port chaplains may find themselves suggesting ways in which communication technologies could enhance and develop the work of chaplains in other sectors in the future.

Chaplaincy and Seafarers: Faith at Work. Helen Sampson, Nelson Turgo, Wendy Cadge, and Sophie Gilliat-Ray, Oxford University Press. © Helen Sampson, Nelson Turgo, Wendy Cadge, and Sophie Gilliat-Ray 2024. DOI: 10.1093/9780198913290.003.0009

Conclusion

In the United Kingdom, the tradition of port chaplaincy goes back almost 200 years. Starting at sea with provision on board vessels, chaplaincy grew out of a desire to minister to, and cultivate, the faith needs of seafarers who were removed from their land-based communities for periods of several years at a time. As services were established ashore, the ministry of chaplains changed from one rooted in a historic sense of 'mission' to one rooted in notions of a 'ministry of presence' and the provision of welfare services to seafarers, including both accommodation and recreation. Port chaplains put their talents to use in a wide variety of capacities, ranging from 'provider of religious services' to 'hospital visitor' and 'social secretary'—organizing, as they did, dances and similar events involving the land-based community and aimed at seafarers' entertainment.

Prior to 1940, voluntary organizations were the only providers of welfare support to seafarers in UK ports. However, a wartime recognition of the value of merchant seafarers resulted in a more structured response to seafarers' welfare needs from the British state, and a welfare board was established to make appropriate decisions about the disbursement of funds originating from personal donations by the public, pension funds, and the shipping industry. As the war drew to an end, there were calls to raise a special tax, which would be used to fund seafarers' welfare services, but these plans failed to come to fruition, and as time marched on, seafarers, once again, became largely reliant on the voluntary sector in relation to their welfare needs.

This situation has persisted, and today, provision for the port-based welfare of seafarers remains very dependent on services provided by religious charities such as Mission to Seafarers and Stella Maris. These services are hugely significant to seafarers, who may rely on chaplains' support and help in times of extreme difficulty, such as when companies stop paying their wages, when they are prevented from going home despite having completed their contracts, and when they face fear on board as a result of the demands of senior officers or as a result of bullying and abuse. In many cases, just talking to a sympathetic outsider is of benefit to seafarers, but chaplains have the option of going beyond this, and in our study, they reported that they sometimes provide direct support (food, for example) and sometimes reach out to shore-based organizations on behalf of seafarers in distress. In some cases, they also instigate monitoring and send requests to chaplains in the next ports listed on a vessel's schedule, asking them to check up on the situation of the specific seafarers in question.

Seafarers also have more prosaic needs, which chaplains provide for. Many chaplains sell SIM cards to seafarers on an almost 'at-cost' basis so that they can remain in touch with their friends and families. Some undertake personal shopping for seafarers, and as such, they became vitally important when the COVID-19 pandemic struck, and seafarers were forced to remain on board their vessels, preventing them from 'nipping ashore' to purchase necessary goods. In seafarers' centres and in the course of ship visits, donated clothes and gifts are passed to seafarers from local port-based communities, and chaplains are available to offer counselling and a limited range of religious services, such as the conduct of a shipboard Mass or a blessing. Seafarers' centres are greatly valued by seafarers, who believe that they offer them a safe haven in unfamiliar ports. In these centres, they feel they are among friends and can trust the staff and volunteers to give them good and safe advice; to look after their belongings, if necessary; and to send remittances home.

In the course of the research, seafarers were identified as universally supporting the work of chaplains, even though there were occasions when some ships would not give permission for chaplains to board (this was generally the decision of the captain or the company and could relate to shipboard concerns about workload or fears about seafarers raising complaints). However, despite this largely supportive context, the work of port chaplains was revealed to be physically and emotionally demanding. It involved a high degree of emotional labour, and it took place in a context where chaplains and volunteers were often relatively isolated. In this respect, our research revealed that the work of seafarers and the work of chaplains had something in common. Their jobs were poorly understood ashore, and their labour received little *public* recognition and was largely experienced as undervalued.

In many respects, were they to come to public attention, port chaplains and seafarers would be likely to be characterized as almost polar opposites—as 'angels' and their antithesis respectively! Port chaplains minister to the welfare and spiritual needs of seafarers and would be likely to be characterized as embodying a spirit of selflessness and generosity. Their emblem, adopted by the Mission to Seafarers (MtS), is a flying angel, which symbolizes the chaplains in action, and in the past, seafarers' centres run by MtS were often known as 'flying angel clubs'. By contrast, stereotypes of seafarers represent them as hard drinking, hard living men, frequenting brothels and bars and earning lots of money (Bhattacharjeee 2019).

Nevertheless, despite these opposing superficial stereotypes, there are many similarities in the situations and behaviour of port chaplains and seafarers. Not only do they work in a realm that is relatively cut off from, and invisible to, mainstream society, but they also work in, and with, multi-faith, multinational environments. Seafarers frequently find themselves on board with colleagues of a variety of nationalities and faiths, while chaplains self-evidently work with multinational and multi-faith seafarers, *and* they also work alongside colleagues from other religious charities, who do not share their faith, in an ecumenical context. In the case of both seafarers and port chaplains, our research revealed that a high degree of tolerance was practiced in relation to working and, in the case of seafarers, living alongside individuals with a different faith. As a representative of the North American Maritime Ministry Association (NAMMA) pointed out (see Chapter 8), port chaplains from different faith backgrounds are 'fairly forgiving with one another'. Similarly, seafarers practice considerable religious tolerance on board their vessels in order to prioritize just 'getting the job done' and then getting home safely without complications. Inevitably, in both contexts, contentious issues do periodically emerge. Sometimes, seafarers were found to disagree about the importance of particular religious teachings and the acceptability of particular behaviours (such as possessing and valuing artefacts and icons), while chaplains were prone to hold different views on matters such as the appropriateness of selling SIM cards and whether Anglican chaplains could, and should, refer to services as 'Mass'.

In some respects, both chaplains and seafarers find themselves working cheek by jowl with others of different faiths because of a need and a desire—in shipping companies and in voluntary organizations—to cut costs. In this context, they have little option but to accept that they need to work with and alongside people with different beliefs. It is interesting that, to different degrees, this has led both groups to place less emphasis on public discussion of faith and more importance on shared goals and objectives—in the case of seafarers, their work and a desire to get home in one piece and, in the case of Christian chaplains, a desire to deliver kindness and welfare to strangers in an effort to emulate Christ.

Beyond the similar circumstances and contexts in which they found themselves working, it became apparent, in our study, that chaplains had developed (over a period of time) a huge sympathy for seafarers. In some respects, this is surprising as seafarers are frequently reasonably paid and often enjoy their work, so to that extent, they would not seem to be candidates for sympathy. Furthermore, they are also known to sometimes engage in behaviours that chaplains are likely to disapprove of (drinking, gambling, commercial sex, for example). However, it was seafarers' longing for their families, the ways in which they became lonely on board, the lack of choice and control available to them, and the shipboard monotony and confinement that chaplains seemed to strongly relate to. They saw at first hand the kinds of conditions that seafarers lived in, and they heard their heart-rending stories of missed births, deaths, marriages, birthdays, Christmases, anniversaries: indeed, of little more or less than lives 'unlived'. Furthermore, the fact that chaplains braved the elements to traverse what could be busy and confusing locations (ports) and that they climbed perilous-looking gangways and hung out in messrooms to visit seafarers all contributed to a sense of belonging in the port and amongst seafarers. This sense of solidarity was also identified amongst volunteers working in support of chaplains or seafarers' centres. Some of them were former seafarers themselves, but many were not, and they all seemed to have developed a degree of empathy in relation to seafarers and their families.

Notwithstanding the considerable effort and dedication of port chaplains and volunteers, it became evident, in our study, that existing services for seafarers' welfare were often at breaking point. Some chaplains had reduced their paid hours in an effort to sustain services, while they continued to work just as much as before, and unpaid volunteers often played an essential role in keeping centres open and in driving seafarers between their vessels and the seafarers' centres or to other destinations. Despite seafarers' centres being universally valued and appreciated by seafarers, their day-to-day reality saw them mostly calling into ports that provided no welfare facilities at all. In this regard, the provisions of the Maritime Labour Convention (MLC) 2006 with regard to port-based welfare services for seafarers would appear to have been largely ignored by ports and governments across the globe. One optimistic finding from the research was the positive impact that the introduction of voluntary port levies on visiting vessels could be seen to have had on funding for some welfare services for seafarers in the United Kingdom. However, the efforts to provide decent port-based welfare services to seafarers across the globe, which might have been anticipated post MLC, seem not to have materialized. As a consequence, it is Christian voluntary bodies that continue to dominate the limited provision of welfare services to the world's multi-faith body of seafarers.

Despite a stated intention amongst many participants to involve personnel from a variety of faiths, and none, in ministering to seafarers' needs, port chaplains remain predominantly Christian, and while our evidence strongly endorses their claims to provide welfare support to seafarers of all faiths, and all cultures and nationalities, they are, nevertheless, best placed to offer spiritual support to seafarers of a Christian persuasion. It may also be that some seafarers themselves regard port chaplains as irrelevant to them because of their faith. We are unable to do more than speculate that this may be the case because of the limitations of the research—both the shipboard and port-based elements of the study.

One of the significant limitations of our shipboard research was that we were unable to select vessels that carried seafarers of particular faiths, and we therefore ended up with Christian seafarers being significantly over-represented.[1] There are two reasons for this. The first, and most significant, is that seafarers' employers have no record of the faith of the seafarers who they deploy on their ships. As a result, nationality was considered to be a proxy guide to the likely faith backgrounds of seafarers on board, but this is an imperfect approximation,

---

[1] Although we do not know the faith backgrounds of the world's seafarers, we do have intelligence on their nationality, which implies that the seafaring labour force is likely to be of much more diverse faith than our sample of seafarers.

which contributed to an over-representation of Christian seafarers amongst the crews that worked on our two vessel 'case studies',[2] The second reason why we were restricted in terms of our vessel (and likely faith) choices is that negotiating access to ships is extremely difficult, many of the world's multinationally crewed vessels employ Filipinos as a significant part of their crew 'mix' and Christianity is the predominant faith in the Philippines. Meanwhile a limitation of our port-based fieldwork is that much of it took place (for obvious, logical, and sound reasons) in seafarers' centres. As a consequence, we self-evidently missed out on any opportunity to access the experiences or attitudes of seafarers who feel that such centres are inappropriate for them or who feel that they are overlooked when it comes to ship visits from port chaplains—should such seafarers exist.

Despite some limitations, the study we have reported on is unusual in its robustness. We were fortunate to be able to conduct ethnography in both ports and on board working cargo ships. This gave us an unprecedented comprehension of both the life and faith of seafarers at sea and their life and faith when briefly ashore. It also provided an opportunity to explore, with chaplains and volunteers, their lives, work, motivations, and beliefs. Further to this, we gained considerable insight from our interviews with seafarers, chaplains, and stakeholders. When put together, these elements of the research allowed us to develop a very deep and thorough understanding of the multitude of ways in which chaplains and volunteers provide welfare support to seafarers, of the context in which this takes place, and of the needs and understandings of seafarers. This insight has allowed us to develop some limited recommendations, which we hope will be of value to both seafarers and chaplains/volunteers working with UK port-based welfare services.

Recommendations

The findings from the study support a small number of others (Palmer and Murray 2016; Montemaggi 2018), which strongly suggest that port-based seafarers' centres make an essential contribution to seafarers' welfare. As a matter of priority, therefore, we urgently recommend that

(1) port authorities, governments, and non-governmental organizations come together to organize, fund, and support the provision of a seafarers' centre in every port, which fully complies with MLC guidance;

(2) consideration be given to a levy providing funding for the provision of welfare services for seafarers in every port;

---

[2] This term is employed loosely, in a non-technical sense, to convey our meaning.

(3) seafarers' centres should provide, at a minimum, sundry items for purchase, café/bar facilities of some sort, free wi-fi, and the contact details of a chaplain/volunteer who can provide assistance if needed;

(4) centres should be staffed to provide seafarers with the opportunity for some social interaction with individuals who are not on board their vessels;

(5) transport should be available from ships to centres;

(6) information should be made available at seafarers' centres regarding local religious provision—churches/mosques/temples—and contact numbers for available religious personnel.

In relation to life on board ship, it appears that seafarers have developed a strong set of occupational cultural norms that assist them in navigating the tricky terrain of religious diversity in their living and working space. We therefore recommend that

(1) companies continue to allow seafarers to manage their own interactions on board without undue intervention or guidance;

(2) managers support positive interactions between all seafarers on board by ensuring that they have anti-discrimination, anti-bullying, and anti-harassment policies in place;

(3) training is provided by companies in support of their anti-discrimination, anti-bullying, and anti-harassment policies.

Recommendations for Further Research

There are two significant areas of further necessary research that are indicated by this work:

(1) Research designed to explore and understand the ways in which individuals may abandon their religious practices when away from their communities without experiencing this as problematic from the point of view of the teachings of their faith would be of interest. In this study, it was fascinating to find that, while they were away at sea, seafarers were often quite content to deviate from norms to which they adhered very closely at home (and sometimes enforced in their households). Gambling, drinking, eating meat of proscribed kinds and on proscribed occasions, and engaging in commercial sex were all practices that seafarers described engaging in, when they said that they would not engage in them in their home communities. While some expressed regret about this and felt they

needed to seek the forgiveness of their God, many seemed, somewhat paradoxically, to simply accept deviance as the norm while away at sea. This warrants further study and greater understanding.

(2) It would be valuable to undertake further study of the value of seafarers' centres and port chaplains to much larger numbers of seafarers, including those of different faiths and none.

Chaplaincy and Seafarers: Faith at Work. Helen Sampson, Nelson Turgo, Wendy Cadge, and Sophie Gilliat-Ray, Oxford University Press. © Helen Sampson, Nelson Turgo, Wendy Cadge, and Sophie Gilliat-Ray 2024.
DOI: 10.1093/9780198913290.003.0010

References

Acejo, I. (2013) 'Filipino Seafarers and Transnationalism', PhD thesis, Cardiff: Cardiff University. https://orca.cardiff.ac.uk/id/eprint/52843/1/0635324%20Iris%20Acejo%20Final%20Thesis.pdf (Accessed 8 March 2024).

Ali, M. and Gilliat-Ray, S. (2012) 'Muslim Chaplains: Working at the Interface of "Public" and "Private"', in Ahmad, W. and Sardar, Z. (eds), *Muslims in Britain: Making Social and Political Space*, London: Routledge, pp. 84–100.

Amante, M. (2003) *Philippine Global Seafarers: A Profile*, Cardiff: Cardiff University Social Issues Research Centre.

Anson, P. (1974) *The Church Maritime 'The Word upon the Waters': Incidents in the History of Christian Missions to Seafarers*. Unpublished Manuscript, ICMA Archives.

AoS (Apostleship of the Sea) (1931–1942) 'Diary/Log', *Records of the Apostleship of the Sea*, Hull: Hull History Centre (HHC).

AoS (1940–1960) 'Reports', *Records of the Apostleship of the Sea*, Hull: HHC.

AoS (1970) 'Report', *Records of the Apostleship of the Sea*, Hull: HHC.

AoS (1977) 'Report', *Records of the Apostleship of the Sea*, Hull: HHC.

AoS (1989) 'Port Chaplain Report', *Records of the Apostleship of the Sea*, Hull: HHC.

AoS (1991) 'Report', *Records of the Apostleship of the Sea*, Hull: HHC.

Avery, W. (1986) 'Toward an Understanding of Ministry of Presence', *Journal of Pastoral Care and Counseling*, 40(4): 342–352. https://doi.org/10.1177/002234098604000408.

Bardarova, S. Jakovlev, Z., Serafimova, M., and Koteski, C. (2013) 'The Role of Amnesty International in Protecting of Human Rights', International Scientific Conference, Promoting Human Rights, 25–27 September, Skopje, North Macedonia.

Beckford, J. (1999) 'The Management of Religious Diversity in England and Wales with Special Reference to Prison Chaplaincy', *International Journal on Multicultural Societies*, 1(2): 55–66.

Beckford, J. and Gilliat, S. (1998) *Religion in Prison: Equal Rites in a Multi-Faith Society*, Cambridge: Cambridge University Press.

Belcher, P., Sampson, H., Thomas, M., Veiga, J., and Zhao, M. (2003) *Women Seafarers: Global Employment Policies and Practices*, Geneva: International Labour Office.

Bhattacharjee, S. (2019) '12 Famous Myths about Merchant Navy People Have', *Marine Insight*, 16 June, https://www.marineinsight.com/life-at-sea/12-famous-myths-about-merchant-navy-people-have (Accessed 11 August 2022).

BIMCO (Baltic and International Maritime Council)/ICS (International Chamber of Shipping) (2021) *Seafarer Workforce Report: The Global Supply and Demand for Seafarers in 2021*, London: BIMCO/ICS.

Boswell, W., Moynihan, L., Roehling, M., and Cavanaugh, M. (2001) 'Responsibilities in the "New Employment Relationship": An Empirical Test of an Assumed Phenomenon', *Journal of Managerial Issues*, 13(3): 307–327, http://www.jstor.org/stable/40604353 (Accessed 22 January 2024).

Brown, A. (2013) 'Hero to Homesick Seafarers. Meet the Leith Docks Chaplain Who Is on a Mission to Help Visiting Crews', *Daily Record* and *Sunday Mail*, 16 December.

Butler, N. and Russell, D. (2018) 'No Funny Business: Precarious Work and Emotional Labour in Stand-Up Comedy', *Human Relations*, 71(12): 1666–1686.

Cadge, W. (2012) *Paging God: Religion in the Halls of Medicine*, Chicago, IL: University of Chicago Press.

Cadge, W. and Skaggs, M. (2018) 'Serving Seafarers in the Boston Harbor: Local Adaptation to Global Economic Change', *International Journal of Maritime History*, 30(2): 252–265.

Cadge, W. and Skaggs, M. (2019) 'Humanizing Agents of Modern Capitalism? The Daily Work of Port Chaplains', *Sociology of Religion*, 80(1): 83–106.

Cadge, W., Calle, C., and Dillinger, J. (2011) 'What Do Chaplains Contribute to Large Academic Hospitals? The Perspectives of Pediatric Physicians and Chaplains', *Journal of Religion and Health*, 50: 300–312.

Cadge, W., Turgo, N., Gilliat-Ray, S., Sampson, H., and Smith G. (2022) 'The Work of Port Chaplains: Views from Seafarers Served', *Journal of Contemporary Religion*, 325–342, https://doi.org/10.1080/13537903.2021.1986311.

Carotenuto, A., Molino, I., Fasanaro, A., and Amente, F. (2012) 'Psychological Stress in Seafarers: A Review', *International Maritime Health*, 63(4): 188–194.

Chapman, P. (1994) 'What the Church Says to Seafarers', *Maritime Mission Studies*, 1(1): 23–26.

Cudahy, B. (2006) *Box Boats: How Container Ships Changed the World*, New York: Fordham University Press.

Devereux, H. and Wadsworth, E. (2021) 'The Forgotten Keyworkers: Challenges Faced by British Seafarers as a Result of the Covid-19 Pandemic', Southampton: Solent University, https://www.solent.ac.uk/research-innovation-enterprise/documents/forgotten-keyworkers-project-report-september-2021.pdf (Accessed 18 May 2022).

DiPietro, R. and Bufquin, D. (2018) 'Effects of Work Status Congruence and Perceived Management Concern for Employees on Turnover Intentions in a Fast Casual Restaurant Chain', *Journal of Human Resources in Hospitality and Tourism*, 17(1): 38–59.

Down, B. (1989) *On Course Together: The Churches' Ministry in the Maritime World Today*, Norwich: The Canterbury's Press.

Down, B. (1999) 'Seafarers', in Legood, G. (ed.), *Chaplaincy: The Church's Sector Ministries*, London: Cassell, pp. 124–131.

Dutt, M. (2015) 'Indian Seafarers' Experiences of Ill-Treatment Onboard Ships, PhD thesis, Cardiff: Cardiff University, https://orca.cardiff.ac.uk/id/eprint/71472/13/Manasi%20Dutt%20Final%20Thesis%20ORCA%20SIGS%20REMOVED.pdf (Accessed 8 March 2024).

Eyerman, R. and Jamison, A. (1989) 'Environmental Knowledge as an Organizational Weapon: The Case of Greenpeace', *Social Science Information*, 28(1): 99–119.

Finch, J. (1980) 'Devising Conventional Performances: The Case of Clergymen's Wives', *Sociological Review*, 28(4): 851–870, https://doi.org/10.1111/j.1467-954X.1980.tb00598.x.

Foster, L. (1975) 'The Chaplain: Patient's Advocate and Institution's Ombudsman', *Journal of Pastoral Care* 29 (2): 106–110.

Gandy, R., Harrison, P., and Gold, J. (2018) 'Criticality of Detailed Staff Turnover Measurement', *Benchmarking: An International Journal*, 25(8): 2950–2967.

Gilliat-Ray, S. (2003) 'Nursing, Professionalism, and Spirituality', *Journal of Contemporary Religion*, 18(3): 335–349.

Gilliat-Ray, S. (2005) ' "Sacralising" Sacred Space: A Case Study of "Prayer Space" at the Millennium Dome', *Journal of Contemporary Religion*, 20(3): 357–372.

Gilliat-Ray, S. Ali, M., and Pattison, S. (2013) *Understanding Muslim Chaplaincy*, Aldershot: Ashgate.

Gilliat-Ray, S., Cadge, W., Sampson, H., Turgo, N., and Smith, G. (2022) 'Here Today, Gone Tomorrow: The Risks and Rewards of Port Chaplaincy', *Journal of Beliefs & Values*, 173–187, https://doi.org/10.1080/13617672.2022.2039982.

Gould, E. (2010) 'Towards a Total Occupation: A Study of UK Merchant Navy Officer Cadetship', PhD thesis, Cardiff: Cardiff University, https://orca.cardiff.ac.uk/id/eprint/55023/1/U585412.pdf (Accessed 8 March 2024).

Goulielmos, A. and Anastasakos, A. (2005) 'Worldwide Security Measures for Shipping, Seafarers and Ports. An Impact Assessment of ISPS Code', *Disaster Prevention and Management*, 14(4): 462–473.

Grillot, S. and Cruise, R. (2010) *Protecting Our Ports: Domestic and International Politics of Containerized Freight Security*, London: Routledge.

Grimell, J. (2020) 'From Theory to Practice When Presenting Core Features of a Swedish Hospital Chaplaincy Identity: A Case Study Analysis', *Health and Social Care Chaplaincy*, 10(2): 165–184.

Hafiz, A. (2015) 'Muslim Chaplaincy in the UK: The Chaplaincy Approach as a Way to a Modern Imamate', *Religion, State and Society*, 43(1): 85–99.

Hall, T. (1997) 'The Personal Functioning of Pastors: A Review of Empirical Research with Implications for the Care of Pastors', *Journal of Psychology and Theology*, 25(2): 240–253, https://doi.org/10.1177/009164719702500208.

Hansen, H. (1996) 'Surveillance of Deaths on Board Danish Merchant Ships 1986–1993: Implications for Prevention', *Occupational and Environmental Medicine*, 53: 269–275.

Hansson, P. and Andersen, J. (2001) 'The Swedish Vicar and Change', *Journal of Empirical Theology*, 14(1): 47–60, https://doi.org/10.1163/157092501X00037.

HMSO (His Majesty's Stationery Office) (1942) 'Welfare Outside the Factory and Seamen's Welfare in Port, August 1941–August 1942', London: Ministry of Labour and National Service.

HMSO (1945) 'Seaman's Welfare in Ports: Report of the Committee Appointed by the Ministry of Labour and National Service and the Minister of War Transport in 1943', London: Ministry of Labour and National Service, Ministry of War Transport, https://babel.hathitrust.org/cgi/pt?id=wu.89073375917&view=1up&seq=6 (Accessed 3 August 2022).

Hochschild, A. ([1983] 2012) *The Managed Heart: Commercialization of Human Feeling*, 3rd edn, Berkeley, CA: University of California Press.

Holm, N. (2009) 'Toward a Theology of the Ministry of Presence in Chaplaincy', *International Journal of Chaplaincy and Education*, 52(1): 7–22, https://doi.org/10.1177/002196570905200103.

Holst, L. (1982) 'The Hospital Chaplain: Between Worlds', in Marty, M. and Vaux, K. (eds), *Health/Medicine and the Faith Traditions*, Philadelphia, PA: Fortress Press, pp. 293–311.

Hovde, D. (1994) 'Sea Colportage: The Loan Library System of the American Seamen's Friend Society, 1859–1967', *Libraries & Culture*, 29: 389–414.

Hystad, S. and Eid, J. (2016) 'Sleep and Fatigue among Seafarers: The Role of Environmental Stressors, Duration at Sea and Psychological Capital', *Safety and Health at Work*, 7(4): 363–371, https://doi.org/10.1016/j.shaw.2016.05.006.

ILO (International Labour Organization) (2006) 'The Maritime Labour Convention, 2006 International Labour Conference', https://www.ilo.org/wcmsp5/groups/public/---ed_norm/---normes/documents/normativeinstrument/wcms_090250.pdf (Accessed 12 August 2022).

Iversen, R. (2012) 'The Mental Health of Seafarers', *International Maritime Health*, 63(2): 78–89.

Jepsen, J., Zhao, Z., and Leeuwen, W. (2015) 'Seafarer Fatigue: A Review of Risk Factors, Consequences for Seafarers' Health and Safety and Options for Mitigation', *International Maritime Health*, 66(2): 106–117.

Jezewska, M. and Iversen, R. (2012) 'Stress and Fatigue at Sea versus Quality of Life', *International Maritime Health* 63(3): 106–115.

Johnston, R. and McFarland, E. (2010a) 'Out in the Open in a Threatening World: The Scottish Churches' Industrial Mission: 1960–1980', *International Review of Social History* 55 (1): 1–27.

Johnston, R. and McFarland, E. (2010b) 'With God in the Workplace: Industrial Chaplains in Scottish Heavy Industry, 1970s–1990', *Oral History*, 38: 55–67.

Kahveci, E. (2007) *Port Based Welfare Services for Seafarers*, Cardiff: Prepared for ITF Seafarers' Trust (Seafarers International Research Centre, Cardiff University).

Kevern, P. and McSherry, W. (2015) 'The Study of Chaplaincy: Methods and Materials', in Swift, C., Cobb, M., and Todd, A. (eds), *A Handbook of Chaplaincy Studies: Understanding Spiritual Care in Public Places*, Aldershot: Ashgate, pp. 47–62.

Kim, H., Kim, J., Choe, K., Kwak, Y., and Song, J. (2018) 'Mediating Effects of Workplace Violence on the Relationships between Emotional Labour and Burnout among Clinical Nurses', *Journal of Advanced Nursing*, 74: 2331–2339.

Kinghorn, W. (2015) 'Critical Response to Psychiatric Case Studies: A Psychiatrist's Perspective', in Fitchett, G. and Nolan, S. (eds), *Spiritual Care in Practice: Case Studies in Healthcare Chaplaincy*, London: Jessica Kingsley, pp. 186–194.

Knickerbocker, W. (2014) *Bard of the Bethel*, Cambridge: Cambridge Scholars Publishing.

Kverndal, R. (1986) *Seamen's Missions: Their Origin and Early Growth*, Pasadena, CA: William Carey Library.

Kverndal, R. (2008) *The Way of the Sea: The Changing Shape of Mission in the Seafaring World*, Pasadena, CA: William Carey Library.

La Grange, H.and Homden, M. (2010) *Successful Seafarers' Centres*, International Christian Maritime Association and the ITF Seafarers' Trust. https://www.yumpu.com/en/document/view/52402143/successful-seafarers-centres-international-christian-maritime (Accessed 11 March 2024).

Lambie-Mumford, H. (2015) *Addressing Food Poverty in the UK: Charity, Rights and Welfare*, Sheffield: Sheffield Political Economy Research Institute, University of Sheffield.

Lamvik, G. (2002) 'The Filipino Seafarer: A Life between Sacrifice and Shopping', PhD thesis, Norwegian University of Science and Technology NTNU Open, The Filipino seafarer: a life between sacrifice and shopping. https://core.ac.uk/download/pdf/30820359.pdf (Accessed 10 October 2023).

Linz, S., Good, L., and Busch, M. (2013) 'Does Worker Loyalty Pay? Evidence from Transition Economies', *Evidenced-Based HRM: A Global Forum for Empirical Scholarship*, 1(1): 16–40.

MAIB (Marine Accident Investigation Branch) (2012) 'Report on the Investigation of the Grounding of Karin Schepers at Pendeen, Cornwall, UK on 3 August 2011', Report No. 10/2012, May 2012, https://assets.publishing.service.gov.uk/media/547c6f83e5274a4290000033/KarinSchepers.pdf (Accessed 8 November 2021).

Markkula, J. (2021) 'Containing Mobilities: Changing Time and Space of Maritime Labour', *Journal of Global and Historical Anthropology*, 89: 25–39, https://doi.org/10.3167/fcl.2021.890103.

Mauno, S., Ruokolainen, M., Kinnunen, U., and De Bloom, J. (2016) 'Emotional Labour and Work Engagement among Nurses: Examining Perceived Compassion, Leadership and Work Ethic as Stress Buffers', *Journal of Advanced Nursing*, 72(5): 1169–1181, https://doi.org/10.1111/jan.12906.

Mazaheri, A. and Ekwall, D. (2009) 'Impacts of the ISPS Code on Port Activities: A Case Study on Swedish Ports', *World Review of Intermodal Transportation Research*, 2(4): 326–342.

McFarland, E. and Johnston, R. (2010) 'Faith in the Factory: The Church of Scotland's Industrial Mission, 1942–58', *Historical Research*, 83(221): 539–564.

McKay, F. and Lindberg, R. (2019) 'The Important Role of Charity in the Welfare System for Those Who Are Food Insecure', *Australian and New Zealand Journal of Public Health*, 43(4): 310–312.

McKinnon, A. (2005) 'Reading "Opium of the People": Expression, Protest and the Dialectics of Religion', *Critical Sociology* 31(1–2): 15–38.

Mellbye, A. and Carter, T. (2017) 'Seafarers' Depression and Suicide', *International Maritime Health*, 68(2): 108–114.

Miller, D. (2007) *God at Work: The History and Promise of the Faith at Work Movement*, Oxford: Oxford University Press.

Miller, D., Ngunjiri, F., and Lorusso, J. (2018) '"The Suits Care about Us": Employee Perceptions of Workplace Chaplains', *Journal of Management, Spirituality & Religion*, 15(5): 377–397.

Miller, J. (2020) 'Religion in the Philippines', Asia Society, https://asiasociety.org/education/religion-philippines (Accessed 3 December 2020).

MNWB (Merchant Navy Welfare Board) (2017) 'UK Seafarers' Centres & Port Welfare Services Study: Analysis of 876 Responses', MNWB. ICMA Archives.

Montemaggi, F. (2018) 'Hospitality and Compassion: The Work and Ethics of Catholic Chaplains Supporting Seafarers', *Journal of Beliefs & Values*, 39(4): 502–515.

Montemaggi, F., Bullivant, S., and Glackin, M. (2018) '"Being There": How Catholic Chaplains Support Seafarers in the UK', St Mary's University. https://www.stmarys.ac.uk/research/centres/benedict-xvi/docs/2018-jun-being-there-report.pdf (Accessed 8 March 2024).

Moody, D. (1877) 'To All People', in McLoughlin, W. G. (ed.), *The American Evangelicals, 1800–1900: An Anthology*, 1986th edn, New York: Harper, pp. 171–185

Mooney, P. (2000) 'Serving Seafarers under Sail and Steam: A Missiological Reflection on the Development of Maritime Missions from 1779 to 1945', *Occasional Papers of the International Association for the Study of Maritime Mission* 2(June). 32 p.

Mooney, P. (2019) *A History of ICMA*, London: International Christian Maritime Association and the North American Maritime Ministry Association.

Morgan, G. (2010) 'Independent Advocacy and the "Rise of Spirituality": Views from Advocates, Service Users and Chaplains', *Mental Health, Religion & Culture*, 13(6): 625–636.

MtS (Mission to Seafarers) (1947) *Archives of the Mission to Seafarers*, Hull: Hull History Centre (HHC).

MtS (1948) 'Senior Chaplain Report', *Archives of the Mission to Seafarers*, Hull: HHC.

MtS (1949) 'Chaplain Report', *Archives of the Mission to Seafarers*, Hull: HHC.

MtS (1954) 'Chaplain Report', *Archives of the Mission to Seafarers*, Hull: HHC.

MtS (1955) 'Chaplain Report', *Archives of the Mission to Seafarers*, Hull: HHC.

MtS (1958) 'Chaplain Report', *Archives of the Mission to Seafarers*, Hull: HHC.

MtS (1960) 'Chaplain Report', *Archives of the Mission to Seafarers*, Hull: HHC.

MtS (1975) 'Chaplain Report', *Archives of the Mission to Seafarers*, Hull: HHC.

MtS (1991) 'Meeting Minutes', *Archives of the Mission to Seafarers*, Hull: HHC.

MtS (1999) 'Meeting Minutes', *Archives of the Mission to Seafarers*, Hull: HHC.

MtS (2000) 'Meeting Minutes', *Archives of the Mission to Seafarers*, HHC.

MtS (2019) 'New Grant to Increase and Diversify Our Volunteer Base', 8 April, https://www.missiontoseafarers.org/news/new-grant-to-increase-and-diversify-our-volunteer-base (Accessed 8 December 2020).

Nielsen, D. and Roberts, S. (1999) 'Fatalities among the World's Merchant Seafarers (1990–1994)' *Marine Policy*, 23(1): 71–80.

Oldenburg, M. and Jensen, H. (2019) 'Stress and Strain among Seafarers Related to the Occupational Groups', *International Journal of Environmental Research and Public Health* 16(7), https://doi.org/10.3390/ijerph16071153.

Oldenburg, M., Jensen, H., Latza, U., and Baur, X. (2009) 'Seafaring Stressors Aboard Merchant and Passenger Ships', *International Journal of Public Health*, 54(2): 96–105.

Oldenburg, M., Jensen, H. and Wegner, R. (2013) 'Burnout Syndrome in Seafarers in the Merchant Marine Service', *International Archives of Occupational and Environmental Health*, 86(4): 407–416.

Otis, P. (2009) 'An Overview of the U.S. Military Chaplaincy: A Ministry of Presence and Practice', *Review of Faith and International Affairs*, 7(4): 3–15, https://doi.org/10.1080/15570274.2009.9523410.

Palmer, T. and Murray, E. (2016) '"Christ Offered Salvation, and Not an Easy Life": How Do Port Chaplains Make Sense of Providing Welfare for Seafarers? An Idiographic, Phenomenological Approach Analysis', *International Maritime Health*, 67(2): 117–124.

Pattison, S. (1994) *Pastoral Care and Liberation Theology*, Cambridge: Cambridge University Press.

Pattison, S. (2015) 'Situating Chaplaincy in the United Kingdom: The Acceptable Face of "Religion"?', in Swift, C., Cobb, M., and Todd, A. (eds), *A Handbook of Chaplaincy Studies: Understanding Spiritual Care in Public Places*, Aldershot: Ashgate, pp. 13–30.

Poulsen, R. and Sampson, H. (2020) 'A Swift Turnaround? Abating Shipping Greenhouse Gas Emissions via Port Call Optimization', *Transportation Research Part D*, 86, https://doi.org/10.1016/j.trd.2020.102460.

Roberts, S. and Marlow, P. (2005) 'Traumatic Work-Related Mortality among Seafarers Employed in British Merchant Shipping 1976–2002', *Occupational and Environmental Medicine*, 62: 172–180.

Roehling, P., Roehling M., and Moen, P. (2001) 'The Relationship between Work–Life Policies and Practices and Employee Loyalty: A Life Course Perspective', *Journal of Family and Economic Issues*, 22: 141–170.

Ross, C. (2012) 'Maintenance and Development of National Welfare Boards and Port Welfare Communities', July, Report for the International Committee on Seafarers' Welfare (ICSW), London: Working Lives Research Institute and London Metropolitan University.

Ryan, B. (2014) *A Very Modern Ministry: Chaplaincy in the UK*, London: Theos/Cardiff Centre for Chaplaincy Studies.

Sajeva, S. (2007) 'Identifying Factors Affecting Motivation and Loyalty of Knowledge Workers', *Economics and Management*, 12: 643–652.

Sampson, H. (2005) 'Left High and Dry? The Lives of Women Married to Seafarers in Goa and Mumbai', *Ethnography*, 6(1): 61–85, https://doi.org/10.1177/1466138105055661.

Sampson, H. (2011) 'Spilling Oil, Spilling Blood: Cost and Corporate Decision Making concerning Safe Working Practices', *Policy and Practice in Health and Safety*, 9(1): 17–32, https://doi.org/10.1080/14774003.2011.11667754.

Sampson, H. (2013) *International Seafarers and Transnationalism in the Twenty-First Century*, Manchester: Manchester University Press.

Sampson, H. (2016) '"Seabirds Matter More Than Us!" Understanding the Complex Exercise of CSR in the Global Shipping Industry', *Journal of Sustainable Mobility*, 3(2):101–119, https://doi.org/10.9774/GLEAF.23502016de.00007.

Sampson, H. (2022) '"Beyond the State": The Limits of International Regulation and the Example of Abandoned Seafarers', *Marine Policy*, 140(105046): 105046, https://doi.org/10.1016/j.marpol.2022.105046.

Sampson, H. (2024) *Sea-Time: An Ethnographic Adventure*, London: Routledge.

Sampson, H. and Acejo, I. (2022) 'Urgent Need for Port-Based Welfare', *The Sea*, 1 March, https://www.missiontoseafarers.org/the-sea/urgent-need-for-port-based-welfare (Accessed 18 May 2022).

Sampson, H. and Ellis, N. (2019) 'Seafarers' Mental Health and Wellbeing, Full Report', Institution of Occupational Safety and Health (IOSH). https://orca.cardiff.ac.uk/id/eprint/127214/1/seafarers-mental-health-wellbeing-full-report.pdf (Accessed 8 March 2024).

Sampson, H. and Wu, B. (2003) 'Compressing Time and Constraining Space: The Contradictory Effects of ICT and Containerisation on International Shipping Labour', *International Review of Social History*, 48: 123–152.

Sampson, H., Ellis, N., Acejo, I., Turgo, N., and Tang, L. (2018) *The Working and Living Conditions of Seafarers on Cargo Ships in the Period 2011–2016*, Cardiff: Seafarers International Research Centre.

Sampson, H., Turgo, N., Acejo, I., Ellis, N. and Tang, L. (2019) 'Between a Rock and a Hard Place': The Implications of Lost Autonomy and Trust for Professionals at Sea', *Work, Employment and Society*, 33(4): 648–665, https://doi.org/10.1177/0950017018821284.

Sampson, H., Turgo, N., Cadge, W., Gilliat-Ray, S., and Smith, G. (2022) 'Overstretched and Under-Resourced': The Corporate Neglect of Port Welfare Services for Seafarers', *Maritime Policy & Management*, https://doi.org/10.1080/03088839.2022.2084788.

Schmid, H. (2020) '"I'm Just an Imam, Not Superman": Imams in Switzerland', *Journal of Muslims in Europe*, 9(1): 64–95, https://doi.org/10.1163/22117954-12341408.

Shepherd, D. and Hammond, D. (2020) 'New Zealand: Under-Funding of Seafarers' Welfare Services and Poor MLC Compliance', *Human Rights at Sea*, https://www.humanrightsatsea.org/sites/default/files/media-files/2022-02/NZ%20MLC%20Welfare%20Failures%20Report%20March%202020.pdf (Accessed 8 March 2024).

Siefert, K., Jayaratne, S., and Chess, W. (1991) 'Job Satisfaction, Burnout, and Turnover in Health Care Social Workers', *Health and Social Work*, 16(3): 193–202.

Slade, R. (2015) *Into the Raging Sea: Thirty-Three Mariners, One Megastorm, and the Sinking of El Faro*, New York: HarperCollins Publishers.

Stam, D. (2012) 'The Lord's Librarians: The American Seamen's Friend Society and Their Loan Libraries, 1837–1967', *Coriolis*, 3: 45–59.

Strhan, A. (2015) *Aliens and Strangers? The Struggle for Coherence in the Everyday Lives of Evangelicals*, Oxford: Oxford University Press.

Sullivan, S. (2006) 'The Work–Faith Connection for Low-Income Mothers: A Research Note', *Sociology of Religion* 67(1): 99–108, https://doi.org/10.1093/socrel/67.1.99.

Sullivan, W. (2014) *A Ministry of Presence: Chaplaincy, Spiritual Care, and the Law*, Chicago, IL: University of Chicago Press.

Swift, C. (2015) *A Handbook of Chaplaincy Studies: Understanding Spiritual Care in Public Places*, Aldershot: Ashgate.

Swift, O. (2011) 'Durban Fieldwork Report' (personal document).

Swift, O. (2013) 'Port Levies and Sustainable Welfare for Seafarers', May, ISWAN. https:// www.seafarerswelfare.org/assets/documents/resources/ISWAN_PortLeviesReport_low-res.pdf (Accessed 8 March 2024).

Swift, O. (2015) 'Social Isolation of Seafarers; What Is It? Why Does It Matter? What Can Be Done?' International Seafarers Welfare and Assistance Network (ISWAN). https:// www.seafarerswelfare.org/assets/documents/resources/Social-Isolation-Article-PDF. pdf (Accessed 8 March 2024).

Taplin, I., Winterton, J., and Winterton, R. (2003) 'Understanding Labour Turnover in a Labour Intensive Industry: Evidence from the British Clothing Industry', *Journal of Management Studies*, 40(4): 1021–1046.

Todd, A. Cobb, M., and Swift, C. (2015) 'Conclusion', in Swift, C., Cobb, M., and Todd, A. (eds), *A Handbook of Chaplaincy Studies: Understanding Spiritual Care in Public Places*, Aldershot: Ashgate, pp. 327–335.

Turgo, N. and Sampson, H. (2021) ' "What Is Immediate and Obvious Feels Real": National Identity and Emotional Vulnerabilities in the Field', *Methodological Innovations*, September–December: 1–11.

Turgo, N., Cage, W., Gilliat-Ray, S., Sampson, H., and Smith, G. (2023) 'Relying on the Kindness of Strangers: Welfare-Providers to Seafarers and the Symbolic Construction of Community', *Journal of Contemporary Ethnography*, 52(2): 92–217, https://doi. org/10.1177/08912416221092001.

UNCTAD (United Nations Conference on Trade and Development) (1990) 'Review of Maritime Transport 1990: Report by the UNCTAD Secretariat', https://unctad.org/ system/files/official-document/rmt1990_en.pdf (Accessed 18 May 2022).

UNCTAD (2017) 'Review of Maritime Transport 2017', https://unctad.org/system/files/ official-document/rmt2017_en.pdf (Accessed 12 August 2022).

UNCTAD (2021) 'Chapter 2: Maritime Transport and Infrastructure: Review of Maritime Transport 2021', https://unctad.org/system/files/official-document/rmt2021ch2_en.pdf (Accessed 18 May 2022).

Uygur, S., Spence, L., Simpson, R., and Karakas, F. (2017) 'Work Ethic, Religion and Moral Energy: The Case of Turkish SME Owner-Managers', *International Journal of Human Resource Management* 28(8): 1212–1235, https://doi.rog/10.1080/09585192.2016.1166790.

Viljoen, C. (2011) 'Mission Work and Pastoral Care in the Port of Durban: A Narrative Hermeneutical Adventure', PhD thesis, Pretoria: University of Pretoria. https://repository. up.ac.za/bitstream/handle/2263/24562/Complete.pdf?sequence=7&isAllowed=y (Accessed 11 March 2024).

Walsh, G. and Bartikowski, B. (2013) 'Employee Emotional Labour and Quitting Intentions: Moderating Effects of Gender and Age', *European Journal of Marketing*, 47(8): 1213–1237.

Woodhead, L. (2015) 'Foreword: Chaplaincy and the Future of Religion', in Swift, C., Cobb, M., and Todd, A. (eds), *A Handbook of Chaplaincy Studies: Understanding Spiritual Care in Public Places*, Aldershot: Ashgate, pp. xvii–xxii.

Zevallos, J., Hulshof, C., Mutsaerts, T., and Sluiter, J. (2014) 'Outcomes of Seafarer Work Fitness Qualifications in the Netherlands', *Occupational Medicine* 64(4): 267–270, https://doi.org/10.1093/occmed/kqu020.

Zuidema, J. and Walker, K. (2020) 'Welcoming the Orphans of Globalisation: The Case for Seafarers' Ministry', *Science et Esprit*, 72(3): 311–324.

Zurcher, L. (1965) 'The Sailor Aboard Ship: A Study of Role Behaviour in a Total Institution', *Social Forces*, 43(3): 389–400.

Index

Since the index has been created to work across multiple formats, indexed terms for which a page range is given (e.g., 52–53, 66–70, etc.) may occasionally appear only on some, but not all of the pages within the range.